MERCY AND GRACE

Previously Published Records of Building Bridges Seminars

The Road Ahead: A Christian–Muslim Dialogue, Michael Ipgrave, editor (London: Church House, 2002)

Scriptures in Dialogue: Christians and Muslims Studying the Bible and the Qur'ān Together, Michael Ipgrave, editor (London: Church House, 2004)

Bearing the Word: Prophecy in Biblical and Qur'ānic Perspective, Michael Ipgrave, editor (London: Church House, 2005)

Building a Better Bridge: Muslims, Christians, and the Common Good, Michael Ipgrave, editor (Washington, DC: Georgetown University Press, 2008)

Justice and Rights: Christian and Muslim Perspectives, Michael Ipgrave, editor (Washington, DC: Georgetown University Press, 2009)

Humanity: Texts and Contexts: Christian and Muslim Perspectives, Michael Ipgrave and David Marshall, editors (Washington, DC: Georgetown University Press, 2011)

Communicating the Word: Revelation, Translation, and Interpretation in Christianity and Islam, David Marshall, editor (Washington, DC: Georgetown University Press, 2011)

Science and Religion: Christian and Muslim Perspectives, David Marshall, editor (Washington, DC: Georgetown University Press, 2012)

Tradition and Modernity: Christian and Muslim Perspectives, David Marshall, editor (Washington, DC: Georgetown University Press, 2012)

Prayer: Christian and Muslim Perspectives, David Marshall and Lucinda Mosher, editors (Washington, DC: Georgetown University Press, 2013)

Death, Resurrection, and Human Destiny: Christian and Muslim Perspectives, David Marshall and Lucinda Mosher, editors (Washington, DC: Georgetown University Press, 2014)

The Community of Believers: Christian and Muslim Perspectives, Lucinda Mosher and David Marshall, editors (Washington, DC: Georgetown University Press, 2015)

Sin, Forgiveness, and Reconciliation: Christian and Muslim Perspectives, Lucinda Mosher and David Marshall, editors (Washington, DC: Georgetown University Press, 2016)

God's Creativity and Human Action: Christian and Muslim Perspectives, Lucinda Mosher and David Marshall, editors (Washington, DC: Georgetown University Press, 2017)

Monotheism and Its Complexities: Christian and Muslim Perspectives, Lucinda Mosher and David Marshall, editors (Washington, DC: Georgetown University Press, 2018)

Power—Divine and Human: Christian and Muslim Perspectives, Lucinda Mosher and David Marshall, editors (Washington, DC: Georgetown University Press, 2019)

A World of Inequalities: Christian and Muslim Perspectives, Lucinda Mosher, editor (Washington, DC: Georgetown University Press, 2021)

Freedom: Christian and Muslim Perspectives, Lucinda Mosher, editor (Washington, DC: Georgetown University Press, 2021)

Naming God: Christian and Muslim Perspectives, Lucinda Mosher, editor (Washington, DC: Georgetown University Press, 2023)

MERCY AND GRACE

CHRISTIAN AND MUSLIM PERSPECTIVES

A Record of the Twentieth Building Bridges Seminar

Hosted by
Georgetown University
Warrenton, Virginia
June 13–17, 2022

Lucinda Mosher, Editor

Georgetown University Press / Washington, DC

Library of Congress Cataloging-in-Publication Data

Names: Building Bridges Seminar (20th : 2022 : Warrenton, Va.), author. | Mosher, Lucinda, editor.
Title: Mercy and grace : Christian and Muslim perspectives / [edited by] Lucinda Mosher.
Description: Washington, DC : Georgetown University Press, [2024] | Papers originally presented at the Twentieth Building Bridges Seminar, held at Airlie Center, Warrenton, Virginia, June 13-17, 2022. | Includes bibliographical references and index.
Identifiers: LCCN 2024020684 (print) | LCCN 2024020685 (ebook) | ISBN 9781647124885 (hardcover) | ISBN 9781647124892 (paperback) | ISBN 9781647124908 (ebook)
Subjects: LCSH: Mercy in the Qur'an—Congresses. | Mercy in the Hadith—Congresses. | God (Christianity)—Mercy—Congresses. | Grace (Theology)—Congresses. | LCGFT: Conference papers and proceedings.
Classification: LCC BP134.M47 B85 2022 (print) | LCC BP134.M47 (ebook) | DDC 234—dc23/eng/20241106
LC record available at https://lccn.loc.gov/2024020684
LC ebook record available at https://lccn.loc.gov/2024020685

∞This paper meets the requirements of ANSI/NISO Z39.48-1992 (Permanence of Paper).

EU GPSR Authorized Representative
LOGOS EUROPE, 9 rue Nicolas Poussin, 17000, LA ROCHELLE, France
Email: Contact@logoseurope.eu

26 25 9 8 7 6 5 4 3 2 First printing

Printed in the United States of America

Cover design by Nathan Putens
Interior design by Paul Hotvedt

Contents

Part Two: Christian Perspectives on Mercy and Grace

Part Three: Reflections

Participants in Building Bridges Seminar 2022

Muhammad Modassir Ali, Hamad Bin Khalifa University, Qatar
Betül Avcı, Ibn Haldun University, Turkey
Mehdi Azaiez, Université catholique de Louvain, Belgium; University of Lorraine, France
Alexandra Brown, Washington and Lee University, USA
Stephen L. Cook, Virginia Theological Seminary, USA
Maria Massi Dakake, James Madison University, USA
Susan Eastman, Duke University Divinity School, USA
Dustin Ellington, Justo Mwale University, Zambia
Ramon Harvey, Cambridge Muslim College, UK
Christopher M. Hays, ScholarLeaders International, USA
Tuba Işık, Humboldt University of Berlin, Germany
Veli-Matti Kärkkäinen, Fuller Theological Seminary, USA / University of Helsinki, Finland
Julia Lamm, Georgetown University, USA
Daniel Madigan, SJ, Australian Catholic University, Australia / Georgetown University, USA
David Marshall, University of Bern, Switzerland / Georgetown University, USA
Mahan Mirza, University of Notre Dame, USA
Younus Mirza, Georgetown University, USA / Shenandoah University, USA
Esther Mombo, St. Paul's University, Limuru, Kenya
Lucinda Mosher, Hartford International University for Religion and Peace, USA
Munjed Murad, United Theological Seminary of the Twin Cities, USA
Kenan Musić, University of Sarajevo, Bosnia and Herzegovina
Abdul Rahman Mustafa, Paderborn University, Germany
Rasoul Naghavi Nia, Mufid Academic Seminary, USA
Martin Nguyen, Fairfield University, USA

Jacob Onyumbe, Université Notre Dame de Tshumbe, Democratic Republic of the Congo
Ermin Sinanović, Shenandoah University, USA
Staff: Samuel Wagner, Georgetown University, USA

Preface: Two Decades of Mutual Theological Hospitality: Reflections on the Twentieth Anniversary of the Building Bridges Seminar

Lucinda Mosher

> We engage with what we believe God has given us to engage with, in holy text and in tradition. And we invite our neighbors and friends to watch us doing that, and to learn a bit about how to share in that as best they can. . . . We've tried to avoid large generalities, so that we can come back again and again to the specifics of what we believe God is saying to us.

Thus Rowan Williams, in his opening remarks to the eleventh convening, described a distinctive aspect of the Building Bridges Seminar. A decade later, that description still holds true. This international gathering of Christian and Muslim scholar-believers that fosters a deep commitment to the practice of dialogical close reading has now sustained itself for two decades. Here, then, is a consideration of its history, practices, and future.[1]

Origins

Of three international Christian–Muslim relations initiatives brought forth in January 2002 by George Carey (then Archbishop of Canterbury), only the Building Bridges Seminar continues. It was conceived out of a sincere desire to foster understanding and cooperation in the wake of the catastrophic attack on the United States the previous September. Its founding event, held at Lambeth Palace (the London offices of the Archbishop of Canterbury), was an international seminar on "bridge-building"—defined as an effort to establish "new routes for information, appreciation and respect to travel freely and safely in both directions between Christians and Muslims, Muslims and

Christians."[2] Christian–Muslim relations scholar David Marshall had become chaplain to the Archbishop of Canterbury in 2000 and was deeply involved in the event's planning. Archbishop Carey shared the role of host with Prime Minister Tony Blair and HRH Prince El Hassan bin Talal of Jordan. By means of paired lectures (one by a Christian, one by a Muslim), formal responses, discussion facilitated by Professor Gillian Stamp of the Brunel Institute of Organisation and Social Studies, and informal conversation over meals, thirty-eight distinguished Muslim and Christian scholars and leaders took note of lessons from one-thousand-plus years of Christian–Muslim interaction. They analyzed present-day challenges and opportunities. They paid heed to the practice of appreciative conversation—an exchange distinguished by "courage, grace, imagination and sensitivity in addressing and retreating from painful issues."[3] Ultimately, they affirmed the notion of a sustained dialogue. Almost immediately, planning commenced for a second seminar.

That second convening took place in April 2003 in Doha, Qatar—very near the staging ground for the US invasion of Iraq. It was chaired by Rowan Williams, successor as Archbishop of Canterbury to George Carey, who had retired some months earlier. Williams prioritized the Building Bridges Seminar, shaped it (with able assistance from David Marshall, who remained on the Archbishop of Canterbury's staff until 2005), and served as its moderator for ten convenings.

Williams once described the Building Bridges Seminar as an exercise in "listening to each other listening to God," which enables the participants to "become better able to listen to each other." Thus, they would form "a virtuous circle" rather than a vicious one.[4] Having stressed the importance of investigating "what is disbelieved in other religious discourses" as a means for finding "appropriate language in which difference can be talked about rather than used as an excuse for violent separation," he frequently asserted that the Seminar's purpose was "to improve the quality of our disagreements."[5]

Georgetown University hosted the Seminar four times during the decade of Rowan Williams's leadership.[6] Playing a key role in forging this relationship was Jane McAuliffe. Now president emeritus of Bryn Mawr College and the inaugural director of national and international outreach at the Library of Congress, she was the dean of Georgetown's College of Arts and Sciences when she attended the 2003 Building Bridges Seminar. "Although I had for many years been active in various forms of Muslim–Christian engagement," she says, "I found this experience to be exceptional. When I returned to Georgetown, therefore, I met with President [John] DeGioia and told him about it in the hope that Georgetown could consider a collaboration with Lambeth Palace. President DeGioia invited Archbishop Williams to convene the Third Building Bridges Seminar at Georgetown in March 2004."[7] The invitation was accepted; the relationship deepened. In fact, the university's president, John DeGioia, attended the Seminar several times.

As Williams prepared for retirement in 2012, he arranged for stewardship of the Seminar to be assumed by Georgetown University. Since then, it has been chaired by Professor Daniel Madigan, SJ, now professor emeritus of Georgetown University and a member of the faculty of Australian Catholic University. Professor Abdul Rahman Mustafa of Paderborn University describes him as "a Jesuit scholar who has studied and taught Islam while also being engaged in Christian ministry throughout the world. But for many, Madigan is first and foremost someone who teaches by example how to live as a person with a deep commitment to a faith tradition, while being receptive, even welcoming, towards a critique of one's religious tradition from outsiders."[8]

Locations

Except for a pause in 2020, necessitated by the global coronavirus pandemic, the Building Bridges Seminar has been convened annually since 2002. It has met seven times in the vicinity of Washington, DC (on the Georgetown University campus exclusively in three instances; with most or all of the work carried out at the Airlie Center in Northern Virginia in four); four times in Qatar; twice in London (with time spent in Canterbury during the second); twice in Sarajevo; and once each in Switzerland, Turkey, Italy, Singapore, and cyberspace. "Our choice of venue has been determined not only positively by the generosity of hosts but also negatively at times by the politics of suspicion and exclusion," Madigan explains. "We have tried to avoid being drawn into that atmosphere of political contentiousness so we may contend with the deeper theological questions that long predate and will just as long outlast our current geopolitical situation."[9]

Indeed, the venue of a convening may have an impact on the "sense of well-being and comfort" of its participants, asserts Tuba Işık, a member of the Seminar since 2015. Rowan Williams had described Qatar as the Building Bridges Seminar's seedbed because participants had come away from the city of Doha believing "that it was possible, desirable, and even necessary that the conversations which we had begun should be continued."[10] We might say that the repeated use of the Airlie Center has, in its own way, nurtured the project. As Işık sees it, "a familiar space like the Airlie Center has a unique character that conveys a sense of belonging to an established tradition and an inherent feeling of togetherness—a shared bond."

"Meetings in different parts of Europe and in several Muslim-majority countries have provided an important counterpoint to DC-based gatherings," Jane McAuliffe observes. "On a practical level, they have facilitated engagement with local scholars and, in some instances, allowed the attendance of scholars who would have struggled to secure US visas. On a psychological and social level, convening in countries that are culturally Muslim has let Muslim colleagues feel an enhanced sense of seminar ownership and of hospitality."

"In my experience," says New Testament scholar Susan Eastman, a veteran of ten convenings, "Sarajevo was by far the best location for the Seminar." In fact, she feels Muslim contexts have had the most significant impact on a convening; "but alas, due to global politics beyond our control, it is increasingly difficult to meet in such locations. That itself is perhaps a topic for discussion."

Indeed, Abdul Rahman Mustafa, for whom the twentieth convening of the Seminar was his first, asserts that xenophobia and racism have made traveling to the United States and Europe "increasingly burdensome not only for Muslims (as expressed in the so called 'Muslim travel ban' of the Trump administration) but also for citizens of Asian and African nations who, even after meeting the onerous, expensive and humiliating set of tests involved in applying for visit visas to Europe and North America, often end up with their travel applications denied."[11]

On the whole, the fact that the Seminar's venue was in some years a predominantly Muslim environment and in others a predominantly Christian space "has a salutary chastening effect," says Bible scholar Christopher Hays. "It reminds us of how situated we are culturally and religiously, which conduces to a greater humility and effort to understand the other in their own right, even as we hope to be known."

Demographics

Since 2002 a total of 234 scholars have participated in the Building Bridges Seminar, with Muslims and Christians in equal number. Given the project's origins and infrastructure, it is not surprising that the majority of participants have had some connection to the United States or the United Kingdom (75 and 73 scholars, respectively). However, the Seminar's geographic reach has been significant. Participants have hailed from, lived, worked in, or have some other deep connection to one or more of forty-six other locales: Algeria, Australia, Austria, Bangladesh, Belgium, Benin, Bosnia and Herzegovina, Brazil, Burkina-Faso, Canada, Chad, Colombia, Côte d'Ivoire, Croatia, Cyprus, Democratic Republic of the Congo, Dubai, Egypt, Finland, France, Germany, Ghana, Gibraltar, India, Indonesia, Iran, Italy, Japan, Jordan, Kenya, Lebanon, Libya, Malaysia, the Maldives, Morocco, Nigeria, Pakistan, Qatar, Serbia, Singapore, South Africa, Sri Lanka, Sudan, Switzerland, Syria, and Turkey.

Participation has always been by invitation only. As Daniel Madigan explains,

> Members from both traditions are invited on the basis of their expertise in their *own* tradition and their willingness to learn from the theological engagement with the other. From the point of view of the Seminar's overall aim, it is much more valuable to introduce a mainstream Christian theologian to the new experience of doing theology in conversation with Muslims than it is to assemble the "usual suspects" for whom this kind of conversation is a regular, often central part of their normal work.[12]

The goal is to create a circle of scholars who are well suited to robust dialogical exploration of the designated topic.

"Finding a week for this exercise every year has been a challenge," says Ahmet Alibasic of Sarajevo. "However," he explains, "the commitment and leadership of Georgetown President DeGioia and the Building Bridges staff have always convinced me that I have no option but to answer their invitations positively whenever possible—and it has been very rewarding."

Professor Alibasic has answered positively nine times. That is unusual. The topic changes year by year; so, therefore, does the invitation list. Of the 234 scholars on the Seminar's cumulative roster, 117 attended only one of the twenty convenings held between 2002 and 2022; another 44 attended twice. Twenty-six individuals have participated in six or more; only six have been at ten or more.[13] If we direct our focus on the last nine meetings of these twenty meetings—that is, those held after stewardship of the project was assumed by Georgetown University (2013–2022)—we find a total of 104 individuals on the summary roster. Eighteen (9 Muslims, 9 Christians) were present at five or more of those nine convenings. From whatever angle we look, repeat participation appears to have been limited yet still sufficient to sustain continuity of method. Certainly, the diversity of the master roster has deepened the Seminar's engagement with each topic.

Turning once more to the project's summary roster, we find that not quite 25 percent of the Building Bridges Seminar's participants (55 of 234) have been women. Yet, significantly, every convening has featured at least one formal presentation by a woman. In all, over the course of twenty years, 31 women (14 Muslim, 17 Christian) gave papers or responses. Six did so in four or more years, thus playing a vital role in orienting the group to the meeting's content.

Themes

The initial seminar focused on dialogue's potential. Each subsequent convening has centered on a theme: scriptures; prophecy; the common good; justice and rights; humanity; revelation, translation, and interpretation; science and religion; tradition and modernity; prayer; death, resurrection, and human destiny; community; sin, forgiveness, and reconciliation; God's creativity and human action; monotheism and its complexities; power; inequalities; freedom; naming God; and mercy and grace. Occasionally, a decision is made to return to a previous theme. For example, in 2008 *Communicating the Word* returned to elements of *Bearing the Word*—which had been the theme in 2004. In 2021 *Naming God* picked up on themes of *Monotheism and Its Complexities* (2016). The 2006 seminar on justice and rights drew upon concerns informing the 2002 and 2005 convenings—among them, religious freedom and political authority. In time these themes would be examined from other angles as the convenings on inequalities and freedom (2018 and 2019) built on the consideration (in 2017) of divine and human power.

Twice a convening's theme has seemed to have diverged from the norm. In each case an external factor was instrumental. In 2009 the choice to examine the intersection of science and religion acknowledged the two hundredth anniversary of the birth of Charles Darwin. In 2005 the choice to consider "the common good" when convening in Sarajevo was informed by that city's recent history of extraordinary suffering. Different from all others, this convening emphasized study of regional cases rather than exegesis of texts as it took up themes of faith, identity, justice, religious freedom, and sharing of responsibilities.

"In particular," says Susan Eastman, "I have enjoyed topics that bring basic theological issues about how our respective traditions think about God and God's relationship to the world, into conversation with questions about how we practice our faith. For me, highlights have been the sessions on mercy and grace, freedom, power—divine and human, and human action within divine creation."

"Although it is hard to choose among the many excellent meetings of the seminar, I particularly recall the tenth one," says Jane McAuliffe. "We were again in Doha, this time at Georgetown's School of Foreign Service, and the topic was prayer. The formal presentations were uniformly excellent; and they prompted an unusual level of candor in the discussion sessions. Participants, both Muslim and Christian, seemed willing to push a bit deeper, to speak more personally about their prayer lives, both the joys and the struggles."

"I loved our seminar on freedom," says Christopher Hays.

> As a Christian from the US, I was primed to interpret freedom in a particular way (downstream of John Locke, focused on personal liberties). But the seminar quickly revealed how much that construal of freedom sat in tension with both Christian and Islamic tradition, both of which emphasized our obligations to God over our autonomous liberties. The work across religions and across cultures helped elevate a more truly Christian (and I trust, Muslim) understanding of what it means to be free.

Method

Tuba Işık's fondest memory is not of a particular topic but of an activity. "The most exciting moment of any seminar is when we get into an intensive exchange, with the participants bringing their personal theological positions to the table. I enjoy these moments of communal theological sharing." With that we have come to the Building Bridges methodology, which has these distinguishing elements: it is an exercise in theological dialogue. Therefore, it depends on a carefully constructed, well-balanced circle of participants who can commit to being present for the entire convening—which may extend to five days. All members of that circle are scholar-believers who are practitioners either of Islam or of Christianity.

"Eating together definitely enhances the experience of the seminars," Susan Eastman notes. "Some of the richest and most provocative conversations happen at meals." Plenary sessions (some of which may be open to the public but most of which are closed) provide opportunities to hear and discuss pairs of learned lectures meant to offer Muslim and Christian perspectives on aspects of the overarching theme or to provide context for the material to be studied.

Central to the Seminar's method is that its primary activity, to which the daily schedule devotes a substantial number of hours, is the dialogical close reading of passages from scripture and (some years) from other relevant texts. This takes place in preassigned "small groups" of seven or eight scholars, one of whom is predesignated as moderator. "Having the honor of chairing a small group has been the most rewarding aspect of my involvement with the Building Bridges Seminar," one of the Muslim scholars has noted. These small-group sessions afford Christians an opportunity to study the Bible with Muslims and for Muslims to study the Qur'an with Christians. It also provides for (and encourages) Christians to sort out issues of interpretation among themselves—and for Muslims to do likewise—with adherents of the other religion looking on. The project has been distinguished by a propensity to seek "understanding of a particular kind," as Rowan Williams explained at the 2012 convening—that is, to practice "a *patience* in dialogue that is fundamentally oriented towards getting to know one another's hearts."[14]

Preparation is expected. Participants go about that in a number of ways. The theme is announced in the letter of invitation; a booklet of texts comes later—ideally, a month before the Seminar is to begin. "When I learn what the theme will be, I find and read at least one to two articles on that subject to get a basic overview and refresh my memory," Tuba Işık explains. "Once I have received the text booklet, I go through all the verses one by one, reading each verse in my native languages and reading a work of *tafsir* on each verse."

Says Susan Eastman, "My preparation for seminars depends on what I will be doing for the seminar. I often am part of the planning team, so preparation includes brainstorming about which scriptural texts to include in the booklet of texts. I also may spend considerable time reflecting on particular texts in my tradition. Each evening of the seminar I read through all the texts for the next day and try to highlight those I find most intriguing or difficult."

"I'm typically part of the team of Christian scholars that selects the biblical texts for study," Christopher Hays explains.

> After that, I write one of the papers to introduce some of the texts to the larger group. Writing that piece is a unique sort of exercise, unlike writing a typical academic article, because you can assume that all of your listeners are at once very astute scholars of religion who simultaneously have very little familiarity with your faith. So I spend a lot of time sifting my data, separating the things that I would need to say to cover my flank academically from the things that are genuinely important for a Muslim scholar to know. That means that, by the time I get to the seminar, I've made an effort to put myself in the shoes of my Muslim friends, which helps me be a better dialogue partner.

The Seminar advocates a particular approach to the small-group process. The members of the group settle themselves. Each person points out a word or phrase (or more) that provokes or delights in some way. The moderator looks for common threads, then posits an agenda. Assuming that the group concurs, someone reads the first selection aloud. (Some groups prefer to hear it in its original language. It is commonplace for a Qur'an passage to be read aloud in Arabic. Only occasionally has someone read a Bible passage aloud in Hebrew or Greek.) Free discussion ensues. At the appointed hour, all groups gather in plenary for a period of sharing their most interesting insights or conundrums.

"Each Seminar enables me to spend several days with more than two-dozen Christian and Muslim scholars who take their traditions seriously, discussing some of our time's most profound theological questions," says Ahmet Alibasic, who has served as a small-group moderator.

> I learn so much about the two traditions and their diversity during those in-depth discussions. During each of the nine seminars I have attended, I have challenged other participants and I myself have been challenged. Often, this has meant that I've had to revisit some of my readings and venture into other ones. I could have done that sort of text studying on my own. However, as a Building Bridges colleague recently noted, the Seminar gives us proximity to other scholars—and that always makes the journey through the texts much shorter.

Younus Mirza (Georgetown University and Shenandoah University), a participant in 2022, quickly saw the value of small-group work. He was appreciative of the intentionality of the Seminar "about understanding texts within an interpretative tradition and how that scripture has a functional role within a society and theology. The texts in many ways 'ground' or 'anchor' the seminar as discussions could go in a myriad of ways."[15] Small-group work, he says, "made me more interested in Christian texts that I had heard of but had not studied in any depth or with scholars of the religion. In particular, I was fascinated by the story of the Prodigal Son. The parable made me reflect on the Islamic tradition where there are similar stories regarding fathers, sons and sibling rivalry."[16]

Where some dialogical projects strive toward the issuance of a common statement, the Building Bridges Seminar has always eschewed that goal. Rather, it has seen itself as an exercise in what Daniel Madigan has termed "mutual theological hospitality," which he defines as "part of a longer-term project of learning to do theology first in the presence of the religiously other and then in conversation with the other."[17]

This has its challenges. "Sometimes, disagreements in a small-group discussion can be quite tough," says one of the Christians. "Yet, frequently, discussing points of disagreement generates the most rewarding conversations, leading to real mutual affection and new insights forged through sometimes exhausting discussions. And that leads me to mention a second challenge: the schedule can feel relentless. We are given time for recharging in the early afternoon, which helps considerably."

"On occasion," a Muslim scholar explains, "theological questions arise which I haven't yet contemplated in depth. These are moments of silence for me; moments when I am unable to contribute to the group discussion. However, the fruitful aspect of the overall concept of Building Bridges is the opportunity to clarify these kinds of questions in personal discussions over dinners or during lunchtime walks."

Outcomes

Over the years adjustments have been made to the Seminar's methodology—primarily, as Madigan explains, "to avoid the tendency to gloss over particularity and difference."[18] For example, in the first convenings, passages from the Bible and the Qur'an tended to be grouped together (or even paired). A small-group session would then involve close reading of material from both the Islamic and Christian traditions. In recent years, especially when considering a theological theme, the schedule calls for focus on one religion per day (or, at least, per session).

Noting that Miroslav Volf has called Islam and Christianity "contending particular universalisms," Daniel Madigan asserts that

> contention is a founding aspect of the relationship between Muslims and Christians in the sense that it could be said that each sees the other as heretical: each recognizes that the other inhabits the same world of religious discourse and appeals to the same history of divine engagement with humanity. Each claims to have the true and correct understanding of who Jesus of Nazareth is and what God intended to do through him. . . . It is difficult to see, therefore, how we can hope to overcome the fundamental contentiousness of our relationship.[19]

Among the Seminar's goals, therefore, is "to make that contention fruitful rather than destructive."[20] As Abdul Rahman Mustafa notes, "the initiative largely privileges theological over overtly political dialogue. This is, it must be said, never an easy distinction to maintain."[21]

Over the years, the Seminar's aptitude for interrogating particularities, for investigating "questions at the very heart of our faith and or our traditions' disagreements," has expanded markedly, Daniel Madigan asserts. The ethos of the Seminar is "to allow others into our own theologizing space. . . . We invite the other into our questioning, not just into our answers."[22] Seminar participants are allowed to witness differences of opinion, not just between Muslims and Christians but between Muslims and Muslims and between Christians and Christians—and that, Madigan believes, is essential to the Building Bridges Seminar process. He explains: "When we acknowledge that neither of us is the proprietor but that we are both guests in God's space, something new in theology can emerge from the openness to mutual questioning."[23] Through the study of texts, participants in the Building Bridges Seminar actually do constructive theology, a point made by Muslim scholar Martin Nguyen of Fairfield University, for whom the 2022 convening was his fifth.[24]

Younus Mirza applauds the ability of the Seminar to give attention to "themes relevant to both Christians and Muslims that will live beyond the current moment."[25] He was pleased that the tone of the 2022 convening was neither apologetic nor polemical. Rather, "real debates emerged between the various participants but not done in a hostile or antagonistic way. Rather the discussions arose out of curiosity and a true desire to understand the different concepts and religious traditions."[26]

It has often been asserted that the Building Bridges Seminar strives not to resolve the differences between Christians and Muslims but rather to improve the quality of our disagreements. Abdul Rahman Mustafa picked up on this, writing that

> Christians and Muslims will always continue to disagree about many things. But there is no reason for this disagreement to be based on a miscommunication, a failure to understand what the other side is actually saying (as opposed to what one side thinks or is told the other is saying) and an arrogance that makes one side think it has nothing to learn from those whose accounts of the world are different from its own. Adopting a posture of receptivity, of an openness to being the object of another's interest, critique, acceptance or rejection, might be considered a vulnerable and undesirable one for believers to inhabit. Perhaps what is required is the cultivation of pious faith rather than nourishing our appetite for skepticism. But for some, the truth of their faith is realized when they are forced to suspend their comfortable and unquestioned ways of thinking and to respond to those whose ways of seeing and living in the world are strange, different, and—perhaps—wrong. There is nothing wrong with thinking that someone else is wrong. But it is better to not have the wrong reasons for thinking so.[27]

Impact

"My twelve years of participation in the Seminar have enhanced my scholarly work both directly and indirectly," says Jane McAuliffe. "I have written and spoken about it as part of my outreach to more general audiences. The varied topics addressed by the seminar and their multifaceted investigation have deepened my understanding of Muslim faith and practice, while simultaneously enriching my experience as a Christian believer."

Tuba Işık says that each time she has attended the Building Bridges Seminar, her theological horizons have been broadened; she has gone home with fresh ideas for the content and structure of the courses she offers; and she has forged new connections that lead to academic collaboration. Many participants would say the same. The Building Bridges Seminar's ripple effect has been far-reaching!

Susan Eastman says that "by far the most rewarding part of my involvement with Building Bridges is the global network of friendships it has generated—both with Muslims and with members of my own Christian faith from very different cultural contexts. This is simply a great and rich gift."

"As I reflect further," she says,

> the quality of our conversations comes to mind—the discussions that happen inside the small groups and also sometimes at meals and elsewhere. It is rare to encounter such depth of theological engagement, which perhaps is intensified and clarified by the fact that it takes place across interfaith lines as well as across disciplines. In the field of New Testament, too often the disagreements about textual interpretation get in the way of talking about the theology in the texts. At the Building Bridges Seminar, we talk about issues of faith that matter. The fact that participants are also practitioners of their faith, and that fellowship of worship and prayer is built into the structure of the seminars seasons and enlivens our discussion. This, in my view, is a key dimension of the relational dynamic of these meetings.

The Seminar, says Christopher Hays,

> has made me more aware of how patient God has been with me—in my own situatedness and despite my own partial and blinkered understanding. It has stretched me to look harder at what I believe and what I assume. So, in that way, I think I now have deeper insights into my own Scriptures and beliefs. Participating in Building Bridges has made me

> want to understand other religions more sympathetically, even affectionately. It also has emboldened me to be clear and kind about what I see, what I don't understand, what I like, and what I find off-putting. That candor, embedded in friendship, has conduced to quicker learning, as our exchanges take place from postures of "faith seeking understanding" as opposed to defensive retrenchment.

The most rewarding aspect of having been a participant, he says, is this:

> I have been loved and cared for by Muslim scholars both during the Seminar and beyond it. When I fell ill one year—I had lost my voice and felt truly like rubbish—a Muslim scholar went out of her way to make me hot tea multiple times a day, even raiding the kitchen at the retreat center for ginger, lemon, and honey to help my sore throat. On another occasion, when my son was visiting Georgetown as a prospective student, a Muslim colleague spent hours showing us around. These were acts of genuine friendship—not mere interreligious performances—and they made deep impressions on me.

Hays continues, "I have also felt moved by the transparency of my Seminar colleagues. Each year, outside of our formal sessions, someone shares their fears, professional struggles, or personal pain with genuine vulnerability. It's an honor to be trusted this way. It speaks to the unique power of how the Building Bridges Seminar structures its work and recruits participants year over year. I know of nothing else like it."

Given increased polarization and radicalization locally and globally, says one participant, the range of places where the Seminar might meet is narrowing; very real external limitations on who can participate are mounting. Yet the bridge-building persists. During the twentieth convening, plans were made for a twenty-first!

In reminiscing about the founding session of the Building Bridges Seminar in January 2002, David Marshall recalled that

> at that point the focus was very much on responding to the events of 9/11 and seeking to offer a model of intelligent and respectful Christian–Muslim conversation in a world where the need for this was urgently felt. Nobody would have guessed how this initiative was going to develop and that it would still be running over twenty years later. The list of those to be thanked is too long to embark upon, but I am deeply grateful to many, many people for their generous contributions to the flourishing of

> Building Bridges. It has been a privilege to play a part. Each seminar is hard work for all those involved, both in the months of preparation and in the intense days of meeting. When we reach the end and go our different ways, it is moving to hear how much the experience has meant and to see the bonds of Muslim–Christian friendship that have grown. Thanks be to God.

Indeed, for two decades, the Building Bridges Seminar has been an exercise in offering and receiving mutual theological hospitality. Sustaining it has been "an act of hope," says Daniel Madigan. However, he stresses, it has also been "an act of love; for the community of scholars that has made up the Seminar is nourished by the friendship that develops when people explore their sacred texts in each other's company."[28]

Notes

Epigraph source: Rowan Williams, Preface to *Death, Resurrection, and Human Destiny: Christian and Muslim Perspectives*, ed. by David Marshall and Lucinda Mosher (Washington, DC: Georgetown University Press, 2014), xxii.

1. For previous retrospectives, see Lucinda Mosher, "A Decade of Appreciative Conversation: The Building Bridges Seminar under Rowan Williams," in *Death, Resurrection, and Human Destiny*, 259–74; and Lucinda Mosher, "Preface: Fifteen Years of Construction: A Retrospective on the First Decade and a Half of the Building Bridges Seminar," in *Monotheism and Its Complexities: Christian and Muslim Perspectives*, ed. by Lucinda Mosher and David Marshall (Washington, DC: Georgetown University Press, 2018), ix–xxiv. Lucinda Mosher, "The Building Seminar: The First Five Years," was composed in late 2007 for a special issue on dialogue planned by an academic journal, then set aside. Instead, in 2010, that essay was posted on the Building Bridges Seminar website and remained there for several years.

2. Michael Ipgrave, ed., *The Road Ahead: A Christian–Muslim Dialogue* (London: Church House, 2002), 1.

3. Gillian Stamp used the term *appreciative conversation* when commenting on the first Building Bridges seminar; see her "And They Returned by Another Route," in *The Road Ahead*, 112, 113.

4. From remarks made by Rowan Williams on March 28, 2006, at a dinner in Washington, DC, during the fifth Building Bridges Seminar.

5. See, particularly, Rowan Williams, "Analysing Atheism: Unbelief and the World of Faiths," in *Bearing the Word: Prophecy in Biblical and Qurʾānic Perspective*, ed. by Michael Ipgrave (New York: Church Publishing, 2005), 1–13.

6. Georgetown University, Washington, DC, was the venue in 2004 and 2006; Georgetown School of Foreign Service–Qatar, in 2010 and 2011.

7. Unless otherwise attributed, this and other comments on the Building Bridges

Seminar are excerpted from correspondence between the editor and members of the Seminar between January and June 2023.

8. Abdul Rahman Mustafa, "Building Bridges," in *BloKK: Der Blog des Zentrums fur Komparative Theologie und Kulturwissenschaften* (blog), September 2, 2022, https://blogs.uni-paderborn.de/zekkblog/2022/09/02/building-bridges/.

9. Daniel A. Madigan, SJ, "The Building Bridges Seminar: Interrogating the Category of Interreligious Studies," in *The Georgetown Companion to Interreligious Studies*, ed. by Lucinda Mosher (Washington, DC: Georgetown University Press, 2022), 335.

10. Rowan Williams, Preface, in *Prayer: Christian and Muslim Perspectives*, eds. David Marshall and Lucinda Mosher (Washington, DC: Georgetown University Press, 2013), xv.

11. Mustafa, "Building Bridges."

12. Madigan, "The Building Bridges Seminar," 340.

13. Regarding the convenings in 2002 through 2022, Daniel Madigan has been present for nineteen of twenty; David Marshall, for eighteen; Jane McAuliffe, for twelve; and Susan Eastman, Lucinda Mosher, and Rowan Williams, for ten. Asma Afsaruddin, Ahmet Alibasic, Michael Ipgrave, and Mona Siddiqui have participated in nine; Lucy Gardner and Recep Senturk, in eight; Michael Nazir-Ali and Philip Sheldrake, in seven; and Jonathan Brown, Maria Massi Dakake, Celia Deane-Drummond, Brandon Gallaher, Mustansir Mir, Esther Mombo, Abdullah Saeed, Christoph Schwöbel, and Tim Winter, in six.

14. Rowan Williams, Preface to *Death, Resurrection, and Human Destiny*, xxii.

15. Younus Mirza, "The Building Bridges Seminar: An Exercise in Relational Theology," in *Maydan*, an online publication of the Abu Sulayman Center for Global Islamic Studies at George Mason University, posted July 28, 2022.

16. Mirza, "The Building Bridges Seminar."

17. Madigan, "The Building Bridges Seminar," 334.

18. Madigan, "The Building Bridges Seminar," 336.

19. Madigan, "The Building Bridges Seminar," 335. See also Miroslav Volf and M. Croasmun, *For the Life of the World: Theology That Makes a Difference* (Grand Rapids, MI: Brazos, 2019), 95–107.

20. Madigan, "The Building Bridges Seminar," 335.

21. Mustafa, "Building Bridges."

22. Madigan, "The Building Bridges Seminar," 335, 338.

23. Madigan, "The Building Bridges Seminar," 336, 339.

24. See Martin Nguyen, "Modern Scripturalism and Emergent Theological Trajectories: Moving Beyond the Qur'an as Text," *Journal of Islamic and Muslim Studies* 1, no. 2 (November 2016): 66–67.

25. As Madigan states, "We have tried to avoid being drawn into that atmosphere of political contentiousness in order to contend with the deeper theological questions that long pre-date and will just as long outlast our current geopolitical situation." Madigan, "The Building Bridges Seminar," 337.

26. Mirza, "The Building Bridges Seminar."

27. Mustafa, "Building Bridges."

28. Madigan, "The Building Bridges Seminar," 335.

Introduction

Without doubt, the themes of divine mercy and graciousness are among the most foundational concepts in the Christian and Islamic traditions and their scriptural witnesses. Mercy might seem more prominent in Islamic discourse than in Christian; grace, more prominent in Christian thought than in Islamic. Yet, in fact, both are present in both. In the Bible's account of pivotal events on Mount Sinai, God passes before Moses and proclaims, "The Lord, the Lord, a God merciful [*raḥūm*] and gracious [*ḥannūn*], slow to anger, and abounding in steadfast love and faithfulness" (Exod. 34:6). In the Qurʾan—which, in the Islamic tradition, is deemed God's speech—the *basmala* ("In the name of God: the compassionate the merciful") is the first verse of the first sura and of each sura thereafter (Sura 9 excepted). It may well function as a reminder that the key to understanding the Qurʾan is mercy.

Indeed, for Christianity and Islam alike, the themes of mercy and graciousness are central to God's self-description. Yet, *within* Christianity and *within* Islam, understandings of mercy and grace are neither straightforward nor univocal, precisely because those concepts are central to Christian and Islamic doctrines of God and the divine–human relationship. It is a small wonder, therefore, that *mercy* and *grace* have generated many a substantial intrareligious theological discussion and dispute. Differences between Christian and Islamic understandings of *mercy* and *grace* might therefore be substantial. Could interreligious examination of these key terms be fruitful?

With this question in mind, the Building Bridges Seminar convened for the twentieth time. Arguably the longest-running international dialogue of Christian and Muslim scholar-believers, the Building Bridges Seminar was initiated in 2002 by George Carey in his role as Archbishop of Canterbury. It was sustained by Rowan Williams, Carey's successor, during his ten years in that office. Since 2012 it has been stewarded by Georgetown University.

For its twentieth convening the Building Bridges Seminar returned to the serene Airlie Center in rural Northern Virginia, a meeting place that had served the project well on three previous occasions (2014, 2016, and 2019). There twenty-six Muslim and Christian scholars spent five days (June 13–17, 2022) engaging in dialogical close reading of preselected passages from the Bible, the Qur'an, and respected hadith collections in preassigned groups of eight. The texts they studied are provided here, along with revised (and, in some cases, expanded) versions of lectures by members of the Seminar, each providing contextualization and clarification of that material.

In a preconvening memo to the Seminar's twentieth roster of scholars, chair Daniel Madigan and academic director David Marshall laid out the concept foundational to the program for that meeting. In it they asserted that one's grasp of the full significance of the terms *mercy* and *grace* will be enhanced if close reading of the scriptures of Christianity and Islam takes cues from key elements of their vocabulary.[1] Investigation of the lexicon and grammar of *mercy* and *grace*, they suggested, benefits from three considerations:

- The terms *mercy* and *grace* apply to the relationship between God and God's creation. This is how God promises to act toward us. All is merciful gift—abundant, gracious, and overflowing. Yet we must be wary of imposing on God our own more constrained and conditioned notions of mercy and gift, but rather seek in what God has revealed of God's self how the graciousness of divine mercy exceeds our own conceptions. Even so, questions remain: are these gifts conditional upon our prior performance? If not, do they at least elicit or even demand a response?
- Christians and Muslims, naturally enough, begin with the gift of mercy they believe God has promised and what that entails for *them*. Yet such an insistently made promise moves us to also consider whether this gracious mercy is more than simply one of God's attributes distinct from others and to be balanced by them, or whether mercy might rather be defining of God's very nature. . . . This might mean considering all of God's attributes as being integral to God's mercy. Mercy always has an object. Mercy is always *for* or *toward* another. So, it cannot be the nature of God in God's self. In the Christian tradition, it is love that is understood to be that essence of God; not just that God is "loving," but that "God is love" (1 John 4:16). Nonetheless, mercy is intimately linked with love; mercy is the

expression in time, directed beyond God to creatures, of that eternal love which is the essence of God.
- Both the Islamic and Christian traditions would recognize that God's gift of mercy aims to transform us so that we too might be merciful, that we might allow our lives to be conformed to the characteristics of God. This third element is the basis—not only of our ethics but also of prayer and the spiritual life.

Those three considerations undergirded the texts studied in 2022, and the essays that introduced them—hence, the contents of this volume.

This book has three sections. In Part One: Muslim Perspectives on Mercy and Grace, the first chapter, "Concepts of Mercy and Grace in the Muslim Tradition: An Overview" by Kenan Musić, orients the reader to the overarching theme. Two exegetical essays follow, each paired with a compendium of the Qur'an passages it has introduced. Thus, we have "Mercy, Grace, and Guidance: The Meccan Suras" by Maria Massi Dakake with "The Meccan Suras on Mercy and Grace: Texts for Study," and Mahan Mirza's "Mercy and Grace in the Medinan Qur'an: An Introduction" with "The Medinan Suras on Mercy and Grace: Texts for Study." Ramon Harvey's "Mercy and Grace in the Islamic Theological Tradition: An Overview" is an orientation to Hadith; in "Mercy and Grace in the Prophetic Tradition: A Close Look at Selected Hadith," Muhammad Modassir Ali introduces those that are provided for study in the final chapter of the section.

This pattern is repeated in Part Two: Christian Perspectives on Mercy and Grace. "Concepts of Mercy and Grace in the Catholic Tradition: An Overview," Julia Lamm's orientational essay, is followed by two exegetical essays paired with collections of the Bible passages they have introduced. Thus we have "Mercy and Grace in the Old Testament: An Introduction" by Jacob Onyumbe with "The Old Testament on Mercy and Grace: Texts for Study," and "Implicit Mercy and Ubiquitous Grace: Examples in the New Testament Gospels and the Letter of James" by Christopher M. Hays with "The Gospels and James on Mercy and Grace: Texts for Study." Veli-Matti Kärkkäinen's "Theology of Grace in the Christian Tradition: Basic Affirmations and Debates" provides further orientation. Finally, Susan Eastman's "Paul on Mercy and Grace: Key Passages; Parallels with Teachings of Jesus" introduces passages provided for study in the chapter to follow.

Most volumes of the Seminar's book series include an essay endeavoring to convey the flavor of the dialogue itself. In this volume that purpose is served by "Mercy and Grace in Virginia: Conversations during the Twentieth

Building Bridges Seminar," a collage of participants' remarks and recollections on themes of the 2022 seminar made available in Part Three: Reflection. Indeed, 2022 was a landmark year for the project, as is acknowledged by this volume's preface: "Two Decades of Mutual Theological Hospitality: Reflections on the Twentieth Anniversary of the Building Bridges Seminar" by rapporteur Lucinda Mosher. The question is often raised: does the impact of the Seminar reach beyond its participants? Part Three includes, therefore, two short pieces by scholars who have never participated in a convening yet have deep interest in this project: Charles Tieszen's "Cultivating Peaceful Proximity: A Scholar-Practitioner's Engagement with the Building Bridges Seminar Book Series" and Syed Atif Rizwan's "A Solid Contribution: An Assessment of a Volume in the Building Bridges Seminar Book Series."

Readers who wish to engage in further exploration of Muslim and Christian perspectives on mercy and grace may find the following resources helpful: *Sin, Forgiveness, and Reconciliation: Christian and Muslim Perspectives*, edited by Lucinda Mosher and David Marshall (Georgetown University Press, 2017); "Sin and Redemption in Christianity and Islam" by Cosmas Ebo Sarbah in *Theological Issues in Christian–Muslim Dialogue*, edited by Charles Tieszen (Pickwick, 2018); *The Vision of Islam* by Sachiko Murata and William C. Chittick (Paragon House, 1994), especially chapters 3 and 5; and *Mercy: The Essence of the Gospel and the Key to Christian Life* by Walter Kasper (Paulist Press, 2014).

Throughout this volume diacritics are employed sparingly. Dates are "CE" unless otherwise indicated. When presenting these essays orally, Muslim scholars were likely to interject the phrase "Peace be upon him" when mentioning Muhammad or any of the other prophets in their tradition. In most instances, this phrase has been edited out. The choice of English translation for Qur'an quotations was left to the discretion of each contributing scholar. Chapter 1 employs Ahmed Ali, *Al-Qur'an: A Contemporary Translation* (Princeton, NJ: Princeton University Press, 1988); chapters 2 and 3, *The Study Quran*; and chapters 4, 5, 6 (to an extent), and 7, M.A.S. Abdel Haleem, *The Quran: English Translation and Parallel Arabic Text* (New York: Oxford University Press, 2004; used by permission; all rights reserved). Throughout, unless otherwise noted, Bible passages are according to the New Revised Standard Version of the Bible, copyright 1989 by the Division of Christian Education of the National Council of the Churches of Christ in the USA (used by permission; all rights reserved).

David Marshall and Daniel Madigan (who, as noted above, are the Seminar's academic director and chair, respectively) were instrumental in establishing the 2022 convening's theme, organizing its roster of scholars, designating the presenters, and (in close conversation with those designees) selecting the texts to be studied. Samuel Wagner, Georgetown University's director of dialogue and Catholic identity, is the Seminar's coordinator—and thus worked closely with the chair, academic director, and rapporteur on a multitude of issues related to the 2022 meeting's planning, conduct, and follow-up.

Gratitude abounds for Georgetown University president John J. DeGioia's steadfast belief in, and ongoing support of, the Building Bridges Seminar. Thanks goes as well to Georgetown University's Berkley Center—which provides a base of operations, an online presence, and an archive for the Seminar, and enables the publication of its proceedings. Finally, thanks are due to Al Bertrand and the staff of Georgetown University Press.

Notes

1. The memo mentions paying particular attention to the Hebrew roots *ḥ-ṣ-d*, *r-ḥ-m*, *ḥ-n-n*, and *ḥ-m-l*; to the Greek terms *chāris*, *didōmi*, *dōrea*, *eleeō*, *oiktiró*, and *splagchnon*; and to the Arabic roots *r-ḥ-m*, *m-n-n*, *n-ʿ-m*, *f-ḍ-l*; *gh-f-r*, ʿ-ṭ-y, *ḥ-n-n*; and *r w ḥ*.

Part One

Muslim Perspectives on Mercy and Grace

1

Concepts of Mercy and Grace in the Muslim Tradition

An Overview

Kenan Music

It is said that during the wanderings of the Israelites in the desert, Musa (Moses)—blessings be upon him—and his people were seized by unbearable thirst. Together they raised their hands to the sky and prayed for rain. Suddenly, to the surprise of Musa and the Israelites, the few clouds that were in the sky parted. The heat increased and their thirst intensified. Musa received revelation that there was a sinner among them who had been in disobedience to God for forty years. It was said to Musa, "Let him stand out from you. Only then will you receive rain." Then Musa addressed everyone: "Among us is a person who has been disobeying dear God for forty years. Let him separate himself from us and we will be saved from dying of thirst."

The sinner to whom Musa was referring was waiting, turning left and right, hoping someone else would answer. When no one answered, he began to sweat, knowing that he was indeed the wrongdoer. If he remained among society, everyone would die of thirst. But if he were cast out, he would be ashamed for the rest of his life. Overwhelmed with a pain he had never before experienced, he tearfully raised his hands to heaven and said to the Creator with sincerity, "My God, have mercy on me! My God, hide my sins! My God, forgive me!"

While Musa and the Israelites were waiting for the sinner to leave them, clouds gathered, and rain descended. Musa asked Allah: "My Allah, you have blessed us with rain, even though the sinner has not come forward!" God answered him: "Musa, due to the repentance of this very person, I have blessed all the people of Israel with rain." Musa wanted to know who this blessed man was, so he asked: "Show me this man, my Allah." And Allah, the Exalted, replied: "O Musa, I have hidden his sins for forty years. Do you think I will expose him now when he has repented?!"[1]

The story I just recounted about Musa, the messenger of God, is from *Kitab At-Tawwabin* by Ibn Qudama. It reflects the general position of grace and mercy in Islamic tradition. Mercy and grace are beyond the capabilities of creatures, although human beings and others are described by them. Divine mercy and grace transcend everything known to us and are absolute in this life. In addition, they are related to happiness and salvation in the hereafter. God, who is Most Merciful and Whose grace is infinite, grants His kindness to humankind first through creation. Guidance to faith provides them with causes of happiness in this life and in the hereafter.[2]

Writing about God's mercy and grace in Islamic tradition is extremely difficult—primarily due to the limits of the human mind, and secondarily because the Creator and the nature of His greatness are beyond human comprehension. Mercy and grace are key Qur'anic concepts in defining the relationship between the Creator and His creation. Within the Islamic tradition, the Qur'an and the Sunnah (lifestyle) of God's Messenger are seen as God's Revelation and are thus considered as the main sources of faith. We can analyze certain terms derived from these sources by observing the frequency of citations and different contexts in which they are mentioned.

Mercy and Grace in the Qur'an

The word *raḥma* is mentioned in the Qur'an more than three hundred times in various forms. All the chapters in the Qur'an, except for the chapter called "Tawba" (repentance), start with "In the Name of God, the Merciful, the Compassionate." Both of God's names mentioned in this opening verse—Raḥman and Raḥim—are derived from the same root. Interestingly, these terms are used in several different contexts. Depending on the context, they may be translated into English as "blessing," "bounty," or "compassion." "Grace" is the English translation of two other terms found in the Qur'an: *niʿma* and *faḍl*. Both *niʿma* and *faḍl* are mentioned in the Qur'an more than one-hundred times, in various contexts and forms. *Faḍl* is sometimes translated as "bounty."

Grace and mercy (*niʿma* or *faḍl* and *raḥma*) are mentioned together in many verses of the Qur'an. Consider, for instance, these four examples, as translated by Ahmed Ali:[3]

- "But God chooses whom He likes for His grace (*raḥma*); and the bounty (*faḍl*) of God is infinite" (Q. 2:105).
- "He may choose whom He likes for His favors (*raḥma*), for great is His bounty (*faḍl*)" (Q. 3:74).

- "And but for the favor (*faḍl*) of God and His mercy (*raḥma*) you would certainly have followed Satan, except a few" (Q. 4:83).
- "So those who believe in God and hold fast to Him shall indeed be received into His mercy (*raḥma*) and His grace (*faḍl*), and be guided to Him the straight path" (Q. 4:175).

In many other verses, grace and mercy are related. However, when we read verses in which they are mentioned separately, their meaning becomes clear. *Raḥma* (mercy), in general, refers to God's blessings, benevolence, and favor bestowed upon His creation. The revelation of the Qur'an, the sending of Muhammad as the last messenger, and his behavior toward his companions are also mercy.

- "What We have sent down of the Qur'an is a healing and a grace (*raḥma*) for the faithful, and adds only loss for the sinners" (Q. 17:82).
- "We have sent you as a benevolence (*raḥma*) to the creatures of the world" (Q. 21:107).
- "It was through God's mercy (*raḥma*) that you dealt with them gently; for had you been stern and hard of heart they would surely have broken away from you. So, pardon them and pray that forgiveness be theirs, and seek their counsel in all affairs, And when you have come to a decision place your trust in God alone, for He loves those who place their trust in Him" (Q. 3:159).
- "Are they the ones who dispense the favor (*raḥma*) of your Lord? It is He who apportions the means of livelihood among them in this world, and raises some in position over the others to make some others submissive. The favors (*raḥma*) of your Lord are better than what they amass" (Q. 43:32).

Alongside the term *mercy* (*raḥma*), the Qur'an sometimes uses the term *guidance* (*hūd*)—as in Q. 6:157, 7:52, 7:203, and 45:20; or *knowledge* (*'ilm*)—as in Q. 40:7. However, these are only two of many possible dimensions. It is important to emphasize that in the Qur'an, mercy embraces everything that exists: "'Enjoin for us good in the world, and good in the world to come. We turn to You alone.' And the Lord said: 'I punish only those whom I will, but My mercy enfolds everything'" (Q. 7:156).

Furthermore, paradise—the reward for faith in God and the performance of good deeds—is described as a *raḥma*. In this context, it may be rendered into English as "mercy," or as "favor," as in the Ahmed Ali translation: "So, those who believed and did good things will be admitted to His favor (*raḥma*) by their Lord. This will be a clear triumph" (Q. 45:30). In the Islamic tradition, to worship God is to wholeheartedly seek His mercy, pray, and stand in front of the Almighty. This is a clear indicator of the highest level of knowledge: knowledge of God: "Can one who prays in the watches of the night, bowing in homage or standing attentive, fearful of the life to come, and hoping for the mercy of his Lord, (be like one who does not)? Say: 'Can those who know, and those who do not know, be equal? Only they think who are wise'" (Q. 39:9).

On the other hand, the term *grace* is mentioned in al-Fātiḥa ("The Opening")—the first chapter of the Qur'an—and is recited by Muslims during the five daily prayers. The path that leads to the Creator and paradise is the path followed by those to whom He has granted His grace (Q.1:7). In many verses of the Qur'an, *ni'ma* (the grace of God and His blessing) and *faḍl* (which has similar meaning) are accompanied by an order from Almighty God to remember them and be aware of them. For example: "O you people, remember the favors of God to you. Is there any creator other than God who gives you food from the heavens and the earth? There is no god but He: how can you turn aside?" (Q. 35:3).[4]

Many of God's gifts are described as grace. For example, spouses and offspring are a special grace and gift from the Almighty: "God has provided mates for you of your own kind, and has bestowed on you sons and daughters from your mates, and has given you good things for food. Will they even then believe in the false and deny God's grace?" (Q. 16:72).

In some cases, Qur'anic verses provide guidance on how to relate and understand God's gifts. This is especially important because God's grace in Islamic tradition is the basis of His relationship with his creation. For example, "If you tried to count God's blessings, you could never take them all in: He is truly most forgiving and most merciful (raḥīm)" (Q. 16:18); and: "Whatever blessings (*ni'ma*) you possess come from God, and when hardship afflicts you, it is to Him alone you cry out for help" (Q. 16:53).[5]

God's gifts are continuous, innumerable, and deserve human gratitude. Therefore, we can say that in the Qur'an, as a source of the Islamic tradition, God's grace is mentioned to remind people to show respect and gratitude for the numerous blessings bestowed upon them: "Indeed God bestows His blessings on people; only most people are not grateful" (Q. 2:243).[6]

Understanding God's grace means not following the paths of evil and Satan. Essentially, Satan's action is focused on human perceptions, but having a firm belief that everything is in God's hands and that His grace is absolute prevents human beings from leaving the right path: "Satan threatens you with want, and orders you (to commit) shameful acts. But God promises His pardon and grace, for God is bounteous and all-knowing" (Q. 2:268).

In Islamic tradition, faith is the ultimate gift and highest blessing from God. Believers should guard and protect this grace from God knowing that it comes only from His divine wisdom and knowledge: "O believers, any one of you who turns back on his faith (should remember) that God could verily bring (in your place) another people whom He would love as they would love Him, gentle with believers, unbending with infidels, who would strive in the way of God, unafraid of blame by any slanderer. Such is the favour of God which He bestows on whomsoever He will. God is infinite and all-knowing" (Q. 5:54).

Mercy and Grace in the Sunnah

A hadith, as a fragment of the Prophet Muhammad's entire life, provides insight into his lifestyle. We have mentioned that he is described in the Holy Qur'an as a "mercy to all the worlds" and that the Qur'an itself is God's mercy. In the modern age, one of the greatest challenges is to look at the life and work of Muhammad through an integral approach that allows us to conclude what is and what is not part of his legacy. This is also the case with the concepts that are the focus of my work, so mercy and grace in this dimension of the Islamic tradition can only be recognized and understood through careful reading and thorough research of the Sunnah. The reason for the creation of humankind, according to the Qur'an, is the worship of God, and in Islamic tradition it is not possible without God's mercy and His grace to achieve this goal. According to a hadith, the Prophet Muhammad described his mission thus: "Indeed, I am a mercy that is gifted!"[7]

Also, his interpretation of the Qur'an and practical guidance emphasized the importance of God's grace and encouraged us to rely on it. It is reported that Muhammad said: "Ask God to grant you His grace! Indeed, the Almighty loves to be asked and the best worship act is waiting for deliverance of harm."[8]

In the Sunnah of the Prophet Muhammad, grace and mercy are the basis of human success and salvation both in this life and in the hereafter. The Sunnah encourages people to do good deeds and to stay away from all that is forbidden and evil. But, ultimately, salvation is not tied to deeds; rather, it is tied to the mercy that the Almighty shows His creatures. Surely, human deeds are essential; but in Islamic tradition they are perceived as a gift from God to people due to the fact He has given us the capability to perform these deeds. Yet, according to one hadith, "Abu Hurayra reported that God's Messenger said: 'There is none whose deeds alone would entitle him to get into Paradise.' It was said to him: 'And, God's Messenger, not even you?' Thereupon he said: 'Not even I, but that my Lord wraps me in Mercy'" (*Sahih* Muslim, 2816c).

Mercy and grace in the Sunnah are related to the will to enjoin good, kindness, and benevolence as well as to getting rid of every affliction or tendency that drives a person to evil while enjoining good to people. Numerous hadiths encourage people to do so. Muhammad recommended people to treat each other in that way because "the believers, in their mutual love, compassion, and sympathy are like a single body; if one of its organs suffers, the whole body will respond to it with sleeplessness and fever."[9]

The environment at the time of Muhammad and his mission was not at all conducive to values such as mercy and grace. Rudeness was unfortunately extremely prevalent among the people; therefore, he suggested in numerous hadiths that this attitude was wrong and needed correction, especially when it came to children and treating them with love and mercy. Some Bedouins came to the Messenger of God and asked: "Do you kiss your children?" He said: "Yes." They then said: "By Allah, we do not kiss them." The Prophet replied: "I cannot help you if God has snatched kindness (*raḥma*) from your hearts" (*Sahih* Muslim 4:1808).

When his son Ibrahim died, the Prophet Muhammad wept and explained that doing so comes from mercy within the heart. He said: "Verily the eyes shed tears and the heart grieves, and we are saddened over your departure oh Ibrahim. But we will not say except that which is pleasing to our Lord."[10]

Since the Sunnah is the practical application of the teachings of the Qur'an, the same meanings we find in the Qur'an can be found in the Sunnah. God's grace has been shown to people, and by God's grace and mercy they can achieve all that is good and beautiful in this world and in the Afterlife. It is especially emphasized that grace and mercy will ultimately be received only by those who have grace in their hearts: "The merciful are shown mercy by al-Raḥmān. Be merciful on the earth, and you will be shown mercy from Who is above the heavens."[11]

Understanding God's Grace and Mercy in Practice

The relationship between God and His creation in Islamic tradition is guided by the Qur'an and Sunnah. Muslim practices are founded on them but remain dynamic as long as they have a general foundation in the Qur'an and Sunnah. For example, in some Muslim communities, before making supplication to God collectively, certain verses are recited, such as "We have sent you as a benevolence (*raḥma*) to the creatures of the world" (Q. 21:107). This is emphasis on mercy—a core value of Islamic tradition—reminds all Muslims that Muhammad was sent as a mercy and benevolence to all creatures.

God's grace is present in the perceptions of Muslims as well as in everyday practices. When Muslims receive blessings, in accordance with Muhammad's practice they say: "Praise be to God by Whose grace good deeds are completed!"[12] So it is crucial to comprehend that all gifts are His and are derived from His divine mercy and grace. In Islamic tradition, God's justice and mercy coexist with balance, at least according to our perception. Muslims view God as immensely merciful but also a just and wise Lord whose commands must be followed. So there is a grace that pervades everything and leaves no one out as well as a grace that is especially intended for those who respond to God and tread the path of devotion to Him.

Additionally, in practice, Muslims experience God's mercy as something that accompanies benefactors. Therefore, when they do good deeds, they become qualified to receive God's grace. This perception and practice is based on the Qur'anic verse "And do not corrupt the land after it has been reformed; and pray to Him in awe and expectation. The blessing of God is at hand for those who do good" (Q. 7:56).

A very important principle in this context, considering mercy and grace, was articulated by a famous scholar and Sufi authority Ibn Ata'illah al-Iskandari when he said: "One of the signs of relying on one's own deeds is the loss of hope when a downfall occurs."[13] This piece of wisdom is the first one in his book of aphorisms and is fundamental in understanding Islam in general. When a person commits sins and feels discouraged, it is a clear sign that they rely on their deeds, not on God's mercy and grace. God's messenger explained this in the hadith mentioned previously: "There is none whose deeds alone would entitle him to get into Paradise. It was said to him: And, Allah's Messenger, not even you? Thereupon he said: 'Not even I, but that my Lord wraps me in Mercy.'"[14]

From everything mentioned above, we can understand that mercy and grace are God's special gifts. They come at times completely undeservedly, sometimes with little effort and at other times with full commitment. Following the guidance of the Qur'an and Hadith, Muslims constantly ask God for His mercy and grace when performing their obligatory prayers, when doing good deeds, or when addressing the Creator in solitude. In Islamic ethics, one's understanding of the notions of mercy and grace is considered a supreme indicator of one's morality and developed awareness of God.

Conclusion

The complexity of the topic of grace and mercy in the Islamic tradition can be greatly mitigated through careful study of the Qur'an and Sunnah. In those sacred sources we see that mercy is an attribute of God that encompasses all of His creatures, while grace is an attribute that can be viewed as a source of special gifts such as faith, trust in God, reliance on Him, and all other noble states of the believer's heart. In the Islamic tradition, human salvation comes through God's grace and mercy, and anything beyond that is simply self-deception. Prayers, good deeds, and human noble states are the condition, not the true reason for human success. Consider the story of a sinner who came to the famous pious woman Rabia and asked, "If I repent to God, will God accept my repentance?" She replied, "If God had accepted your repentance, you would have repented!"[15]

Besides God's love, grace and mercy are core issues in the relationship between God and human beings, and that is why we find it most appropriate to conclude this article with a hadith of the Prophet Muhammad: "God Almighty allotted character between you as He divided provision between you. God Almighty bestows wealth on those He loves and those He does not love. He bestows faith only upon those who He loves."[16]

Notes

1. Muwaffaq al-Din Abu Muhammad 'Abd Allah ibn Ahmad ibn Qudamah, *Kitab At-Tawwabin* (Beirut: Dar Ibn Hazm, 2003), 55.

2. Abu Hamid al-Ghazali, *Al-Maqsad al-Asna* (Cyprus: Al-Gifan, 1987), 63.

3. In this chapter, unless otherwise noted, all Qur'an quotations in English are rendered according to Ahmed Ali, *Al-Qur'an: A Contemporary Translation* (Princeton, NJ: Princeton University Press, 1988).

4. See also Q. 2:47; 2:122; 5:20; 93:11.

5. Q. 16:18 and 53 are rendered according to M.A.S. Abdel Haleem, *The Quran: English Translation and Parallel Arabic Text* (New York: Oxford University Press, 2004).

6. Ahmed Ali translation, edited slightly.

7. Bayhaqi, *Shuab al-iman*, vol. 2 (Riyad:Maktaba ar-rushd, 2002), 372.

8. Tabarani, *Al-Mu'jam al-ewsat*, vol. 3 (Qahire: Dar al-haramayn, 1995), 224.

9. Bukhari, *Sahih*, vol. 10 (Bayrut: Dar Ihya at-turas, 2001), 8.

10. Bukhari, *Sahih*, vol. 2 (Beirut: Dar tawq an-najat), 83.

11. Tirmizi, *Sunan*, vol. 3 (Beirut: Dar al-gharb al-islami, 1998), 388.

12. Tabarani, *Al-Mu'jam al-ewsat*, vol. 6 (Qahire: Dar al-haramayn, 1995), 375.

13. Ibn 'Ata'illah, *The Book of Wisdom* / Kwaja Abdullah Ansari, *Intimate Conversations*, introductions, translations, and notes for *The Book of Wisdom* by Victor Danner and for *Intimate Conversations* by Wheeler M. Thackston (Ramsey, NJ: Paulist, 1978).

14. Muslim, *Sahih*, vol. 4 (Bayrut: Dar Ihya al-turas), 216.

15. Abu'l-Qasim al-Qushayri, *Al-Risala al-Qushayriyya fi 'Ilm al-Tasawwuf*, vol. 1 (Qahire: Dar al-ma'arif), 214.

16. Muhammad al-Bukhāri, *al-Adab al-Mufrad*, no. 275 (Bayrut: Dar al-bashair, 1989).

2

Mercy, Grace, and Guidance

The Meccan Suras

Maria Massi Dakake

In common, nontechnical, religious parlance the terms *mercy* and *grace* are often used more or less interchangeably to connote divine beneficence, favor, blessing, respite, or deliverance. Theologically, of course, the two terms are related, in that grace—if we define it generally as a free and undeserved gift from God—is one way in which God manifests his essential quality of mercy toward human beings. Yet while the concept of mercy pervades the Islamic message at every level and is essential in both traditions, the concept of grace is a fundamental theological term in the Christian context in a way that it is not in the Islamic.

While the meaning of grace has been the topic of important theological disputes in Christianity and is inescapably connected with the Christian doctrine of Christ's sacrifice for the sake of human salvation, the term has no specific theological definition in the Islamic tradition. It does not figure significantly or directly in historical or contemporary theological constructions or debates, and there is not even a singular corresponding Arabic term for it but, rather, multiple terms that approximate it. Although grace is not a theologically specific concept in Islam—and is nowhere near as central in Islam as it is in Christianity—a comparison of the concept of "God's abundant, undeserved gift" as it is found in the two traditions is hardly without merit and is likely to yield some important insights. In this brief article, then, I would like to begin with some general statements about mercy and grace in their Qur'anic context and then offer some more specific thoughts about how these concepts manifest in some of the Meccan Qur'anic passages we will study later.

Regarding mercy, I would argue that the concept of mercy (*raḥma*, and related terms) is so pervasive and "all-encompassing" in the Qur'an that one can take it to be the primary hermeneutical key with which the Qur'an itself suggests we should understand its words. While grace is not tied to a single technical or theological terminology in the Qurʾan, the English word *grace* may be used to render the Qurʾanic Arabic term *niʿma* (closer to "blessing"), and some English translations of the Qurʾan will occasionally use the term *grace* to translate the Qurʾanic term *mercy* (*raḥma*) itself. However, in my view, the Qurʾanic term that most closely approximates grace in the sense of God's abundant and undeserved gifts to his creatures is *faḍl* (a term more typically translated as favor or bounty). The etymological root of *faḍl* has to do with abundance and surplus—the connotation is of something that not only fulfills a need but gives beyond what is needed or deserved or warranted. The Qurʾan tells its audience to seek God's *faḍl* both through their own efforts in the world and through supplication to him (for whatever one attains in the world, regardless of one's own effort, should be seen as the *faḍl* of God; see Q. 4:36, 62:10, 73:20). As the Qurʾan says elsewhere, "Truly *faḍl* is in God's Hand. He grants it to whomever He will" (Q. 3:74)—emphasizing God's complete freedom in granting his bounty and that it is not necessarily tied to what human beings deserve or have earned.

The Qurʾan brings the terms *raḥma* (mercy) and *faḍl* together in various places, telling its audience repeatedly that if it were not for God's *faḍl* and *raḥma*, or "grace and mercy," people would surely have gone astray.[1] This particular formulation, which is mentioned several times in the Qurʾan, suggests that the real spiritual fruit of both grace and mercy is the right guidance that keeps people from "going astray." In fact, I have long thought that the Islamic theological counterpart to divine *grace* in the Christian economy of human salvation is divine guidance (*hudā*, *rushd*). Like grace in the Christian sense, divine guidance is made universally accessible to all human beings, according to the Qurʾan, and is the key to human salvation. Moreover, like grace, the salvific potential of divine guidance requires that it be gratefully received, trusted in, and responded to by human beings. However, while grace in Christian theology is understood as having the potential to liberate human beings from an innate sinfulness, "divine guidance" in the Islamic context saves not by restoring or redeeming human nature (as all human beings are understood to be born pure according to the Islamic concept of *fiṭra*) but by dispelling the illusions of self-sufficiency and independence from God to which all human beings are prone. These false illusions, rather than an innately sinful nature, lead to the arrogance, self-satisfaction, and ingratitude that the Qurʾan presents as the root of human sin and error. In offering the possibility of deliverance from this false consciousness toward a right understanding of God's uniqueness and beneficence and of the corresponding weakness and need of human beings, divine guidance can be understood from an Islamic perspective as God's ultimate mercy and free gift to human beings. All other mercies and graces can be seen as ultimately connected to, and serving the purpose of, guidance.

Mercy as a "Key" to the Qurʾan

One of the names for God in the Qurʾan is al-Wāsiʿ ("The Encompasser"), and throughout the Qurʾan God is said to encompass all things in knowledge but also to encompass all things "in mercy" (see Q. 40:7 and 7:156). Thus, the concept of mercy itself both "encompasses" and pervades every part of the Qurʾan. Mercy and Compassion (both from the same root, *r-ḥ-m*) are the two qualities most commonly predicated of God, and used to name God, in the Qurʾan. Of the many names for God in the Qurʾan, al-Raḥīm (the Merciful) is by far the most common descriptive name of God in the Qurʾan, while al-Raḥmān ("the Compassionate," from the same root) is the only name other than Allāh that the Qurʾan uses as a proper name for God in the grammatical sense.[2] It is sometimes said that the name al-Raḥmān pertains to the universal mercy that God shows to all human beings and is therefore often associated with the gift of creation itself; whereas the name al-Raḥīm refers to the mercy God will show exclusively to the believers on the day of judgment.[3]

As is well known, these two divine names of mercy are invoked along with the name Allāh at the beginning of each Qurʾanic sura with one exception. This invocatory opening formula, *bismi'Llāh al-Raḥmān al-Raḥīm* ("In the Name of God, the Compassionate, the Merciful"), referred to as the *basmalah*, precedes every Qurʾanic sura, with the sole exception of Sura 9 (which is discussed with the Madinan suras). Not only do the individual suras open with an invocation of God as merciful and compassionate, but the Qurʾan as a whole opens with the Fātiḥa, the first Qurʾanic sura, which reads and functions as the fundamental Muslim prayer and in which God's qualities of mercy and compassion are repeatedly invoked. In this sura the *basmalah* is not only a benediction preceding the sura (as it is for other suras) but actually constitutes its first numbered verse, and the divine names Al-Raḥmān and Al-Raḥīm (Compassionate and Merciful) are then repeated again for emphasis in verse 3. It is true that this sura also alludes to God's potentially harsh judgment: in verse 4 he is called the "Master of the Day of Judgment," and in verse 7 a reference is made to those who "incur anger" (presumably, God's anger). But even so, the second half of this short sura takes the form of a hopeful supplication for God's help, guidance, and blessing. The fact that all individual suras (but one) open with the invocation of God as "The Merciful," and that the Qur'an as a whole opens in this way as well with the Fātiḥa, suggests to me that mercy is the lens—the very hermeneutical key—through which the whole of the Qur'an can and should be read.

In many passages of the Qur'an such a reading seems straightforward. God's mercy is repeatedly emphasized in the Qur'an not only through his particular names but also in the myriad acts of mercy and grace or bounty that he is said to show toward his creatures. Indeed, as the Qur'an tells us in two different passages: "God has *prescribed* mercy for himself (*kataba ʿala nafsihi'l-raḥma*)" (Q. 6:12, 6:54)—that is, he has made mercy incumbent upon himself, freely committing himself to approach human beings and all his creatures with compassion. His mercy and compassion are manifest in the Qur'an, in part through the repeatedly mentioned worldly gifts that God provides to human beings—the water from the sky that nourishes them and the animals and plants on which they depend for their sustenance; the cattle that bear their burdens; the day and the night that provide human beings with opportunity and rest by turns; or their spouses "like unto themselves" in whom they find affection and mercy again (Q.30:21). And his mercy is also found in the spiritual favors he grants to human beings, according to the Qur'an—the gift of life itself; patient and repeated warnings against wrongdoing before punishment; forgiveness for those who sincerely repent, even of the greatest sins; and an approach to the judgment of human actions that takes account of human weakness, affording greater weight to good deeds than evil ones.

As I suggested above, however, the greatest of these spiritual gifts is divine guidance and the intellectual capacity to understand it; it is this "gift" and "mercy" that allows human beings to travel safely from the blessings and bounties of this world to the blessings and bounties of the hereafter. Given the importance of guidance as God's gift to humanity, the agents and embodiments of this guidance—the prophets and the scriptures—are often referred to as mercies in themselves. The Prophet Muhammad, especially, is described in the Qur'an as a "mercy to the worlds" (Q. 21:107; 28:46), and Jesus, too, is referred to as a "sign" and a "mercy" for humankind (Q. 19:21). The Qur'an as well as the Torah and the Gospels, are repeatedly said to contain mercy as well as guidance and light (see Q. 6:154–157, 7:52, 7:154, 7:203, 11:17, 12:111, 16:64, 17:86–87).

Yet, as we know, the Qur'an also contains accounts of God's punishing destruction of whole communities who did not heed the warnings of the messengers sent to them, as well as his threats to individuals who refuse to believe, or who associate other deities with him, or who act as corrupt oppressors toward others. And while paradise is elaborately described as a beautiful garden filled with joys and pleasures of all kinds, hell is described in equally elaborate terms as a place of myriad tortures and punishments. One of the peculiar features of the Qur'an is that explicit assertions of God's mercy often sit side by side with passages referencing God's punishment. The last verse of sura 6, for example, says "Truly your Lord is Swift in Punishment [*sarīʿ al-ʿiqāb*] and truly he is Forgiving, Merciful [*ghafūr*[un], *raḥīm*]" (Q. 6:165). In another passage, Abraham tells his idolatrous father that if he persists in his unbelief, he fears that a terrible punishment will befall him from al-Raḥmān, from "the Compassionate" (Q. 19:45). And in Qur'an 7:156, God says: "I cause My punishment to smite whomever I will, though My mercy encompasses all things. I shall prescribe it for those who are reverent and give the alms, and those who believe in Our signs." This verse not only juxtaposes the greatness of God's punishment and the greatness of his mercy, but it also juxtaposes the universality of God's mercy (it encompasses "all things") with its exclusivity (it is specifically prescribed for "the reverent").

An extended example of juxtaposition of divine mercy and punishment is found in Sūrat al-Raḥmān, which is included in full among our readings. As indicated by its name, this sura's thematic focus is the many ways in which God's mercy to human beings (and *jinn*) is manifested through the bounteous gifts (here "boons," *alāʾ*) that he gives to them in both this world and the next. The well-known sura has a distinctive structure, with the rhythmic and rhetorical refrain "which, then, of your Lord's blessing do you two deny? (*fa bi-ayya alāʾi rabbikumā tukadhdhibān*)" repeated after every one or two verses throughout nearly the entire sura. For much of the sura the refrain follows descriptions of the many blessings that God provides both in this world (verses 1–25) and for the pious in the hereafter (from verse 46 to the end).

Sandwiched between descriptions of blessings in this world and those in the next are a set of verses detailing the terrifying events of the last day: the unleashing of fire and smoke, a sky torn apart, the "guilty . . . seized by their foreheads and feet," and finally a hell of flames and scalding water (verses 35–45). Each frightening detail is followed, almost ironically, with the same rhetorical question: "Which, then, of your Lord's blessings do you both deny?" This refrain, suddenly alternating with terrifying images of judgment rather than images of natural beauty, effectively changes the tone of the refrain itself. Instead of being reassuring, it takes on the tone of warning and rebuke: will you continue to deny God's blessings, even when you know that such denial can lead to these terrible consequences?

However, this is the Sūrat al-Raḥmān, the sura of "The Compassionate," and like the other suras, it opens with the invocation of God as merciful and compassionate. How, then, might we read this sura, and these harsh passages within it, using the hermeneutical key of mercy? There are some simple answers that might be suggested. The Qur'anic threat of divine punishment for oppressors and those who commit evil deeds insofar as it may discourage such behavior would obviously be a mercy for human society. The promise that wrongdoers will suffer the consequences of their evil deeds may satisfy the yearning for justice among the oppressed and the victimized. In this way, even these harsh passages can be said, in some way, to serve the cause of mercy.

But, perhaps more fundamentally, we should note that in this sura, the discussion begins and ends with mercy. The mercies and gifts that all human beings enjoy on earth open the sura, while the mercies and gifts that the pious will enjoy in the hereafter draw the sura to its close. The opening and concluding sections describing God's mercies and gifts are longer and more detailed than those describing punishment, accounting for the majority of the sura's verses. Moreover, they completely envelope or encompass the sura's discussion of the terrifying events of apocalypse, judgment, and hellfire. If we attempt to read this sura with mercy as the key, we might understand its frightful descriptions of apocalypse and hell primarily as a warning but meant as a mercy, to ensure that those who take it to heart will steer clear of error and journey safely from the divine gifts in this world to the greater (but more exclusive) ones in the hereafter—to ensure that they remain on the "straight path," the path of divine "blessings," and not the path that goes "astray"—which is the fundamental supplication of all Muslims as they recite the Fātiḥa. The ultimate manifestation of God's mercy, then, is not the divinely provided trees and gardens and rivers (either here or in the hereafter) but rather the opportunity that God's various mercies and gifts provide for human gratitude and for guidance, particularly when paired with warnings about the consequences of denying these gifts.

We see a similar pattern in the short pericope found in the Qur'anic passage from Sūrat al-Isrā' in our readings. In the opening of this passage there is reference to God's mercy in providing human beings with the ability to traverse the seas for their livelihood. The passage opens with a statement of God's mercy and his "bounty" (*faḍl*). It reads: "It is your Lord who makes ships go smoothly for you on the sea so that you can seek His bounty [*faḍl*]: He is most merciful [raḥīm^{an}] to you" (Q. 17:66). This hopeful beginning, referencing both God's bounty and his mercy, is then followed by a divine chastisement. For when the ships fail to "go smoothly" and suddenly experience danger at sea, the false gods worshiped by human beings "desert them" (that is, they are shown to be nothing at all) and it is only God who brings them safely back to land. But instead of being grateful for their deliverance, they "turn away." The image of a ship sailing upon calm waters and then suddenly in distress is one that the Qurʾan invokes multiple times (see Q. 10:22–23, 31:31–33; 29:65), and it serves as a potent symbol for the false sense of security human beings have in the world and how easily it can be shaken. While the ship's passengers traverse calm waters, the water's power and destructive potential can easily be forgotten, allowing them to see the limited space of the ship itself as a secure home: steady, certain, protected, and protective. But once the storm comes, they realize how fragile and impermanent the ship (like the world) truly is, how incapable it is of protecting them, and they turn to the one God alone who can save them. The temporary safety of the ship has created the illusion of self-sufficiency and thus forgetfulness of God. Once this false sense of security is shattered by the tempest, they are terrified but also disabused of their illusions and able to see clearly again. At least, that is, until they have been safely returned to shore, whereupon they quickly fall back into their state of heedlessness. God's merciful deliverance in their moment of desperation has not in itself engendered lasting guidance, it would seem. And so the passage doubles down on its warning: do you think you are safe now that you are on land, it chides the ungrateful passengers; could not the earth itself swallow you up, might you not be overrun by a vicious sandstorm? What if you were to go back out to sea and God were to send a violent storm against you as a punishment for the ingratitude you showed the first time he delivered you? This time, the Qurʾan warns, "you will find no helper against Us" (Q. 17:69).

Immediately after this warning, however, the Qurʾan resumes its discussion of God's gifts to human beings, saying: "We have honored the children of Adam and carried them by land and sea: We have provided good sustenance for them and favored them (*faḍḍalnāhum*) above many of those We have created" (Q. 17:70). As in Sūrat al-Raḥmān, the dire warnings about God's destructive and punitive capability in this passage are preceded and followed by assurances of God's mercy and *faḍl*. The threats of divine punishment are *textually* enveloped and encompassed by assertions of God's mercy, reflecting and reinforcing the Qurʾanic assertion that God's mercy encompasses all things, in reality.

Grace and Guidance

The mercy and *faḍl* (bounty/grace) that God grants to human beings includes, as noted above, both worldly gifts that provide sustenance and comfort, and spiritual gifts, including prophetic messengers and revelatory books.

Both, however, are ultimately sources of guidance—the first indirectly, by making people aware of God's beneficence and their indebtedness to him, and the second more directly, by guiding them toward a clear understanding of the relationship between God and human beings, and human beings' obligation to him. As the Qur'an repeatedly reminds us, though, both forms of guidance—direct and indirect—are frequently rejected or ignored by human beings, to their own detriment and peril. While these "gifts" may seem freely given, they are also opportunities for guidance that require appropriate human responses. Should they be rejected or ignored, they may not only be taken away (like the safety on the ship), they may also serve as damning testaments to a person's ingratitude in the face of these freely given gifts.

This is clearly seen in the parable of the two gardeners from Sūrat al-Kahf 18:32–45. In this passage one man is given a garden of tremendous abundance—two gardens, in fact!. Like the two gardens of paradise described in Sūrat al-Raḥmān, this doubling can be understood to signify abundance (*faḍl*), the presence of more than is needed, and effortless propagation. The man's response to this gift, however, is exactly the wrong one. He imagines that the garden will "never perish," and he even assures himself that if he were to die, God would certainly give him even more in the hereafter—a delusion rooted in the false but perennially tempting assumption that good fortune in this world is a sign of divine approval and therefore portends even greater reward in the next. He sees the garden not as an undeserved gift for which he should be grateful (and which might be taken away at any moment) but as something he rightly deserves and will always have. Moreover, he deepens his wrongdoing by arrogantly lording his abundant gifts over his poorer neighbor. What his poorer neighbor lacks in wealth, however, he more than makes up for in gratitude and the discernment that whatever he has—a lot or a little—is from God. He has hope that his Lord "may well give [him] something better" than his neighbor's garden, but he never assumes it is something he deserves or can expect. He chastises his wealthy neighbor for his ingratitude and warns that all he has been given might be taken away—and so it is. At the end of this parable, the wealthy gardener's fruit is "completely destroyed," and as he watches it "droop on the trellises" he "wrings his hands"—a gesture of his own helplessness, finally realized. His fruit withering on the vine serves as a potent symbol for divine gifts squandered and blighted through arrogance, self-delusion, and ingratitude.

The Qur'an also offers examples of those who, like the poorer gardener, begin with gratitude for the worldly blessings and guidance they have been given and then beseech God for more but with an attitude of humility and trust rather than arrogance and entitlement. In Sūrat al-Kahf, for example, the youths (sleepers) in the cave have already been properly guided to belief in God and bravely resist the king's efforts to turn them toward polytheism. Facing persecution, they call upon God to show them "mercy" and to provide them with the guidance to escape their ordeal. God delivers them in an extraordinary way while also "increasing them in guidance (*wa-zidnāhum hud*[an])" as a reward for their faithfulness.

Finally, in Sūrat Maryam, in which God is referred to by the name al-Raḥmān (the Compassionate) more than anywhere else, we find Zachariah praying to God for the gift of an heir to succeed him in his old age. He prays with desperation, for he is old and fears there is not much time left, but he also prays with deep trust in God's power and beneficence, and gratitude for what he has already been given by God, prefacing his request with the statement: "never, Lord, have I prayed to You in vain." In this sura the already blessed, pious, and rightly guided lives of both Zachariah and Mary yield the further, unexpected gift of prophetic sons—born to Zachariah's wife when she seems too old and to Mary when she seems too young. God's gift is free and unconstrained, even by the normal limits of nature. Moreover, Zachariah's son John is a true *faḍl*, an abundant grace—not only because he is a suitable heir, endowed with wisdom and devotion, according to this passage, but also because he is tender, obedient, and kind to his parents. Mary's son, Jesus, is born through great trial to herself, but this son, too, is an abundant gift—not only a prophet and a "mercy" to all humankind but also a devoted and loving son toward his mother. Zachariah and especially Mary are granted important sons with weighty prophetic missions for the guidance of humanity, but they are also granted loving and tender sons who bestow upon them the more ordinary kinds of comfort that parents hope for from their children. John and Jesus are abundant gifts, sources of guidance for humankind but also sources of filial delight for their parents. Such mundane blessings, the Qur'an assures us, no matter how small or ordinary they may seem, are never too trivial to be beyond the concern of a merciful God. Mercy, grace, and guidance redound upon one another, and are bound up with one another inextricably—certainly in the lives of the prophets and the saints, according to the Qur'an, but also potentially in the lives of all those who respond with gratitude.

Notes

1. Q. 2:64, 105, 3:74, 4:83, 4:175, 10:58, 24:10, 24:14, 24:20, 24:21. Some Arabic philologists have indicated that God's mercy (*raḥma*) toward human beings refers to the blessing

and *faḍl* he grants them. See, for example, the eleventh-century work by al-Rāghib al-Iṣfahānī, *Muʿjam mufradāt alfāẓ al-Qurʾān* (accessed at altafsir.com).

2. The name al-Raḥīm is found 125 times in the Qurʾan specifically as a quality of God. The only names that come close to al-Raḥīm in frequency are "the Forgiving (al-Ghafur)," which occurs 96 times, and "the Mighty (al-ʿAziz)," which occurs 87 times. On al-Raḥmān as a proper name, see Q. 13:30, 17:110, 19:18, 19:26, 19:45, 19:58, 19:75, 19:78, 19:87–93, 19:96, 20:5, 20:90, 20:108–9, 21:26, 21:36, 21:112, 25:26, 25:59–60, 25:63, 27:30, 36:11, 36:15, 36:23, 36:52, 41:2, 43:17–20, 43:33–36, 43:45, 43:81, 50:33, 55 (*sura* title and v. 1), 59:22, 67:19–20, 67:29, 78:37–38.

3. The Andalusian mystic, Ibn ʿArabi, for example, understands the whole of the cosmos as being generated by "the Breath of the All-Merciful" (*nafas al-Raḥmān*), which also, of course, recalls the Qurʾanic accounts of the creation of Adam and Jesus. For a discussion of this, see William C. Chittick, *The Self-Disclosure of God: Principles of Ibn ʿArabi's Cosmology* (Albany: State University of New York Press, 1998), 69–70. On al-Raḥīm as the mercy God will show exclusively to the believers on the day of judgment, see al-Raghib al-Isfahani, *Muʿfam mufradat alfaz al-Qurʾan*.

3

The Meccan Suras on Mercy and Grace

Texts for Study

The Qur'an passages presented here are according to the translation by M.A.S. Abdel Haleem (Oxford: Oxford University Press, 2004).

al-Fātiḥa (1) 1–7

[1]In the name of God, the Lord of Mercy, the Giver of Mercy! [2]Praise belongs
to God, Lord of the Worlds, [3]the Lord of Mercy, the Giver of Mercy, [4]Master
of the Day of Judgement. [5]It is You we worship; it is You we ask for help.
[6]Guide us to the straight path: [7]the path of those You have blessed, those who
incur no anger and who have not gone astray.

al-Anʿām (6) 12

Say, "To whom belongs all that is in the heavens and earth?" Say, "To God. He has taken it upon Himself to be merciful. He will certainly gather you on the Day of Resurrection, which is beyond all doubt. Those who deceive themselves will not believe."

al-Anʿām (6) 54

When those who believe in Our revelations come to you [Prophet], say, "Peace be upon you. Your Lord has taken it on Himself to be merciful: if any of you has foolishly done a bad deed, and afterwards repented and mended his ways, God is most forgiving and most merciful."

al-Isrā' (17) 66–70

[66][People], it is your Lord who makes ships go smoothly for you on the sea so that you can seek His bounty: He is most merciful towards you. [67]When you get into distress at sea, those you pray to besides Him desert you, but when He brings you back safe to land you turn away: man is ever ungrateful. [68]Can you be sure that God will not have you swallowed up into the earth when you are back on land, or that He will not send a sandstorm against you? Then you will find no one to protect you. [69]Or can you be sure that He will not send you back out to sea, and send a violent storm against you to drown you for being so ungrateful? You will find no helper against Us there. [70]We have honored the children of Adam and carried them by land and sea; We have provided good sustenance for them and favored them specially above many of those We have created.

al-Kahf (18) 9–25

[9][Prophet], do you find the Companions in the Cave and al-Raqim so wondrous, among all Our other signs? [10]When the young men sought refuge in the cave and said, "Our Lord, grant us Your mercy, and find us a good way out of our ordeal," [11]We sealed their ears [with sleep] in the cave for years. [12]Then We woke them so that We could make clear which of the two parties was better able to work out how long they had been there.

[13][Prophet], We shall tell you their story as it really was. They were young men who believed in their Lord, and We gave them more and more guidance. [14]We gave strength to their hearts when they stood up and said, "Our Lord is the Lord of the heavens and earth. We shall never call upon any god other than Him, for that would be an outrageous thing to do. [15]These people of ours have taken gods other than Him. Why do they not produce clear evidence about them? Who could be more unjust than someone who makes up lies about God? [16]Now that you have left such people, and what they worshipped instead of God, take refuge in the cave. God will shower His mercy on you and make you an easy way out of your ordeal."

[17]You could have seen the [light of the] sun as it rose, moving away to the right of their cave, and when it set, moving away to the left of them, while they lay in the wide space inside the cave. (This is one of God's signs: those people God guides are rightly guided, but you will find no protector to lead to the right path those He leaves to stray.) [18]You would have thought they were awake, though they lay asleep. We turned them over, to the right and

the left, with their dog stretching out its forelegs at the entrance. If you had seen them, you would have turned and run away, filled with fear of them.

[19]In time We woke them, and they began to question one another. One of them asked, “How long have you been here?” and [some] answered, “A day or part of a day,” but then [others] said, “Your Lord knows best how long you have been here. One of you go to the city with your silver coins, find out where the best food is there, and bring some back. But be careful not to let anyone know about you: [20]if they found you out, they would stone you or force you to return to their religion, where you would never come to any good.”

[21]In this way We brought them to people’s attention so that they might know that God’s promise [of resurrection] is true and that there is no doubt about the Last Hour, [although] people argue among themselves. [Some] said, “Construct a building over them: their Lord knows best about them.” Those who prevailed said, “We shall build a place of worship over them.” [22][Some] say, “The sleepers were three, and their dog made four,” others say, “They were five, and the dog made six”—guessing in the dark—and some say, “They were seven, and their dog made eight.” Say [Prophet], “My Lord knows best how many they were.” Only a few have real knowledge about them, so do not argue, but stick to what is clear, and do not ask any of these people about them; [23]do not say of anything, “I will do that tomorrow,” [24]without adding, “God willing,” and, whenever you forget, remember your Lord and say, “May my Lord guide me closer to what is right.” [25][Some say], “The sleepers stayed in their cave for three hundred years,” some added nine more.

al-Kahf (18) 32–45

[32]Tell them the parable of two men: for one of them We made two gardens of grape vines, surrounded them with date palms, and put corn fields in between; [33]both gardens yielded fruit and did not fail in any way; We made a stream flow through them, [34]and so he had abundant fruit. One day, while talking to his friend, he said, “I have more wealth and a larger following than you.” [35]He went into his garden and wronged himself by saying, “I do not think this will ever perish, [36]or that the Last Hour will ever come—even if I were to be taken back to my Lord, I would certainly find something even better there.” [37]His companion retorted, “Have you no faith in Him who created you from dust, from a small drop of fluid, then shaped you into a man? [38]But, for me, He is God, my Lord, and I will never set up any partner with Him. [39]If only, when you entered your garden, you had said, ‘This is

God's will. There is no power not [given] by God.' Although you see I have
less wealth and offspring than you, [40]my Lord may well give me something
better than your garden, and send thunderbolts on your garden from the sky,
so that it becomes a heap of barren dust; [41]or its water may sink so deep into
the ground that you will never be able to reach it again." [42]And so it was: his
fruit was completely destroyed, and there he was, wringing his hands over
what he had invested in it, as it drooped on its trellises, and saying, "I wish
I had not set up any partner to my Lord." [43]He had no forces to help him
other than God—he could not even help himself. [44]In that situation, the
only protection is that of God, the True God: He gives the best rewards and
the best outcome.

[45]Tell them, too, what the life of this world is like: We send water down
from the skies and the earth's vegetation absorbs it, but soon the plants turn
to dry stubble scattered about by the wind: God has power over everything.

Maryam (19) 1–33

[1]*Kaf Ha Ya Ayn Sad*

[2]This is an account of your Lord's grace towards His servant, Zachariah,
[3]when he called to his Lord secretly, saying, [4]"Lord, my bones have weak-
ened and my hair is ashen grey, but never, Lord, have I ever prayed to You
in vain: [5]I fear [what] my kinsmen [will do] when I am gone, for my wife is
barren, so grant me a successor—a gift from You—[6]to be my heir and the
heir of the family of Jacob. Lord, make him well pleasing [to You]." [7]"Zachariah, We bring you good news of a son whose name will be John—We have
chosen this name for no one before him." [8]He said, "Lord, how can I have
a son when my wife is barren, and I am old and frail?" [9]He said, "This is
what your Lord has said: 'It is easy for Me: I created you, though you were
nothing before.'"

[10]He said, "Give me a sign, Lord." He said, "Your sign is that you will not
[be able to] speak to anyone for three full [days and] nights." [11]He went out
of the sanctuary to his people and signaled to them to praise God morning
and evening.

[12][We said], "John, hold on to the Scripture firmly." While he was still
a boy, We granted him wisdom, [13]tenderness from Us, and purity. He was
devout, [14]kind to his parents, not domineering or rebellious. [15]Peace was on
him the day he was born, the day he died, and it will be on him the day he
is raised to life again.

[16]Mention in the scripture the story of Mary. She withdrew from her

family to a place to the east [17]and secluded herself away; We sent Our Spirit to appear before her in the form of a perfected man. [18]She said, "I seek the Lord of Mercy's protection against you: if you have any fear of Him [do not approach]!" [19]but he said, "I am but a Messenger from your Lord, [come] to announce to you the gift of a pure son." [20]She said, "How can I have a son when no man has touched me? I have not been unchaste," [21]and he said, "This is what your Lord said: 'It is easy for Me—We shall make him a sign to all people, a blessing from Us.'" And so it was ordained: she conceived him. She withdrew to a distant place [23]and, when the pains of childbirth drove her to [cling to] the trunk of a palm tree, she exclaimed, "I wish I had been dead and forgotten long before all this!" [24]but a voice cried to her from below, "Do not worry: your Lord has provided a stream at your feet [25]and, if you shake the trunk of the palm tree towards you, it will deliver fresh ripe dates for you, [26]so eat, drink, be glad, and say to anyone you may see: 'I have vowed to the Lord of Mercy to abstain from conversation, and I will not talk to anyone today.'"

[27]She went back to her people carrying the child, and they said, "Mary! You have done something terrible! [28]Sister of Aaron! Your father was not an evil man; your mother was not unchaste!" [29]She pointed at him. They said, "How can we converse with an infant?" [30][But] he said: "I am a servant of God. He has granted me the Scripture; made me a prophet; [31]made me blessed wherever I may be. He commanded me to pray, to give alms as long as I live, [32]to cherish my mother. He did not make me domineering or graceless. [33]Peace was on me the day I was born, and will be on me the day I die and the day I am raised to life again." [34]Such was Jesus, son of Mary.

[This is] a statement of the Truth about which they are in doubt.

al-Raḥmān 55

[1]It is the Lord of Mercy [2]who taught the Qur'an. [3]He created humankind [4]and taught [humankind] to communicate. [5]The sun and the moon follow their calculated courses; [6]the plants and the trees submit to His designs; [7]He has raised up the sky. He has set the balance [8]so that you may not exceed in the balance: [9]weigh with justice and do not fall short in the balance. [10]He set down the Earth for His creatures, [11]with its fruits, its palm trees with sheathed clusters, [12]its husked grain, its fragrant plants. [13]Which, then, of your Lord's blessings do you both deny?

[14]He created humankind out of dried clay, like pottery, [15]the jinn out of smokeless fire. [16]Which, then, of your Lord's blessings do you both deny?

[17]He is Lord of the two risings and Lord of the two settings. [18]Which, then, of your Lord's blessings do you both deny?

[19]He released the two bodies of [fresh and salt] water. They meet, [20]yet there is a barrier between them they do not cross. [21]Which, then, of your Lord's blessings do you both deny?

[22]Pearls come forth from them: large ones, and small, brilliant ones. [23]Which, then, of your Lord's blessings do you both deny?

[24]His are the moving ships that float, high as mountains, on the sea. [25]Which, then, of your Lord's blessings do you both deny?

[26]Everyone on earth perishes; [27]all that remains is the Face of your Lord, full of majesty, bestowing honor. [28]Which, then, of your Lord's blessings do you both deny?

[29]Everyone in heaven and earth entreats Him; every day He is at work. [30]Which, then, of your Lord's blessings do you both deny?

[31]We shall attend to you two huge armies [of jinn and humankind]. [32]Which, then, of your Lord's blessings do you both deny?

[33]Jinn and humankind, if you can pass beyond the regions of heaven and earth, then do so: you will not pass without Our authority. [34]Which, then, of your Lord's blessings do you both deny?

[35]A flash of fire and smoke will be released upon you and no one will come to your aid. [36]Which, then, of your Lord's blessings do you both deny?

[37]When the sky is torn apart and turns crimson, like red hide. [38]Which, then, of your Lord's blessings do you both deny?

[39]On that Day neither humankind nor jinn will be asked about their sins. [40]Which, then, of your Lord's blessings do you both deny?

[41]The guilty will be known by their mark and will be seized by their foreheads and their feet. [42]Which, then, of your Lord's blessings do you both deny?

[43]This is the Hell the guilty deny, [44]but they will go round between its flames and scalding water. [45]Which, then, of your Lord's blessings do you both deny?

[46]For those who fear [the time when they will] stand before their Lord there are two gardens. [47]Which, then, of your Lord's blessings do you both deny?

[48]With shading branches. [49]Which, then, of your Lord's blessings do you both deny?

[50]With a pair of flowing springs. [51]Which, then, of your Lord's blessings do you both deny?

[52]With every kind of fruit in pairs. [53]Which, then, of your Lord's blessings do you both deny?

54 They will sit on couches upholstered with brocade, the fruit of both gardens within easy reach. 55 Which, then, of your Lord's blessings do you both deny?

56 There will be maidens restraining their glances, untouched beforehand by man or jinn. 57 Which, then, of your Lord's blessings do you both deny?

58 Like rubies and brilliant pearls. 59 Which, then, of your Lord's blessings do you both deny?

60 Shall the reward of good be anything but good? 61 Which, then, of your Lord's blessings do you both deny?

62 There are two other gardens below these two. 63 Which, then, of your Lord's blessings do you both deny?

64 Both of deepest green. 65 Which, then, of your Lord's blessings do you both deny?

66 With a pair of gushing springs. 67 Which, then, of your Lord's blessings do you both deny?

68 With fruits—date palms and pomegranate trees. 69 Which, then, of your Lord's blessings do you both deny?

70 There are good-natured, beautiful maidens. 71 Which, then, of your Lord's blessings do you both deny?

72 Dark-eyed, sheltered in pavilions. 73 Which, then, of your Lord's blessings do you both deny?

74 Untouched beforehand by man or jinn. 75 Which, then, of your Lord's blessings do you both deny?

76 They will all sit on green cushions and fine carpets. 77 Which, then, of your Lord's blessings do you both deny? 78 Blessed is the name of your Lord, full of majesty, bestowing honor.

4

Mercy and Grace in the Medinan Qurʾan

An Introduction

Mahan Mirza

Mecca and Medina are distinct contexts for revelation, a historic fact that has been recognized in both traditional Islamic and modern Western scholarship. The hijra, or emigration from Mecca to Medina, marks the beginning of the Islamic calendar (622 CE). Muhammad's role in Mecca contrasts with Medina, described as prophetic in one, political in the other.[1] The Meccan Qurʾan has its own flavor when compared to the Medinan Qurʾan: rhythmic and apocalyptic in the former, prosaic and legalistic in the latter.

It has been said that mercy is a hermeneutic key for interpreting Muslim scripture in every context, and for good reason. The first sura of the Qurʾan, al-Fatiha, foregrounds al-Raḥmān and al-Raḥīm—translated varyingly as "the Compassionate, the Merciful" (Nasr et al.); "Lord of Mercy, Giver of Mercy" (M.A.S. Abdel Haleem); "the Beneficent, the Merciful" (Pickthall); "Most Gracious, Most Merciful" (Yusuf Ali); "the Mercygiving, the Merciful" (T. B. Irving)[2]—repeating these names/attributes of God in the second verse after already having them appear in the *basmalah*, the formula "In the Name of God, al-Raḥmān, al-Raḥīm" that appears at the beginning of every sura, except for one.

Al-Ḥashr, a Medinan sura that offers the largest number of God's attributes in a single cluster, also foregrounds these two attributes of mercy (Q. 59:22–24). The Meccan Anʿām explicitly says: "He has prescribed Mercy for Himself" (Q. 6:12). A verse in al-Isrāʾ, a late Meccan sura, proclaims: "Call upon God, or call upon the Compassionate (al-Raḥmān). Whichever you call upon, to Him belong the Most Beautiful Names" (Q. 17:110).

In a paper titled "Mercy: The Stamp of Creation," Dr. Umar Faruq Abd-Allah writes that God's mercy "constitutes his primary relation to the world from its inception through eternity, in this world and the next."[3] In this chapter, I introduce the texts from the Medinan Qurʾan that were selected for study by the 2022 Building Bridges Seminar and are available for further study here as chapter 5. The terms *mercy* (*raḥma*) and *grace* (*faḍl*) are prominent in each, of course. Additionally, these selections address seven broad themes.

Polemics

Sura 4, al-Nisāʾ, presents a highly charged polemic against Christian theology: "O People of the Book! Do not exaggerate in your religion, nor utter anything concerning God save the truth. Verily, the Messiah, Jesus son of Mary, was only a messenger of God, and His Word, which He committed to Mary, and a Spirit from Him. So believe in God and His messengers, and say not 'Three.' Refrain!" (Q. 4:171). This admonition soon gives way to a conciliatory note: "Then, as for those who believe and did good works He will give due rewards and more of His bounty (*faḍl*)" (Q. 4:173). And "God will admit those who believe in Him and hold fast to Him into His mercy (*raḥma*) and favor (*faḍl*); He will guide them towards Him on a straight path" (Q. 4:175).

Contrast the exclusivist polemic with a softer—if not altogether inclusivist—approach in al-Baqara, absent any hint of theological denunciation: "Truly those who believe, and those who are Jews, Christians, and the Sabians—whosoever believes in God and the Last Day and works righteousness shall have their reward with their Lord . . . were it not for God's Bounty upon you, and His mercy, you would have been among the losers" (Q. 2:62–64). And further, in a shorter Medninan sura, al-Ḥadīd: "We sent Jesus, son of Mary, and We gave him the Gospel and placed kindness and mercy in the hearts of those who follow him," followed by a reference to "a twofold portion of His Mercy" for the believers (Q. 57:27–28).

What does it mean for the Qurʾan to be simultaneously polemically charged and conciliatory in theological engagement with Christians? How were these verses received by the Qurʾan's original audience, and how should they be read today in historical hindsight? What is the meaning of the "twofold portion" of God's mercy? While much ink has been spilled in pondering "the salvation of the other" over the ages, these questions are always worth revisiting, especially through the prism of God's mercy and grace.

The Hereafter

Vivid descriptions of the hereafter pervade both Meccan and Medinan Qurʾan. The "final hour" is a pivotal moment for God's mercy and grace but also his wrath: "On the day when you see the believing men and the believing women with their light spreading before them and on the right . . . a wall with a gate will be set down between them [true believers and hypocrites], the inner side of which contains mercy, and the outer side of which lies punishment" (Q. 57:12–14).

Another scene appears in Āl 'Imrān: "On the day when faces whiten and faces blacken. And as for those whose faces whiten, they will be in the Mercy of God, abiding therein" (Q. 3:106–8). Are the "whitening" and "blackening" obvious metaphors? Does our heightened awareness of implicit bias and racism today render the Qur'anic choice of vocabulary discussable in new ways? Moving from the "hereafter" to the "herebefore," so to speak, our readings visit the creation story in a time before time when God's mercy plays a key role in human origins, where it connects to the theme of guidance (*hudā*) (Q. 2:35–37).

Divine Law

One of the distinguishing features of the Prophet's life in Medina is his role as community leader and lawgiver. God's laws, we are told, are merciful, even when they may appear to be otherwise. Retributive justice and the regulation of sexuality feature prominently: "O you who believe! Retribution is prescribed for you in the matter of the slain. . . . That is an alleviation from your Lord, and a mercy" (Q. 2:178). We are told that "in retribution there is life for you O possessors of intellect" (Q. 2:179). What is the life-giving aspect of retribution? Is this privileging a kind of communal life over and above individual life? How do we think about the dignity of a community in relation to the dignity of individuals who comprise a community?

Islamic law regulates how allegations of infidelity are to be managed as an aspect of God's bounty (*faḍl*) and mercy (Q. 24:6–10). If it comes to "my word against yours," adjudication in courts becomes impossible, and the jurisdiction transfers to the divine courts of the hereafter. Justice is not always possible to achieve in this world. Every society has individuals who wield outsized influence on account of their wealth and political connections. Sūrat al-Nūr (24) contrasts God's bounty and mercy with the so-called bounty of people who use their influence to spread indecency (Q. 24:19–22). Elsewhere, we are told to be godlike in our ways: "[Our life] takes its color from God" (Q. 2:138).[4]

Supplication

A prophetic prayer reads: "O God! I seek refuge in Your pleasure from Your wrath, I seek refuge in Your forgiveness from Your punishment, I seek refuge in You from You. I cannot praise You enough. You are as You have praised Yourself."[5] This prayer calls attention to attributes of God that are in tension with each other: mercy versus wrath, forgiveness versus punishment. In *The Tao of Islam*, Sachiko Murata explores the dyadic nature of divine attributes—their yin and yang—which in Islamic mysticism have been expressed as God's *jamāl* and *jalāl*, beauty and majesty, coming together in God's perfection, *kamāl*.[6] Murata relates *jamāl* to the feminine and *jalāl* to the masculine, where the former takes precedence over the latter in the divine nature, as in the hadith: "My Mercy overcomes my Wrath."[7]

The Building Bridges Seminar selections made available here in chapter 5 include two prayers from the two longest Medinan suras. The verses that conclude al-Baqara, the longest sura of the Qur'an, were revealed, according to Muslim tradition, on the Prophet's night journey and ascent into heaven as a gift from beneath God's throne: "Our Lord, lay not upon us a burden like Thou Laid upon those before us. Our Lord, impose not upon us that which we have not the strength to bear! And pardon us, forgive us, and have mercy upon us!" (Q. 2:286).

Another prayer for mercy appears in the beginning of the sura that follows, Āl 'Imrān: "Our Lord, make not our hearts swerve after having guided us, and bestow upon us a mercy from thy presence" (Q. 3:8). The prior verse elaborates on "those whose hearts are given to swerving" as followers of the symbolic and ambiguous parts of revelation, instead of following that which is clear and determined: "the Mother of the Book." The "swerving of the hearts" verse—which points to verses that are clear or determined—contrasts sharply with verses that are ambiguous or symbolic. Its meaning has been debated extensively in Islamic thought. Perhaps it is worth taking a fresh look at it through the lens of mercy. Can we learn to see and experience God's mercy in revelations composed of a healthy blend of clarity and ambiguity?

Struggle

Struggle is another theme of the Medinan Qur'an in which mercy plays a role. Mercy is an element in the tests that one endures in the path to God: "And We will indeed test you with something of fear and hunger, and loss of wealth, souls, and fruits; and give glad tidings to the patient. . . . They are those upon whom come the blessings from their Lord, and compassion (*raḥma*)" (Q. 2:155–57). And: "Truly those who emigrate and strive in the way of God—it is they who hope for the Mercy of God" (Q. 2:218). The word for "strive" is jihad, which in the Medinan context includes, but is not limited to, armed struggle against the disbelievers that requires the sacrifice of hard-earned wealth, and even of one's life.

Believers Versus Unbelievers

In fact, the struggle between believers and unbelievers is a major theme of the Medinan Qur'an. It is on this note that Sūrat al-Baqara concludes with a prayer: "Thou art our Master, so help us against the disbelieving people."

Many of the Qur'an's suras come in pairs.[8] One hadith presents al-Baqara and Āl 'Imrān, suras 2 and 3, as a pair that will come on the day of judgment to advocate for those who acted in accordance with their teachings: "They will come as if they are two shades between which there is illumination, or as if they are two shady clouds, or as if they are shadows of lines of birds arguing on behalf of their people."[9] A mark of the pair relationship is similarity in style and structure with contrast and complementarity in meaning. Al-Baqara, for example, references circumstances leading up to the first major battle between the Prophet Muhammad and his Meccan adversaries that took place at Badr. Āl 'Imrān addresses circumstances in the aftermath of the second major military encounter at Uhud. The chronology of revelation is evident as Āl 'Imrān alludes to what came before: "God certainly helped you at Badr" (Q. 3:123–29). The tables turned from the first encounter to the second; defeat at Uhud followed victory at Badr. Those who sacrifice themselves are promised God's mercy: "And indeed if you die or are slain in the way of God, truly forgiveness and mercy from God are better than what they amass" (Q. 3:157).

There are, of course, hypocrites in Medina, ostensibly allying with the Prophet in the wake of his political ascent—unlike in Mecca, where association with God's messenger came with no worldly benefit. Al-Nisā', another lengthy Medinan sura, addresses the hypocrites: "Do they not contemplate the Qur'an?" (Q. 4:82–83) while at the same time consoling and reassuring the Prophet: "Were it not for God's Bounty (*faḍl*) toward thee, and His mercy, a party of them would have plotted to lead thee astray" (Q. 4:110–13).

Struggling in God's way leads not only to success in the hereafter but also in this world. As the Medinan sūrat al-Nūr tells us, those who struggle in God's path have been promised that they will be made vicegerents (literally, "caliphs") on earth, a sign of which will be that they will "perform the prayer, and give the alms, and obey the Messenger, that haply you may receive mercy" (Q. 24:55–56). Al-Nūr is a lone Medinan sura that appears after a long string of Meccas suras. Al-Ahzab follows a similar pattern in the structure of Qur'anic arrangement, promising the believers that if they were to die in God's path, they will have been true to that which they pledged unto God (Q. 33:23–24).

Brotherhood between believers is a hallmark of God's mercy, and that mercy flows through the Prophet: "Muhammad is the messenger of God. Those who are with him are harsh against the disbelievers, merciful to one another" (Q. 48:28–29). "The believers are but brothers; so make peace between your brethren, and reverence God, that haply you may receive mercy" (Q. 49:9–10). The solidarity of believers who struggle in God's path is among both men and women: "But the believing men and believing women are protectors of one another. . . . They are those upon whom God will have mercy" (Q. 9:71).

What do these numerous Qur'anic verses on the conflict between believers and unbelievers tell us about the nature and scope of God's mercy?

How to Interpret an Omission

Every sura but one, al-Tawba, begins with the *basmala*. Why this omission? *The Study Quran* offers two possible explanations: first, that the sura is actually not a stand-alone sura at all but rather a continuation of the previous sura, Al-Anfāl; and second, that the omission signifies the lifting of God's mercy.

Since Sūrat al-Tawba has been transmitted as a separate sura and is recited as such, it is worth proceeding with more thought about the second explanation. Al-Tawba was one of the last suras in the Qur'an to be revealed. What explains the absence of the Qur'an's hermeneutic key at the tail end of God's revelation to humanity? The absence of the key, as it turns out, is another key. Far from confounding the issue, the omission could also be profoundly clarifying.

Al-Tawba is a case study for historical context, chronology, and abrogation in the Qur'an. Its opening verses announce the breaking of treaties with "idolators" (*mushrikin*), their expulsion from the Arabian Peninsula, and the wholesale slaughter of those who would choose to remain behind unless they were to accept Islam and submit to the authority of the Prophet (Q. 9:1–6).

The theory of abrogation (*naskh*) in the reading of scripture creates room for chronological and context-relevant interpretations. It also creates the theological problem of God having changed his mind—or, of historical constraints imposing themselves on a revelation that is supposed to serve guidance for humanity until the end of history. Verse 5, known as the "sword verse" that commands believers to slay the *mushrikīn* if they persist in their rejection of Islam, has been read as an abrogator (*nāsikh*) of other verses in the Qur'an that are more inclusive and tolerant. In other words, God permits Muslims to be pluralistic and tolerant for expedience, not out of principle. Such a reading threatens to render meaningless the ethical teachings of the Qur'an that are conducive to peaceful coexistence.

As one of the shortest *tafsīrs* ever written, *Tafsīr al-Jalālayn* is read in Madrasas around the world as a primer or introduction to the science of tafsir.[10] Note the following exegetical glosses from that ninth/fifteenth-century *tafsīr* in relation to the sword verse:[11]

> So be forgiving, with gracious forgiveness (Q. 15:85). *This was abrogated by the "sword" verse.*
>
> Those who have sundered their religion, and have become differing parties, you have no concern with them at all. Their case will go to God, then He will inform them of what they used to do (Q. 6:159). *This was abrogated by the "sword" verse.*
>
> If they deny you, then say: "Unto me is my work, and to you your work; you are innocent of what I do, and I am innocent of what you do" (Q. 10:41). *This was abrogated by the "sword" verse.*
>
> Except those who attach themselves to a people between whom and you there is a covenant; or, come to you with their breasts constricted about the prospect of fighting you, or fighting their people—*this statement and what follows was abrogated by the "sword" verse.* Had God willed, He would have given them sway over you, so that assuredly they would have fought you. And so if they stay away from you and do not fight you, and offer you peace, then God does not allow you any way against them (Q. 4:90).
>
> So because of their breaking their covenant, We cursed them, and made their hearts hard; they pervert words from their contexts; and they have forgotten a portion of what they were reminded of; and you will never cease to discover some treachery on their part, except for a few of them. Yet pardon them, and forgive; surely God loves the virtuous (Q. 5:13). *This was abrogated by the "sword" verse.*
>
> And if they incline to peace, then incline to it—*Ibn 'Abbās said, "This has been abrogated by the 'sword verse'"*—truly He is the Hearer, the Knower, of actions (Q. 8:61).

On the surface, it looks like Qur'anic injunctions from the earlier revelations to live and let live have given way to a violent, exclusivist, and supremacist doctrine. There are, however, other ways to read the same verses. There is no universal understanding of abrogation in Islamic thought. Its meaning has evolved over time, ranging from a type of clarification or restriction of an earlier verse by a later one, to an outright "substitution"—that is, "the removal or annulment of one legal ruling by a subsequent legal ruling."[12]

Given that a legal norm is contingent on circumstances, another way to read the verses is through social context. In other words, the earlier verses have been abrogated for the Prophet, not for all believers at all times. According to Faraz Rabbani and the team of scholars at the online Sunni portal *Seekers Guidance*, "The verse of the sword by no means abrogated the verses of peace—rather, each is to be implemented in its appropriate situation."[13] Yasir Qadhi, academic dean at the Islamic Seminary of America, cites a range of traditional sources with varying views on abrogation: from none to no fewer than seventy-five verses as abrogated by the "sword verse."[14]

Rabbani's team corroborates Qadhi but offers a wider perspective in reference to other traditional authorities: "all the early Meccan verses of peace and forbearance with respect to non-Muslims remain in effect and are not abrogated with respect to all peoples other than the Arab polytheists. And with respect to all the later verses commanding Muslims to fight the polytheists, they abrogate the early verses of peace only with respect to the Arab polytheists."[15]

All these readings are influenced by juristic hermeneutics that, drawing on an internal chronology in the text, aim to transcend historical context in search of God's timeless will. In speaking about legal hermeneutics as applied to the Qur'anic text, John Burton notes that "with its final official canonization, the Qur'an had become de-historicized[;] . . . as arbitrarily selected texts could be extracted from their sura context . . . passages thus became decontextualized, stripped of tension that had characterized them within their original units."[16]

In contrast to the chrono-juristic approaches that have tended to dominate the tradition are readings that adopt literary and narrative approaches. Carl Ernst, for example, explains that his interest in the study of the Qur'an is from a post-orientalist perspective that views the Qur'an as literature that belongs to the global heritage of humanity.[17] His approach, following pioneering scholars like Theodor Nöldeke and, more recently, Angelika Neuwirth, presumes the sura to be a "literary whole, rather than a random assortment of unrelated verses" that are to be tied together through legal or theological frames that are imposed on it through an extraneous authoritative tradition.[18]

Ernst calls the theory of abrogation a "prominent example of an external interpretive model that is brought to bear upon the text of the Qur'an . . . in order to deal with apparent inconsistencies within the text."[19] He refers to the sword verse as "the most notorious example of abrogation in the Qur'an" but unfortunately does not elaborate further.[20]

Recent and contemporary scholars from within the Islamic tradition have also gravitated toward literary approaches, either independently or through mutually enriching interaction with Western scholarship. Amin Ahsan Islahi, for example, not only analyzes every sura as a literary unit, he goes further by positing that the structure of the Qur'an revolves around clusters of Meccan and Medinan suras linked together as thematic clusters.[21] According to Islahi, the *naẓm* or thematic coherence of the Qur'an takes precedence in interpreting the Qur'an whenever possible.

Islahi interprets the sword verse simply as the enactment of "the Sunnah of God" toward a people who have rejected a messenger who was sent to them, in accordance with a narrative pattern that threads together Qur'anic accounts on the annihilation of peoples who rejected prophets of yore. The sword verse thus becomes an enactment of the Qur'an's annihilation motif, limited entirely to a prophetic context through a chrono-literary reading, without recourses to the chrono-juristic tool of abrogation.

There are further textual indicators that support such a restrictive reading: (1) The *barā'a* (freedom of obligation to abide by treaties) at the beginning of the sura is stipulated only on behalf of God and His messenger—not on behalf of the entire body of believers (*barā'atun min Allāhi wa-rasūlihi*); (2) Verses 3 and 7 again speak of the broken pacts as having been contracted exclusively by God and His messenger; (3) Verse 13 poses a rhetorical question: why would the collective body of believers *not* fight a people who have expelled the messenger of God?; and (4) Verse 14 commands the believers to "Fight them!" because "God will punish them by means of your hands."

Paradoxically, the approach that concerns itself with abrogation of what came historically prior by that which followed—what I am calling chrono-juridic—sends up with a timeless ruling that dehistoricizes the text, whereas a literary approach that concerns itself with narrative in the Qur'an results in a historicization of the text that limits its practical import to a specific time and place.

What would it mean for Muslims to enter into open-ended and mutually enriching conversations on "how to read the Qur'an" with non-Muslims? What does it mean for readers of the Qur'an, through such encounters, to discover new thematic connections and new literary structures in the Qur'an that enable them to read it in ways it has never been read before? Is it acceptable to adopt new approaches only if literary readings merely corroborate and enrich teachings in the established legal and theological tradition; or should Muslims be open to revisions to that tradition in light of fresh readings? In short: is the Muslim tradition able to absorb a shifting authority in scholarship on the Qur'an from traditional and devotional settings to academic and interreligious ones and to be normatively influenced by them, or must such shifts be resisted as inauthentic and dubious?

I happen to think that these questions are beside the point. We should feel free to engage all approaches to the interpretation of scripture so long as the engagement is genuine and respectful. First, has not the Prophet Muhammad himself said that the Qur'an's wonders will never cease to amaze?[22] Second, Muslims should always keep in mind the age-old principle for Qur'an interpretation, as the eminent Mufti Taqi Usmani reminds us: good old common sense.[23]

To conclude, let us return to the omission of "mercy" at the beginning of Sura 9 that led to our lengthy excursus. While mercy—as attributed to God—is omitted in the beginning, it is very much present in the middle and at the end of the sura through the Prophet as a vessel carrying that mercy, but its scope is restricted to the sphere of the believers: "he is a mercy to those among you who believe" (Q. 9:61). And: "A Messenger has indeed come to you from among your own. Troubled is he by what you suffer, solicitous of you, kind and merciful unto the believers" (Q. 9:128–29).

Notes

1. William Montgomery Watt, *Muhammad: Prophet and Statesman* (Oxford: Oxford University Press, 1961).

2. S. H. Nasr, Caner K. Dagli, Maria Massi Dakake, Joseph E. B. Lumbard, and Mohammed Rustom, eds., *The Study Quran* (New York: HarperOne, 2015); M. A. S. Abdel Haleem, trans., *The Qur'an* (Oxford: Oxford University Press, 2004); Mohammed Marmaduke Pickthall, *The Meaning of the Glorious Koran* (New York: Knopf, 1930); Abdullah Yusuf Ali, *The Holy Qur-ān: English Translation & Commentary* (Kashmiri Bazar, Lahore: Shaik Muhammad Ashraf, 1934); and Thomas Ballantyne Irving, trans., *The Qur'an: The First American Version* (Brattleboro, VT: Amana, 1985). In this chapter, Nasr and colleagues' *The Study Quran* is the source of all Qur'an translations, except where otherwise noted.

3. Umar Faruq Abd-Allah, "Mercy: The Stamp of Creation," A Nawawi Foundation paper posted on *The Oasis Initiative* (2014), https://www.theoasisinitiative.org/nawawi-mercy.

4. Translation according to Abdel Haleem, *The Qur'an*. Interestingly, *The Study Quran* translates the first part of 2:138 as "The baptism of God."

5. *Musnad Ahmad*, Book 5, Hadith 3. Translation: https://sunnah.com/ahmad:751.

6. Sachiko Murata, *The Tao of Islam: A Sourcebook on Gender Relationships in Islamic Thought* (Albany: State University of New York Press, 1992).

7. For the full text of this hadith, see chapter 8.

8. See Neal Robinson, *Discovering the Qur'an: A Contemporary Approach to a Veiled Text* (Washington, DC: Georgetown University Press, 2004).

9. *Jami' al-Tirmidhi*, Book 45, Hadith 9, https://sunnah.com/tirmidhi:2883.

10. Jalal al-Din al-Suyuti and Jalal al-Din al-Mahalli, *Tafsīr al-Jalālayn*, trans. Feras Hamza (Louisville, KY: Fons Vitae, 2008).

11. I have included only the translation of the verses and truncated the commentary for brevity, with modest modifications to punctuations to accord with the edits; emphasis mine.

12. See "Jihad, Abrogation in the Quran & the 'Verse of the Sword,'" https://seekersguidance.org.

13. "Jihad, Abrogation in the Quran."

14. Yasir Qadhi, *An Introduction to the Sciences of the Qur'aan* (Birmingham, UK: Al-Hidaayah, 1999), 251.

15. "Jihad, Abrogation in the Quran."

16. Angelika Neuwirth, "Form and Structure," in *Encyclopaedia of the Qur'an*, vol. 2, ed. Jane Dammen McAuliffe (Leiden: Brill Academic, 2003), 248.

17. Carl Ernst, *How to Read the Qur'an: A New Guide, with Select Translations* (Durham: University of North Carolina Press, 2011).

18. Ernst, *How to Read the Qur'an*, 12.

19. Ernst, *How to Read the Qur'an*, 65ff.

20. Ernst, *How to Read the Qur'an*, 66f. He speculates that apparently contradictory verses may simply reflect differences of opinion among the early Muslim community on how to handle conflict, or that further analysis through "ring composition" may reveal counterintuitive results that affirm religious pluralism even while being couched in a frame of conflict.

21. For more on Islahi's approach, see Mustansir Mir, *Coherence in the Qur'ān: A Study of Iṣlāḥī's Concept of Naẓm in Tadabbur-i Qur'ān* (Kuala Lumpur: Islamic Book Trust, 2011).

22. *Jami' al-Tirmidhi*, Book 45, Hadith 32, https://sunnah.com/tirmidhi:2906.

23. Mufti Muhammad Taqi Usmani, *An Approach to the Quranic Sciences* (Karachi: Darul Isha'at, 2007).

5

The Medinan Suras on Mercy and Grace

Texts for Study

The translation provided in this chapter is according to S. H. Nasr, Caner K. Dagli, Maria Massi Dakake, Joseph E. B. Lumbard, and Mohammed Rustom, eds., The Study Quran *(New York: HarperOne, 2015). Used by permission.*

al-Baqara (2) 35–37

[35]And when We said to the angels, "Prostrate unto Adam," they prostrated, save Iblīs. He refused and waxed arrogant, and was among the disbelievers. We said, "O Adam, dwell thou and thy wife in the Garden and eat freely thereof, wheresoever you will. But approach not this tree, lest you be among the wrongdoers." [36]Then Satan made them stumble therefrom, and expelled them from that wherein they were, and We said, "Get you down, each of you an enemy to the other. On the earth a dwelling place shall be yours, and enjoyment for a while." [37]Then Adam received words from his Lord, and He relented unto him. Indeed, He is the Relenting, the Merciful.

al-Baqara (2) 62–64

[62]Truly those who believe, and those who are Jews, and the Christians, and the Sabeans—whosoever believes in God and the Last Day and works righteousness shall have their reward with their Lord. No fear shall come upon them, nor shall they grieve. [63]And when We made a covenant with you, and raised the Mount over you, "Take hold of what We have given you with strength, and remember what is in it, that haply you may be reverent." [64]Then you turned away thereafter, and were it not for God's Bounty upon you, and His Mercy, you would have been among the losers.

al-Baqara (2) 155–157

[155]And We will indeed test you with something of fear and hunger, and loss of wealth, souls, and fruits; and give glad tidings to the patient—[156]those who, when affliction befalls them, say, "Truly we are God's, and unto Him we return." [157]They are those upon whom come the blessings from their Lord, and compassion, and they are those who are rightly guided.

al-Baqara (2) 178–179

[178]O you who believe! Retribution is prescribed for you in the matter of the slain: freeman for freeman, slave for slave, female for female. But for one who receives any pardon from his brother, let it be observed honorably, and let the restitution be made to him with goodness. That is an alleviation from your Lord, and a mercy. Whosoever transgresses after that shall have a painful punishment. [179]In retribution there is life for you, O possessors of intellect, that haply you may be reverent.

al-Baqara (2) 218

Truly those who believe and those who emigrate and strive in the way of God—it is they who hope for the Mercy of God. And God is Forgiving, Merciful.

al-Baqara (2) 285–286

[285]The Messenger believes in what was sent down to him from his Lord, as do the believers. Each believes in God, His angels, His Books, and His messengers. "We make no distinction between any of His messengers." And they say, "We hear and obey. Thy forgiveness, our Lord! And unto Thee is the journey's end." [286]God tasks no soul beyond its capacity. It shall have what it has earned and be subject to what it has perpetrated. "Our Lord, take us not to task if we forget or err! Our Lord, lay not upon us a burden like Thou laid upon those before us. Our Lord, impose not upon us that which we have not the strength to bear! And pardon us, forgive us, and have mercy upon us! Thou art our Master, so help us against the disbelieving people."

Āl ʿImrān (3) 7–8

[7]He it is Who has sent down the Book upon thee; therein are signs determined; they are the Mother of the Book, and others symbolic. As for those

whose hearts are given to swerving, they follow that of it which is symbolic, seeking temptation and seeking its interpretation. And none know its interpretation save God and those firmly rooted in knowledge. They say, "We believe in it; all is from our Lord." And none remember, save those who possess intellect. [8]"Our Lord, make not our hearts swerve after having guided us, and bestow upon us a mercy from Thy Presence. Truly Thou art the Bestower."

Āl ʿImrān (3) 106–8

[106]on the Day when faces whiten and faces blacken. As for those whose faces blacken, "Did you disbelieve after having believed? Then taste the punishment for having disbelieved." [107]And as for those whose faces whiten, they will be in the Mercy of God, abiding therein. [108]These are God's signs which We recite unto thee in truth, and God desires no wrong for the worlds.

Āl ʿImrān (3) 123–29

[123]God certainly helped you at Badr, when you were lowly. So reverence God, that haply you may give thanks. [124]Remember when thou saidst unto the believers, "Is it not enough for you that your Lord should support you with three thousand angels sent down?" [125]Yea, if you are patient and reverent, and they come at you immediately, your Lord will support you with five thousand angels bearing marks. [126]God made it not save as a glad tiding for you, and that your hearts may repose thereby—and there is no victory save from God, the Mighty, the Wise—[127]that He may cut off a faction of those who disbelieve or abase them, so that they be turned back disappointed. [128]Naught is thine in the matter, whether He relent unto them or punish them, for truly they are wrongdoers. [129]Unto God belongs whatsoever is in the heavens and whatsoever is on the earth. He forgives whomsoever He will and punishes whomsoever He will, and God is Forgiving, Merciful.

Āl ʿImrān (3) 157–60

[157]And indeed if you are slain or die in the way of God, truly forgiveness and mercy from God are better than what they amass. [158]And indeed if you are slain or die, truly unto God shall you be gathered. [159]Then [it was] by a mercy from God that thou wert gentle with them. Hadst thou been severe [and] hard-hearted they would have scattered from about thee. So pardon them, ask forgiveness for them, and consult them in affairs. And when thou

art resolved, trust in God; truly God loves those who trust. [160]If God helps you, none shall overcome you. And if He forsakes you, who then can help you thereafter? And in God let the believers trust.

al-Nisāʾ (4) 82–83

[82]Do they not contemplate the Qurʾan? Had it been from other than God, they would surely have found much discrepancy therein. [83]And whenever tidings come unto them, whether of security or fear, they spread it about, whereas had they referred it to the Messenger and to those in authority among them, those of them whose task it is to investigate would have known it. Were it not for God's Bounty toward you, and His Mercy, you would surely have followed Satan, save a few.

al-Nisāʾ (4) 110–13

[110]Whosoever does evil or wrongs himself, and then seeks forgiveness of God, he will find God Forgiving, Merciful. [111]And whosoever commits a sin, commits it only against his own soul, and God is Knowing, Wise. [112]And whosoever commits an offense or a sin, and then casts it upon one who is innocent, bears the burden of calumny and a manifest sin. [113]Were it not for God's Bounty toward thee, and His Mercy, a party of them would have plotted to lead thee astray, but they lead astray only their own souls, and they can do thee no harm in the least. God has sent down unto thee the Book and Wisdom, and has taught thee what thou knewest not; God's Bounty toward thee is great indeed.

al-Nisāʾ (4) 171

O People of the Book! Do not exaggerate in your religion, nor utter anything concerning God save the truth. Verily the Messiah, Jesus son of Mary, was only a messenger of God, and His Word, which He committed to Mary, and a Spirit from Him. So believe in God and His messengers, and say not "Three." Refrain! It is better for you. God is only one God; Glory be to Him that He should have a child. Unto Him belongs whatsoever is in the heavens and whatsoever is on the earth, and God suffices as a Guardian.

al-Nūr (24) 6–10

[6]And as for those who accuse their wives and have no witnesses but themselves, then the testimony of one of them shall be four testimonies, swearing

by God that he is among the truthful, [7]and the fifth shall be that the curse of God be upon him if he is among the liars. [8]And the punishment shall be averted from her should she give four testimonies, swearing by God that he is among the liars, [9]and the fifth that God's Wrath shall come upon her if he is among the truthful. [10]And were it not for God's Bounty upon you, and His Mercy, and that God is Relenting, Wise!

al-Nūr (24) 19–22

[19]Truly those who desire that indecency be spread among those who believe, theirs shall be a painful punishment in this world and the Hereafter. God knows, and you know not. [20]And were it not for God's Bounty toward you, and His Mercy, and that God is Kind, Merciful! [21]O you who believe! Follow not the footsteps of Satan! And whosoever follows the footsteps of Satan, truly he enjoins indecency and wrong. And were it not for God's Bounty toward you, and His Mercy, not one of you would ever be pure. But God purifies whomsoever He will, and God is Hearing, Knowing. [22]And let not the men of bounty and means among you forswear giving to kinsfolk and the indigent and those who emigrated in the way of God. And let them pardon and forbear. Do you not desire that God forgive you? And God is Forgiving, Merciful.

al-Nūr (24) 55–56

[55]God has promised those among you who believe and perform righteous deeds that He will surely make them vicegerents upon the earth, as He caused those before them to be vicegerents, and that He will establish for them their religion, which He has approved for them, and that He will surely change them from a state of fear to [one of] security. They will worship Me, not ascribing any partners unto Me. And whosoever disbelieves thereafter, it is they who are iniquitous. [56]And perform the prayer, and give the alms, and obey the Messenger, that haply you may receive mercy.

al-Aḥzāb (33) 23–24

[23]Among the believers are men who have been true to that which they pledged unto God. Among them are those who have fulfilled their vow, and among them are those who wait, and they have not changed in the least, [24]that God may recompense the truthful for their truthfulness and punish the hypocrites if He will, or relent unto them. Truly God is Forgiving, Merciful.

al-Fatḥ (48) 28–29

[28]He it is Who sent His Messenger with guidance and the Religion of Truth to make it prevail over all religion. And God suffices as a Witness. [29]Muhammad is the Messenger of God. Those who are with him are harsh against the disbelievers, merciful to one another. You see them bowing, prostrating, seeking bounty from God and contentment; their mark upon their faces is from the effect of prostration. That is their likeness in the Torah. And their likeness in the Gospel is a sapling that puts forth its shoot and strengthens it, such that it grows stout and rises firmly upon its stalk, impressing the sowers, that through them He may enrage the disbelievers. God has promised forgiveness and a great reward to those among them who believe and perform righteous deeds.

al-Ḥujarāt (49) 9–10

[9]If two parties among the believers fall to fighting, make peace between them. If one of them aggresses against the other, fight those who aggress until they return to God's Command. And if they return, make peace between them with justice and act equitably. Truly God loves the just. [10]The believers are but brothers; so make peace between your brethren, and reverence God, that haply you may receive mercy.

al-Ḥadīd (57) 12–14

[12]On the Day when you see the believing men and the believing women with their light spreading before them and on their right, "Glad tidings unto you this Day: Gardens with rivers running below, therein to abide. That is the great triumph." [13]On the Day when the hypocrites, men and women, will say to those who believe, "Wait for us that we may borrow from your light," it will be said, "Turn back and seek a light!" Thereupon a wall with a gate will be set down between them, the inner side of which contains mercy, and on the outer side of which lies punishment. [14]They will call unto them, "Were we not with you?" They reply, "Indeed! But you tempted yourselves, bided your time, and doubted; and false hopes deluded you till the Command of God came, and the Deluder deluded you concerning God.

al-Ḥadīd (57) 25–29

[25]We have indeed sent Our messengers with clear proofs, and We sent down the Book and the Balance with them, that the people would uphold justice.

And We sent down iron, wherein are great might and benefits for mankind, and so that God may know those who will help Him and His messengers unseen. Truly God is Strong, Mighty. [26]And indeed We sent Noah and Abraham and established prophethood and the Book among their progeny. And among them is he who is rightly guided; yet many of them are iniquitous. [27]Then We sent Our messengers to follow in their footsteps, and We sent Jesus son of Mary, and We gave him the Gospel and placed kindness and mercy in the hearts of those who follow him. And monasticism they invented—We did not ordain it for them—only to seek God's Contentment. Yet they did not observe it with proper observance. So We gave those of them who believed their reward, yet many of them are iniquitous. [28]O you who believe! Reverence God and believe in His Messenger; He will give you a twofold portion of His Mercy, make a light for you by which you may walk, and forgive you—and God is Forgiving, Merciful—[29]such that the People of the Book may know that they have no power over any of God's Bounty, and that the Bounty is in God's Hand; He gives it unto whomsoever He will; and God is Possessed of Tremendous Bounty.

From an introduction to Surat al-Tawba (9) in *The Study Quran*

This is the only *sūrah* of the Quran that does not begin with the *basmalah*, the formula *In the Name of God, the Compassionate, the Merciful.* It is reported that Ibn ʿAbbās asked ʿAlī ibn Abī Ṭālib why there was no *basmalah* at the start of this *sūrah*. He responded that the *basmalah* is a statement of security, and this *sūrah* begins with the severing of a covenant and a declaration of conflict, which indicate the opposite of a state of security. When it was pointed out to him that the Prophet sent letters beginning with the *basmalah* to call various hostile groups to embrace Islam, ʿAlī ibn Abī Ṭālib responded that this was precisely a call to God, not the rescinding of a pact; the former leads to peace, the latter to war. Commentators note that it was a custom, even in pre-Islamic times, to omit *In the Name of God* in a message breaking a treaty (Q).[1]

al-Tawbah (9) 61

And among them are those who torment the Prophet, and say, "He is an ear." Say, "An ear that is good for you. He believes in God and he has faith in the believers, and he is a mercy to those among you who believe." And [as for] those who torment the Messenger of God, theirs shall be a painful punishment.

al-Tawbah (9) 71

But the believing men and believing women are protectors of one another, enjoining right and forbidding wrong, performing the prayer, giving the alms, and obeying God and His Messenger. They are those upon whom God will have Mercy. Truly God is Mighty, Wise.

al-Tawbah (9) 128–129

[128]A Messenger has indeed come unto you from among your own. Troubled is he by what you suffer, solicitous of you, kind and merciful unto the believers. [129]But if they turn away, say, "God suffices me. There is no god but He. In Him do I trust, and He is the Lord of the mighty Throne."

Note

1. Seyyed Hossein Nasr, Caner K. Dagli, Maria Massi Dakake, Joseph E. B. Lumbard, and Mohammed Rustom, eds., introductory remarks regarding "9 Repentance al-Tawbah" in *The Study Quran: A New Translation and Commentary* (New York: HarperOne, 2015), 503–4. The letter Q in parentheses at the end of this passage is shorthand for the source *al-Jāmi' li-aḥkām al-Qur'ān* by Abū 'Abd Allāh Muḥammad ibn Aḥmad al-Qurṭubī (d. 671/1272). See the editors' explanation of their citation method in their prefatory essay titled "Understanding the Citations in the Commentary" (liii–lv), which in turn refers the reader to their "Commentator Key" (lvii–lix).

6

Mercy and Grace in the Islamic Theological Tradition

An Overview

Ramon Harvey

Mercy (*raḥma*) and grace (*faḍl*) play a significant dual role within Islamic scripture. Yet they are not usually of central focus within classical Islamic theology, the discourse known as *ʿilm al-kalām*. This may seem less curious once it is recognized that *kalām*, which focused on the explication and justification of Islamic creed, usually circled questions of controversy within the community. God's mercy and grace were universally accepted, and thus as concepts only erupt from the Qur'an and Hadith corpus into *kalām* at certain fissures, those places defining alternative theological frameworks. Herein, I will trace some of the main debates over these concepts, seeking to expose in an accessible way what is at stake in the disagreements between Islamic theologians as well as mapping some of the underlying commonalities.

My point of departure is a hadith within *ṢaSḥīḥ Muslim*, one of the foremost canonical collections of reports on what the Prophet Muhammad said and did.

> Ibn Masʿūd reported:
>
> The Messenger of God, may God bless him and grant him peace, said: the last to enter Paradise will be a man who will walk once and stumble once and be burnt by the Fire once. Then when he gets beyond it, he will turn to it and say: blessed is He Who has saved me from you. God has given me something He has not given to anyone from the first to the last.
>
> Then a tree will be raised up for him and he will say: O my Lord, bring me near this tree, so that I may shelter in its shade and drink of its water. God Mighty and Majestic will say: O son of Adam, perhaps if I grant you this, you will ask Me for something else. He will say: no O Lord, and he will promise Him that he will not ask for anything else. His Lord will

> excuse him because he sees that with which he lacks steadfastness, so He will bring him near it, and he will shelter in its shade and drink from its water.
>
> Then, a tree more beautiful than the first will be raised up for him and he will say: O my Lord, bring me near this tree, so that I may drink from its water and shelter in its shade—I shall not ask You for anything else. He (God) will say: O son of Adam, did you not promise me that you would not ask Me for anything else? His Lord will excuse him because he sees that with which he lacks steadfastness, so He will bring him near to it, and he will shelter in its shade and drink from its water.
>
> Then a tree will be raised up for him at the gate of Paradise, more beautiful than the first two. He will say: O my Lord, bring me near this (tree) so that I may shelter in its shade and drink from its water. I shall not ask You for anything else. He (God) will say: O son of Adam, did you not promise Me that you would not ask Me anything else? He will say: yes, my Lord, this [is true]. I shall not ask You for anything else. His Lord will excuse him because He sees that with which he lacks steadfastness. He (God) will bring him near to it, and when He does so he will hear the voices of the people of Paradise.
>
> He will say: O my Lord, enter me into it. He (God) will say: O son of Adam, what will cut short your requests to Me? Will it please you if I give you the world and its like along with it? He will say: O my Lord, are You mocking me, though You are the Lord of the worlds?
>
> [And at this point] Ibn Masʿūd laughed and said: Will you not ask about what I am laughing? They said: about what do you laugh? He said: it is in this way that the Messenger of God, may God bless him and grant him peace laughed. They (the companions of the Prophet) asked: about what do you laugh O Messenger of God? He said: on account of the laugh of the Lord of the worlds, when [it is said to Him]: are You mocking me though You are the Lord of the worlds? He will say: I am not mocking you, but I have power to do whatever I will.[1]

What can we glean from this hadith? No doubt it is an illustration of the neediness of the human being contrasted with the power of God. This, in fact, is the liminal case, the final person to enter into Paradise. This figure no sooner makes a promise before he breaks it, yet God continues to give from His bounty. Second, God laughs. What does that mean? It raises a significant series of questions about the modality of our language in its reference to the divine nature, the divine actions, and the degree of transcendence to be applied within our theology. On the more traditionalist side of the spectrum, some Islamic theologians will tell us to take such an expression in its apparent sense: God laughs, but not in such a way to make it comparable to human laughter. Others will say that we must affirm yet pass over a text like this in silence—we cannot imagine what it means. As we move toward more transcendent theologies, we may find theologians providing a figurative interpretation to the idea of divine laughter, or even to reject the authenticity of this hadith because of its inclusion of this unacceptable anthropomorphism. If this text is informative about the divine nature, perhaps it suggests that God laughs in wonder at the paucity of His servant's imagination of the divine mercy. We will see that these options in the interpretation of God's laughter parallel to some extent those available in the wider debate over divine mercy.

In what follows, I touch on and sketch answers to two distinct questions that this hadith implicitly raises:

1. A question of theology: what does it mean for God to be merciful (and gracious)?
2. A question of theological anthropology: what does it mean for human beings to receive God's grace and mercy?

I should also put in a caveat that as I discuss these questions through a theological lens, I am attempting to give a map to a vast and complex terrain. I am therefore providing a representative reading of the "ideal school positions" of the main Islamic theologies of the classical period—that is, the views that one will mainly find within the tradition of *'ilm al-kalām.* My approach will smooth over idiosyncrasies that, if one begins to look at the theological systems of individual scholars, then inevitably one begins to find.

The Most Gracious, the Most Merciful

God is al-Raḥmān al-Raḥīm, which could be translated as "the Most Gracious, the Most Merciful."[2] The two aspects are usually distinguished by the all-encompassing grace that is shown toward all created beings and a specific mercy that is shown to believers. There is a question that arises about the name itself: it clearly points toward God's mercy, but should the name be reified as an ontic reality in the divine nature, or is this only appropriate for the attribute of mercifulness itself? Alternatively, perhaps the name *Merciful* and the attribute of mercy are both to be parsed on the side of created human language, with God as transcendentally beyond. Although I will not be detained on this point here, I think it allows us to see that, whereas all Islamic theologians agree that God is merciful, they disagree on how that apparently simple idea is to be theologically construed.

I shall distinguish two broad tendencies: those that understand God as merciful because He is the creator of mercy, and those that understand Him as merciful through the intrinsic possession of mercy. The first tendency is that of the Muʿtazilī and Ashʿarī. Who are these groups? The Muʿtazilī are an early and very prominent theological school of thought that is known for its focus on divine transcendence and justice. They were influential for a time but ultimately died out as an independent movement. Many of their ideas were adopted in Shiʿi theology, where their focus on justice was a good fit. The Ashʿarī became one of the major Sunnī schools. They are known for their emphasis on God's absolute divine sovereignty.

The Muʿtazilī and Ashʿarī are often presented in at least semi-opposition to each other, so it may seem puzzling that they can be classed together on this question. The reason is that Ashʿarism adopts key features of a Muʿtazilī theology of creation, explaining divine actions (*ṣifāt al-fiʿl*) in terms of the creation of things within the world. On this reading, what it means for God to be merciful is nothing but His creation of mercy. The motivation for both of these positions is a kind of rationalism that rejects the coherency of attributing actions to the eternal divine. Of course, the Ashʿarī and Muʿtazilī do differ substantially on how they understand the divine nature.

The classical Muʿtazilī hold to a doctrine of divine simplicity. This means that, although, of course, God is acknowledged to be knowing and powerful, there is some debate over how this is to be explained. One of the most common views is to identify God's knowledge and power with His essence. Another option is to treat these properties according to a kind of concept nominalism: God has the property of knowledge because He says in the Qurʾan that He is knowing. According to either theory, God's mercy is explained as something imputed to Him because of the mercy that He creates. The question is then to account for the conditions under which God exercises mercy. For the Muʿtazilī, the idea of God's justice is a core principle alongside His oneness, and it is divine justice that strictly regulates divine mercy: God necessarily acts according to a scale of justice extrapolated from the worldly realm. For them, this meant that whereas the major sinner who repents before death could be forgiven, the one who is unrepentant could not.

The Ashʿarī argue that God has distinct eternal divine attributes, which they understand as neither identical to nor separate from God's essence. But mercy is not one of those attributes. Instead, they emphasize that all aspects of creation, including the creation of mercy, are decided by divine will. This means that, although the Ashʿarīs share the idea that mercy is a creation, they end up in a very different theological position from that of the Muʿtazilī. What God creates goes back to His will and is unencumbered by a humanly understandable principle of justice. This means that God can provide whatever mercy He wishes to whomsoever He wishes. Hence, God's mercy is unlimited, but it is not guaranteed—at least in theory. For example, God could choose to condemn the prophets and saints to Hell and place the disbelievers in Paradise. All is His decision. There is some mitigation in that, even if this is rationally possible, it seems that the promises made within the Qurʾan limit it. The problem is that on such a radical conception of divine freedom, it seems hard to theologically require that God even be bound to what we read in scripture.

Let us now consider two further groups that understood mercy as in some sense integral to the divine nature. God is not only merciful because He creates mercy, but mercifulness is a distinct property possessed by Him. Both of these groups take a cue from the way that divine attributes are conveyed within the Qurʾan and the Hadith, and together with the Ashʿarī, we can see that the majority position in Islamic theology is against the idea of divine simplicity. So, my third grouping consists of the Ḥanafī Māturīdī, some of the people of Hadith, and the transcendence-focused Ḥanbalīs. The Māturīdī school is another important group within Sunnism that is often considered parallel to Ashʿarism and emphasizes divine wisdom ahead of the unconstrained divine will. For my present purposes, however, the distinctive aspect of this grouping is that it treats all of God's actions as eternal. The final group, which we can perhaps call "Traditionalism" for want of a better name, is represented by other people of Hadith, Ḥanbalīs (such as Ibn Taymiyya), and the Karrāmīs. This grouping tends to take the pronouncements of scripture at their apparent meaning and is distinguished by allowing God to have temporal and spatial properties.

So the third position, which is most distinctively taken by the Māturīdī, understands divine mercy to be one of God's eternal actions. That is, God's mercy is not to be placed at the times of its effects within the world, but rather it is a single act (or perhaps multiple acts) in eternity, or at the very least an effect of an eternal attribute of creative action. What decides the mercy that is given? This depends on wider considerations, but, at least in the case of the Māturīdīs, it is regulated by divine wisdom. This means that there are certain definite consistencies within divine action that can be known by human reason.[3]

The final position, which is invested in a more direct (and, to the others, more anthropomorphic) reading of scripture, takes mercy as a temporal divine act. In other words, God possesses a genuine property of mercy at those moments in which He acts with mercy. This position allows for scriptural language to be taken in its outward sense regarding the responsiveness of divine mercy in time and even its spatial direction (descending from above).

Grace and the Human Being

Some connections between the theological positions that I have been exploring and the conception of grace have already emerged. It is useful to provide further clarity on the status of human beings in relation to divine grace according to these four paradigmatic positions. A shared concept is that of the natural disposition (*fiṭra*), which appears in Q. 30:30. The idea of the *fiṭra* is somewhat contested, but it clearly refers to some kind of natural faculty or state that a human is born into in the absence of other influences. The concept gives the idea that, at least in principle, the human being naturally possesses everything that he or she needs to act rightly and come to know God. In other words, in Islam, although Adam and Eve both ate from the tree and descended to the earth, there was no Fall.

The Muʿtazilī have a very strong version of *fiṭra*, believing that the human possesses immediate knowledge of what is good and bad and can easily reason to the existence and properties of God, including His justice. This view of justice impacts the conception of grace. It would be unjust for one person to be given divine guidance ahead of another. Rather, all are equal in ability to use their intellects. So justice requires a flattening of grace. This connects with the Muʿtazilī approach to the question of free will. Human beings act with complete freedom; so any grace must be construed in terms of the general features of the human condition. In the same manner, some of the Muʿtazilī held that God must always do what is best for humanity—which is again understood in a collective way through the prism of justice. So the sending of prophets can be construed as necessary on account of divine justice.

The Ashʿarī, on the other hand, very much weaken the notion of *fiṭra* as a moral property. *Fiṭra*'s role is to allow human beings the potential to believe in a prophet or in the transmission of a prophet's message if it reaches them. In terms of morality, the person who has not received such a message is held to act naturalistically according to what appears good and beneficial or bad and harmful, but without that having any impact on morality—which is defined with reference to God's commands. This allows a great freedom for the operation of grace—as guidance is understood as purely a divine gift. In fact, on the question of freedom, the paradigmatic Ashʿarī position is that human beings merely earn their actions; the power that they are granted to act with is only suitable for the act that they in fact are destined to perform. Prophets here are purely God's free act of grace to humanity.

The Māturīdī sit on the spectrum of thought on this question at a point between the Muʿtazilī and Ashʿarī. *Fiṭra*, for them, provides a faculty that inclines toward coming to know good and bad. Rather than having immediate knowledge, the human being is able to reason to moral judgments and the existence of God. Yet this means that these are binding necessities, even in the absence of revelation. Grace still has considerable leeway when compared to the position of the Muʿtazilī: God in His wisdom can make the path for one person easy and for another hard, yet the approach to free choice (*ikhtiyār*) of the Māturīdī means that a person always has a genuine decision between alternative options to make. The sending of prophets here is understood as necessary by virtue of God's own wisdom.

Finally, the position of Ibn Taymiyya can be taken as an illustrative example of the fourth camp: Traditionalism. However, his position is not necessarily representative of the others that I have been conveniently grouping with him. He holds that *fiṭra* provides direct insight into good and bad as well as belief in God so that such beliefs will well up in the person who approaches the world when in an uncorrupted state. The difference from the position of the Muʿtazilī is that human beings need not have an understanding of rational arguments to underpin their beliefs. This view sees grace in the provision of *fiṭra* and in the degree to which it functions well for any individual. The question of the sending of prophets returns, in a way reminiscent of the Māturīdī, to a necessity bequeathed by the divine wisdom.

Mercy and Grace in Prophecy and Divine Speech

Despite the relevance of concepts of mercy and grace for the human being in their natural state, they are only fully realized when they are made to speak to the election of prophets as conveyors of God's mercy and His self-revelation through speech to them. Hence, when divine favors are recounted in Sūrat al-Raḥmān for the *thaqalān*—the two beings weighing heavy with moral responsibility: the humans and the jinn—they are prefaced with a recognition of this reality: "The Most Gracious, taught the Qurʾan, created the human being, taught him speech" (Q. 55:1–4).

Islamic schools of thought that fight bitterly over their theological territory share an affirmation of the divine mercy and grace expressed through the sending of the prophets—and none more so than the final messenger, the Prophet Muhammad, may God bless him and grant him peace, who was "Only sent as a mercy to all the worlds" (Q. 21:107). Thus, the Prophet is envisaged as the greatest outpouring of mercy from God. In what sense is the Prophet so merciful? He is, of course, a universal prophet who is not just sent to his own people but to all of humanity as well as the jinn. And he is sent with a universal law and code of ethics, one that is to be the final guidance until the Day of Judgment. So he is the Seal of the Prophets (Q. 33:40). And he is understood as the great intercessor, the one whose intercession allows the events of that great day to begin and the one who is able to intercede with God to forgive the grave sinner.

The common thread of the Prophet's role within history, then, is as the final culminating messenger in the chain of messengers that have gone before. He is the last recipient of the divine message—and this message is through speech. That God spoke to His prophets is absolutely central to Islamic theology. But again, we come to a point of divergence: what exactly it means for God to speak is explained differently by the various theological groups. For the Mu'tazila, God speaks through His creation of speech (the Arabic Qur᾿an) in the world. The Ashʿarīs and Māturīdīs broadly agree that God's speech is an eternal attribute and that the Arabic Qur᾿an is an expression or indication to it. Traditionalists would see God's speech as literally the Arabic Qur᾿an that is able to inhere within the divine nature.

Turning to the theme of the reception of divine speech, all schools of *kalām* agree that God spoke to Adam, and thereafter to many prophets via angelic intermediaries. Especially important is the Prophet Moses, to whom God spoke directly (Q. 4:164)—and, of course, who received the Torah. In the Qur᾿an, God says: "We inscribed all for him in the Tablets which taught and explained everything" (Q. 7:145).[4] This provides a very important distinction for Moses in the Islamic tradition and the title *kalīm allāh*, the Addressed of God. It is by virtue of this distinction that the hadith collector al-Bukhārī includes a specific hadith about the Heavenly Ascension. This hadith puts Moses in the seventh and highest heaven and has him saying: "Lord, I did not think that You would elevate anyone above me!"[5]

Within the Islamic tradition, this elevation becomes perhaps the supreme moment of grace and of greatest intimacy between God and His beloved. As this hadith goes on to state, "Then Gabriel ascended with him above that as only God knows until he reached the Lote-Tree of the Furthest Boundary, and the Compeller, the Lord of Might approached and descended until He was the distance of two bow spans from him or nearer" (that is, from the top to the bottom of a bow). This final phrase on the apparent descent and proximity of God quotes Sūrat al-Najm (Q. 53:8–9), making clear in this version of the hadith that God is meant.[6]

This event also raises a powerful debate over whether the Prophet saw God during the Ascension or merely a light that veiled Him. For those who hold that he did indeed see Him, this becomes a second way in which he outdoes his prophetic brother Moses, who was sent into a swoon by the divine manifestation on the mountain. The tryst between God and the Prophet becomes the moment at which the daily prayers are instituted. In his audience with the divine, the Prophet receives the obligation of fifty prayers a day. He submits to this and heads down the mountain—only to bump into Moses. Moses tells Muhammad that he knows from bitter experience that his community will not be able to cope with so many prayers; hence, Muhammad should go back to God. After this is repeated several more times, the number is set as the familiar five prayers daily, although the reward, as for many good deeds, is set at ten times that, in other words the original fifty. Here Moses becomes a willing support to the Prophet Muhammad in his reception of divine mercy for his community.

Moreover, in further hadiths, there is an emphasis on the divine speech of the Qur'an connected with the events of the Ascension. In relation to the present theme, the final two verses of Sūrat al-Baqara are named in some reports as a treasure from beneath the throne that is revealed at the same time. These verses read:

> The Messenger believes in what has been sent down to him from his Lord, as do the faithful. They all believe in God, His angels, His scriptures, and His messengers. "We make no distinction between any of His messengers," they say. "We hear and obey. Grant us Your forgiveness, our Lord. To You we all return!" God does not burden any soul with more than it can bear: each gains whatever good it has done, and suffers its bad. "Lord, do not take us to task if we forget or make mistakes. Lord, do not burden us as You burdened those before us. Lord, do not burden us with more than we have strength to bear. Pardon us, forgive us, and have mercy on us. You are our Protector, so help us against the disbelievers" (Q. 2:285–86).[7]

So in tandem with perhaps the most taxing individual obligation on the follower of the Prophet Muhammad, the five daily prayers, are these verses that provide both powerful prayers for mercy as well as the promise that no one is taxed with more than they can bear. This is a treasure because it is a treasure of mercy, from the Lord of Mercy: the one who can be said to laugh—granting all possible nuance in how that should be understood—because His believing servants fall short in comprehending how encompassing that mercy is for them.

Notes

1. Collected in Muslim, *Ṣaḥīḥ*, *Kitāb al-īmān, Bāb ākhir ahl al-nār khurūjan.*

2. Of the well-known English translations, this combination is chosen by Yusuf Ali.

3. This position is unlike that of the Ashʿarīs, although the extent that God's wisdom can be known is limited. An example is that there are certain minimum standards for eschatological mercy, such as belief in God.

4. As translated by M.A.S. Abdel Haleem, *The Qurʾan: English Translation and Parallel Arabic Text* (New York: Oxford University Press, 2004; used by permission; all rights reserved).

5. For the text of this hadith, see chapter 8 herein.

6. Another interpretation takes this to refer to Gabriel coming close to the Prophet.

7. As translated by Abdel Haleem, *The Qurʾan.*

7

Mercy and Grace in the Prophetic Tradition

A Close Look at Selected Hadiths

Muhammad Modassir Ali

In the chapter entitled "Maryam," God states: "Does humankind not remember that We created it before, when it was nothing?" (Q. 19:67).[1] Contextually, the verse occurs as evidence for the possibility of resurrection for humankind. Yet, in its literal sense, it also establishes an existential truth: that humankind—and, by extension, creation itself—was nonexistent. The fact that God created and, in the process, drew human beings from nonexistence to existence, from nothingness to being, is an act both of mercy and grace.

The theme of mercy is a foundational cosmological principle in the Islamic scheme of things and is elaborately discussed and written about in all genres of Islamic literature. The theme of grace seems to take a back seat. Yet grace is represented with considerable vigor and emotional and spiritual depth in the supplications of the Prophet (peace be upon him). In both the Qur'an and the Hadith, mercy and grace are so seamlessly wed to each other that one hardly makes sense without the other—but God knows best. This state of affairs is reflected in the texts from Islam's Prophetic tradition that were selected for study by the 2022 Building Bridges Seminar—all of which are provided in this volume's chapter 9. In what follows, I offer explanations of many of those selections.

Raḥma and *Faḍl*: Shades of Meaning; Subtleties of Usage

It needs to be mentioned at the very outset that, in the Islamic scheme of things—whether for academic purposes or for practical day-to-day affairs—Hadith (the compendium of records of the spoken word or actions or tacit approval of Prophet Muhammad) is understood as an elaboration and commentary of the Qur'anic message. It might thus seem beneficial to enumerate the various shades of meaning associated with the two words *mercy* and *grace* as they occur in the Qur'an so that one understands how the terms are used in the Prophetic tradition.

According to Abū ʿAbd Allāh al-Dāmaghānī (AH 398–478 / 1007–1085 CE), the term *raḥma* occurs with fourteen different connotations in the Qur'an.[2] They are Islam/submission (Q. 76:31), paradise (Q 2:118; 3:107), rain (Q. 7:57), prophethood (Q. 43:32), blessing (Q. 19:2; 18:65), the Holy Qur'an (Q. 12:111), provision and subsistence (Q. 17:100), protection and opening (Q. 33:17), wellness/well-being (Q. 39:38), love (Q. 57:27; 48:29), faith (Q. 11:28), grace (*minnah*) (Q. 4:83), Prophet ʿĪsā (Jesus) (Q. 19:21), and Prophet Muhammad (Q. 21:107). Al-ʿAskarī adds to that list "replenishment of wealth" (whether in this world or the Hereafter).[3]

As for *faḍl*, its occurrences bear seven different shades of meanings. These are Islam (Q. 3:73), prophethood (Q. 4:113; 17:87), sustenance in this world (including trade, profits, and spoils of war) (Q. 62:10; 4:73; 73:20), provisions of paradise (Q. 4:175; 3:171), replenishment of wealth (whether in this world or the Hereafter) (Q. 2:268), bounty/grace (Q. 4:83; 12:38), and paradise (Q. 33:47).[4] As we shall see, the selected Prophetic traditions use the words *mercy* and *grace* to allude to similar concepts and share several common meanings.

Synonyms for *Raḥma* and *Faḍl*

In addition to *raḥma* and *faḍl*, the Qur'an and hadith literature employ a number of synonymous terms—which, as scholars have explained, also carry subtle differences of meaning. These additional terms are mentioned here merely to acquaint the reader with the richness of these concepts.

Ra'fah (compassion and mercy) derives from the triliteral root *ra-a-fa*, which means to show mercy. God's name al-Ra'ūf derives from the same root. Scholars (linguists, grammarians, theologians, and so on) differ on which of the two terms is more hyperbolic in conveying the meaning of mercy. However, they seem to agree that *ra'fah* is deeper in the "quality of mercy" as it conveys the transfer of compassion and blessings without any pain, whereas *raḥma* is absolute compassion, which might be accompanied with discomfort and pain as in the case of "severing the organ of a leper" to protect him/her from death.[5]

Riqqah (tenderness) comes from the root *r-q-q*, which means "to become tender" and is the opposite of coarseness (*ghilẓah*); it is considered to be the reason for which mercy (*raḥma*) is shown toward others.[6]

Minnah (bestowing a favor), from the root *m-n-n*, literally means "to cut a portion off something or reduce it from the sides." It is used to signify a blessing, the bestowal of a favor without seeking any reward in return, and a gift that requires no effort from the recipient. The sense is that the bestower cuts or takes away from his wealth to transfer it to a beneficiary without seeking any recompense from him. At times, however, it also connotes a favor for which one demands gratitude, and in this sense has been expressly forbidden by certain hadiths.[7] From this word also derives one of God's names—al-Mannān—which means "the bestower of blessings without pretentions" but also indicates one who wants the beneficiary to realize that God has done him a favor.[8]

Al-hannān/hanān (mercy) comes from the triliteral root *ḥ-n-n*, meaning mercy, blessing, and subsistence. It is another of God's names.[9] The difference between al-Ḥannān and al-Mannān is that the former signifies that God turns toward him who has turned away from Him, while the latter signifies that He bestows blessings without being asked for them.[10]

Niʿma (blessing), from the root *n-ʿ-m*, literally means to be in a state of wellness and happiness. According to Rāghib al-Aṣfahānī, when used to mean the conferral of blessing upon another being, the beneficiary has to be a rational being. So one cannot say that one has conferred a certain *niʿma* on a camel.

Ālā' (favor/gift/blessing) occurs more than thirty times in Sūrat al-Raḥmān alone. Linguists differ as to whether the word derives from *w-l-y* or *ʾ-l-y*. Al-ʿAskarī thinks it derives from *w-l-y*, in which case it means a blessing that closely follows another. If derived from *ʾ-l-y*, however, it means a great blessing.[11] Most exegetes and linguists consider *ālā'* to be synonymous to *niʿma*.[12]

Other terms may be included here—among them, *ʿaṭā'* (giving/gift), *barakah* (blessing), *jūd* (generosity), *rawh* (mercy), and *jamāl* (beauty).

Hadiths Introduced

The "Starting" Hadith

"The merciful are shown mercy by the Merciful (al-Raḥmān). Be merciful on the earth." So begins a saying of the Prophet known as *al-ḥadīth al-awwaliyyah* (the first or starting hadith). It was common practice among traditional scholars (a practice that continues today) to commence the study of the Prophetic tradition with this particular hadith, owing to its paramount significance in the Islamic worldview. Its first sentences may be rendered in English as "The merciful are shown mercy by the Merciful (al-Raḥmān).

Be merciful on the earth, and you will be shown mercy from one who is in the heavens." If we are more precise, we will note that the command is: "Be merciful to *man fī' l-Arḍ.*" Hence, a literal translation might be: "Have mercy on the rational beings on earth." This hadith occurs, with slight variations, in many collections. One such variation is "Be merciful to *Ahl al-Ard* (the inhabitants of earth)"—which includes all living things. This version of *al-ḥadīth al-awwaliyyah* is best read alongside the hadith that tells of a man whose seemingly insignificant act of quenching the thirst of a dog led to his acceptance by God.[13]

The *ḥadīth al-awwaliyyah* also explains the etymology of the term *raḥma*, which is largely feminine in nature and is packed with the qualities of love, generosity, protection, and selflessness. It reads well with this verse of the Qur'an: "Say [to them], 'Call on Allāh, or on al-Raḥmān—whatever names you call Him, the best names belong to Him'" (al-Isrā' 17:110). The meaning here is that mercy is so intrinsic to divine nature that God's Name of Essence (Allāh) may be substituted for His most incumbent attribute (Rahmān / "the Merciful").

Creation as Mercy

We turn now, in the hadith collection *Sahih Muslim*, to a report from Abu Hurayra that God's Messenger said: "When God created the creation, He wrote in His Book, which was by Him upon the Throne: 'Verily, My mercy overcomes My wrath.'" A variant of this tradition says: "When God created the creation, He wrote in His Book *with His own Hand*, which was by Him upon the Throne: 'Verily, My mercy *precedes* My wrath."[14]

Commentaries on this hadith, more often than not, tend to focus on its anthropomorphic aspects: its references to God's Book, God's Hand, God's being "upon the Throne," and so on. More important for our purposes is to note how this hadith suggests that God's qualities include *both* mercy and wrath, and that both qualities arise out of God's will (*irādah*). It is thus God's will that the effects of His mercy encompass His creatures more profoundly than that of His wrath—which is restricted to those who stand in sheer defiance of the Merciful Lord. In any case, this hadith is best read in the light of this verse from Sūrat Al-A'rāf: "'Grant us good things in this world and in the life to come. We turn to You.' God said, 'I bring My punishment on whoever I will, but My mercy encompasses all things. I shall ordain My mercy for those who are conscious of God and pay the prescribed alms; who believe in Our Revelations'" (Q. 7:156).

Rain as God's Mercy

A well-known hadith asserts: "The Messenger of God led us in the morning prayer at al-Hudaybiyya after rain." Another hadith states: "A man came to the Prophet on a Friday while he (the Prophet) was delivering a sermon." Both texts depict the mercy of God through rain. Although the context of the former hadith is quite clear, it does not inform us why the Prophet should turn around after the dawn prayer and inform his companions what the Lord had said. While recounting the Hudaybiyya incident in his *Maghāzī*, Al-Wāqidī tells us:

> 'Ibn Abī Sabra related to me on the authority of Ishāq bin ʿAbd Allāh (and he) on the authority of Abū Salama al-Ḥaḍramī, who said: I heard Abū Qatāda say, (who said) I heard Ibn Ubayy say, "As we were in al-Ḥudaybiyyah it rained upon us there." And then Ibn Ubayy said, "This is the *naw'* of Autumn [that is, the period during which one or a set of stars would be setting in the west while another set of stars was rising with the sun in the East.[15]] We were blessed with rain because of Sirius!"[16]

What the reader must understand is that ʿAbd Allāh ibn Ubayy was the head of the hypocrites (*munāfiqūn*)—those who outwardly professed Islam yet remained unbelievers in their hearts and who never missed an opportunity to create confusion in the Madinan community. Of course, the Prophet felt obliged to offer the people a better explanation.

As mentioned earlier, in the Qur'an, rain was one of the connotations of *raḥma*. The Prophet's wife ʿĀ'ishah (may God be pleased with her) is reported to have said that when it rained, the Prophet would say, "(This is) Mercy."[17]

This text may be read in tandem with a hadith wherein a Bedouin requests the Prophet for rain due to the lack of rain in Madina and adjacent areas. While rain is no doubt a source of God's mercy, too much of it can be a cause for discomfort. Hence, the Prophet taught his companions different forms of prayers for rain. Here are two examples: "O God, provide rain to your servants and beasts and spread your mercy and bring forth life in your lifeless land"[18]; and "O God, I beseech you for the best of [rain], and the good therein, and the good with which it is sent and I seek refuge in you from its evil and the evil therein and the evil with which it is sent."[19] Furthermore, when the Prophet prayed for intense rain, he qualified his request by saying "O God, make it a downpour which is beneficial (*ṣayyiban nāfiʿan*)."[20] At times he would say "make it a downpour which is pleasant and enjoyable (*ṣayyiban hanī'an*)."[21]

The Insufficiency of Good Deeds

One hadith declares: "None amongst you can get into Paradise by virtue of his deeds alone." It displays the well-known tension, present in Islam—but more so in Christianity—relating to the primacy of works versus the primacy of grace for salvation. Instead of commenting on the theological discussion that ensues around this tradition, it might be more rewarding to relate a somewhat lengthy and authentic tradition of the Prophet that explains the issue through an anecdote.

It was narrated by Jābir bin ʿAbd Allāh (may God be pleased with him) that once the Prophet came out to us and said:

> My friend Gabriel just left me; he said: O Muhammad, by Him who sent you with the truth, God has a servant from among His servants, who worshipped Him—the Most High—for five hundred years atop a mountain thirty cubits wide and thirty cubits long in the middle of the sea. The sea surrounds the mountain by 4,000 leagues from all the sides. God brought forth for him a sweet-watered spring, the width of a finger, gushing with fresh water, and it collects at the foot of the mountain and (brought forth for him) a pomegranate tree which produces a pomegranate each night that feeds him during the day. When he comes down in the evening, he performs ablution and partakes of that pomegranate, and then stands in prayer to Him. He always beseeches His Lord to seize him in the state of prostration and not permit neither soil nor anything else to spoil his posture until he is resurrected . . . and not for anything that would spoil him. God did so; and we passed by him when we come down or rise. We have come across in the knowledge that he would be resurrected on the Day of Judgement and would be made to stand before God. And the Lord shall say to him: "Enter into Paradise with my mercy," and he would reply: "Lord! Rather, by my work"; and the LORD shall say: "Enter into Paradise with my mercy," and he would reply: "Lord, rather by my work," the Lord shall say to him: "Enter into Paradise with my mercy," and he would reply: "Lord! Rather, by my work"; At that, God will say to the angels: Compare my blessings upon my servant with his works; it will be found that the gift of sight alone accounts for the worship of five hundred years and the gift of the whole body remained unaccounted for. God will then say: "Throw my servant into hell fire." As he is dragged to hell fire, he will cry out, "My Lord, by Your Mercy, admit me to Paradise." God will say, "Bring him back," and he will be made to stand in front of the Lord. Then God will say to him: "My servant! Who created you while you were nothing?" He will reply: "You, my Lord." God will ask him: "Was that by you or by My

> Mercy?" He will reply: "Rather by Your Mercy." God will ask: "Who gave you the strength to worship Him for five hundred years?" He will respond: "You, my Lord." God will ask: "Who brought you to the mountain in the middle of the deep sea and brought forth fresh water out of salt water for you, and produced for you a pomegranate every night when its tree bears fruit once a year only? And you have besought me to take you while you were prostrate, didn't I do that for you?" He will reply: "You, my Lord." The Almighty Lord will say: "All that was through My Mercy and by My Mercy I will admit you to Paradise. Admit my servant to Paradise for you were an excellent servant O My servant." Thus, God will admit him to Paradise. Gabriel said, "Undoubtedly, all affairs are by the Mercy of God, O Muhammad."[22]

In short, in the Islamic tradition, both works and grace have their respective roles to play. Works are just a reason for salvation, while grace and God's mercy are absolutely incumbent. Hence, the Prophetic prayer: "O God! Your Forgiveness is more expansive than my sins; and Your Mercy is more worthy of being sought than my work."[23]

God's Mercy versus God's Wrath

In addition to highlighting the unfathomable expanse of God's mercy, traditions provide, at times, a distressing reminder of man's unwholesome desire of insisting on His majesty rather than His mercy and in the process end up restricting God's mercy to their limited understanding of it.[24]

While God's attributes of majesty and wrath are as inherent in His divinity as His mercy, Muslims have been commanded to focus on His attributes of mercy (for His mercy takes precedence over His majesty) rather than those of His majesty and wrath. To this end, the Prophet has taught us a supplication in which he would pray: "O God I seek refuge in Your pleasure from Your wrath, and in Your pardoning/forgiveness from Your punishment; and I seek refuge in You from You."[25]

The Mercy of the Prophet's Night Journey

The selection of hadiths in this volume includes an account of the nocturnal journey of the Prophet to the heavens and back. The context is important. His wife Khadījah (may God be pleased with her) and uncle who was his fortress, Abū Ṭālib, had passed away leaving him virtually defenseless against the relentless attack of the disbelievers. The Prophet had also just returned from the hilly Ṭā'if, chased away and stoned. He would later recount to his wife ʿĀ'ishah (may God be pleased with her) that he had not faced a more difficult time than the one he experienced in Ṭā'if. In the wake of this painful experience, God invited his beloved Prophet to His presence to console him and make him witness His loving mercy and splendor.

Among the myriad issues raised by this tradition, a prominent one is God's eagerness to engage with humankind despite our frailty and shortcomings. The Prophet is commanded to pray fifty prayers during the day, but thanks to the continuous interventions of the prophet Moses, the fifty prayers were reduced to five, but the reward remained that of fifty. In another tradition, the Prophet, assuming this divine attribute in turn, makes a similar statement when comparing his companions to later generations. He says: "You live in a time when whoever leaves a tenth of what he is being commanded to do will be ruined; then a time shall come when whoever performs a tenth of what he has been commanded to do shall be saved."[26]

Conclusion

It should now be clear that, as an extension of the Qur'anic revelation, the Prophetic tradition presents mercy and grace in more or less the same shades of meaning as are found in the Qur'an. It should also be clear that, in their connotations, *raḥma* and *faḍl* are largely interchangeable. Just as in the Qur'an, where both the terms *faḍl* and *raḥma* quite often occur together—with *faḍl* usually preceding *raḥma*, so the Prophet, in keeping with His *adab ma' Allāh* (customary behavior before God) adheres to the same sequence with *faḍl*, more often than not, preceding *raḥma* both in his everyday use of the term and in his prayers. Again, in accordance with the Qur'an, the Prophetic language is unmistakably embedded in the semantics of mercy.

The Prophet is reported to have said: "Indeed God has ninety-nine names; he who enumerates them shall enter paradise."[27] Several scholars have concluded from this and other prophetic injunctions that, while the enumeration of God's names is of itself an act of virtue, what is meant here is to conduct one's life by the requirements of these names or what the Prophet called "assuming the attributes of God." While understanding the linguistic significance and sociological implications of these attributes has its own benefits, what matters first and foremost is to what extent have we been "god-like" in our interaction with God Himself and His creatures.

Notes

1. This and all subsequent Qur'an quotations in this chapter are according to the translation by M.A.S. Abdel Haleem, *The Quran* (Oxford: Oxford University Press, 2004), adapted slightly in some cases.

2. See Abū ʿAbd Allāh al-Dāmaghānī, *al-Wujūh wa'l-Naẓā'ir li-Alfāẓ Kitāb Allāh al-ʿAzīz*, ed. ʿArabī ʿAbd al-Ḥamīd Āzīz (Beirut: Dār al-kutub al-ʿIlmiyyah, n.d.), 224–27; also see Muqātil bin Sulaymān, *al-Wujūh wa'l-Naẓā'ir fī'l-Qur'ān al-ʿAẓīm*, ed. Ḥātim Ṣāliḥ al-Ḍāmin (Riyadh: Maktabat al-Rushd—Nāshirūn, 2011), 44–47, who mentions eleven meanings for mercy.

3. Abū Hilāl al-Ḥasan bin ʿAbd Allāh al-ʿAskarī, *Muʿjam al-Furūq al-Lughawiyyah*, ed. Bayt Allāh Bayāt and Mu'assasat al-Nashr al-Islāmī (Qum: Mu'assasat al-Nashr al-Islāmī, AH 1412), 386.

4. Al-ʿAskarī terms provisions of paradise as "reward." See his *al-Wujūh wa'l-Naẓā'ir*, edited with commentary by Muḥammad ʿUthmān (Cairo: Maktabah al-Thaqāfah al-Dīniyyah, 2007), 385–87.

5. al-ʿAskarī, *Muʿjam al-Furūq al-Lughawiyyah*, 246–47.

6. al-ʿAskarī, *Muʿjam al-Furūq al-Lughawiyyah*, 259.

7. al-ʿAskarī, *Muʿjam al-Furūq al-Lughawiyyah*, 515.

8. Ibn Manẓūr, *Lisān al-ʿArab* (Beirut: Dār Ṣādir, AH 1414), 13/418; also *m-n-n*.

9. Ibn Manẓūr, *Lisān al-ʿArab*, 13/128–33; also *ḥ-n-n*.

10. al-ʿAskarī, *Muʿjam al-Furūq al-Lughawiyyah*, 204.

11. al-ʿAskarī, *Muʿjam al-Furūq al-Lughawiyyah*, 6.

12. Ḥamīd al-Dīn Farāhī has compellingly questioned this notion that *ālā'* means a gift or favor, claiming that neither the Qur'an nor Arab poetry vindicate this opinion; *ālā'*, rather, means *qudrah* or power. See his *Mufradāt al-Qur'ān*, ed. Muḥammad Ajmal Iṣlaḥī (Beirut: Dār al-Gharb al-Islāmī, 2002), 125–33.

13. For the text of the hadith about quenching the thirst of a dog, see chapter 9.

14. Emphasis mine.

15. In pre-Islamic times, Arabs invoked the stars, among other gods, for rain.

16. Muḥammad bin ʿUmar al-Waqidī, *Kitāb al-Maghāzī*, ed. Marsden Jones (London: Oxford University Press, 1965), 2/590.

17. Muslim bin Ḥajjāj, *Ṣaḥīḥ Muslim*, ed. Muḥammad Fu'ād ʿAbd al-Bāqī (Beirut: Dār Iḥyā' al-Turāth al-ʿArabī, 1991), 2/616.

18. Abū Dā'ūd, *Sunan Abī Dā'ūd*, ed. Shuʿayb al-Arna'ūṭ and Muḥammad Kāmil Qarra-ballī (Beirut: Dār al-Risālah al-ʿIlmiyyah, 2009), 2/376.

19. Muslim bin Ḥajjāj, *Ṣaḥīḥ Muslim*, 2/616.

20. Muḥammad bin Ismāʿīl al-Bukhārī, *al-Jāmiʿ al-Ṣaḥīḥ* (Beirut: Dār Ṭawq al-Najāt, 2001), 2/32.

21. Abū Dā'ūd, *Sunan Abī Dā'ūd*, 7/428.

22. Al-Ḥākim al-Naysābūrī, *al-Mustadrak ʿala al-Ṣaḥīḥayn*, ed. Muṣṣafa ʿAbd al-Qādir ʿAṭā (Beirut: Dār al-kutub al-ʿIlmiyyah, 1990), 4/278.

23. Al-Ḥākim al-Naysābūrī, *al-Mustadrak ʿala al-Ṣaḥīḥayn*, 1/728.

24. See, in chapter 9, the hadith beginning, "The Prophet said, 'Amongst the men of the Children of Israel there was a man who had murdered ninety-nine persons'"; see also the hadith beginning "There were two men among the Children of Israel, who were striving for the same goal. One of them would commit sin."

25. Ibn Mājah, *Sunan Ibn Mājah*, ed. Muḥammad Fu'ād ʿAbd al-Bāqī (Cairo: Dār Iḥyā' al-kutub al-ʿilmiyyah, n.d.), 2/1262.

26. Muḥammad bin ʿĪsā al-Tirmidhī, *Sunan al-Tirmidhī*, ed. with commentary by Aḥmad Muhammad Shākir and Muḥammad Fu'ad ʿAbd al-Bāqī (Cairo: Maṭbaʿat Muṣṭafā Ḥalabī, 1975), 4/530.

27. Ibn Mājah, *Sunan Ibn Mājah*, 2/1269.

8

Selected Hadiths on Mercy and Grace

Texts for Study

Unless otherwise noted, the translation and numbering of these selections accord with sunnah.com.

Jami al-Tirmidhi, Book 27, Hadith 30

Abdullah bin ʿAmr narrated that the Messenger of God said: "The merciful are shown mercy by the Merciful (al-Rahman). Be merciful on the earth, and you will be shown mercy from one who is in the heavens. The womb (*al-rahim*) is named after the Merciful (al-Rahman), so whoever maintains a connection with it, God maintains a connection with him, and whoever breaks off relation with it, God breaks off relation with him."

Sahih Muslim, Book 37, Hadith 6631

Abu Hurayra reported God's Messenger as saying: There are one hundred [parts of] mercy with God and of these He has sent down one part of mercy upon the jinn and human beings and animals and the insects, and it is because of this [one part] that they love one another, show kindness to one another, and even the beast treats its young with affection. God has reserved ninety-nine parts of mercy with which He will treat His servants on the Day of Resurrection.

Sahih Muslim, Book 37, Hadith 6626

Abu Hurayra reported that God's Messenger said: When God created the creation, He wrote in His Book, which was by Him upon the Throne: "Verily, My mercy overcomes My wrath."

Sunan Abi Dawud, Hadith 3897

Narrated by . . . Zayd bin Khalid al-Juhani: The Messenger of God led us in the morning prayer at al-Hudaybiyya after rain which had fallen during the night, and when he finished, he turned to the people and said: "Do you know what your Lord has said?" They said: "God and His Apostle know best." He said: "This morning there were among my servants one who believes in Me and one who disbelieves. The one who said: 'We have been given rain by God's grace and mercy' is the one who believes in Me and disbelieves in the star; but the one who said: 'We have been given rain by such and such a star,' is the one who disbelieves in Me and believes in the star."[1]

Sahih Muslim, Book 6, Hadith 82

Abu Usayd reported that the Messenger of God said: When any one of you enters the mosque, he should say: "O God! open for me the doors of Thy mercy"; and when he steps out he should say: "O God! I beg of Thee Thy grace."

Jami al-Tirmidhi, Book 1, Hadith 147

Abu Hurayra narrated: A Bedouin entered the mosque while the Prophet was sitting. He prayed, then when he was finished, he said: "O God! Have mercy upon me and Muhammad, and do not have mercy on anyone along with us." The Prophet turned, toward him and said: "You have restricted something that is vast." It was not long before the man was urinating in the mosque. So the people rushed at him. But the Prophet said: "Pour a bucket of water over it—or a tub of water over it." Then he said: "You have been sent to make things easy [for people]; you have not been sent to make things difficult for them."

Sahih al-Bukhari, Book 80, Hadith 39

Narrated by Anas Bin Malik: A man came to the Prophet on a Friday while he [the Prophet] was delivering a sermon at Medina, and said, "There is lack of rain, so please invoke your Lord to bless us with rain." The Prophet looked at the sky and no cloud could be detected. Then he invoked God for rain. Clouds started gathering together and it rained till the Medinan valleys started flowing with water. It continued raining till the next Friday.

Then that man (or some other man) stood up while the Prophet was delivering the Friday sermon, and said, "We are drowned! Please call on your Lord to withhold it (rain) from us." The Prophet smiled and said twice or thrice, "O God! Please let it rain round about us but not upon us." The clouds started dispersing over Medina to the right and to the left, and it rained round about Medina and not upon Medina. God showed them the miracle of His Prophet and His response to his invocation.

Sahih Muslim, Book 39, Hadith 210

Abu Hurayra reported God's Messenger as saying: A person was suffering from intense thirst while on a journey, and he found a well. He climbed down into it and drank (water) and then came out and saw a dog lolling its tongue on account of thirst and eating the moistened earth. The person said: "This dog has suffered from thirst as I had suffered from it." He climbed down into the well, filled his shoe with water, then held it in his mouth while he climbed up and made the dog drink it. So God appreciated this act of his and pardoned him. Then [the Companions around him] said: "Messenger of God, is there a reward for us even for [serving] such animals?" He said: "Yes, there is a reward for service to every living animal."

Sahih al-Bukhari, Book 60, Hadith 137

Abu Sa'id Al-Khudri narrated that the Prophet said: Amongst the Children of Israel there was a man who had murdered ninety-nine persons. Then he set out asking [whether his repentance could be accepted or not]. He came upon a monk and asked him if his repentance could be accepted. The monk replied in the negative and so the man killed him. He kept on asking till a man advised him to go to a certain village. [So he left for it] but death overtook him on the way. While dying, he turned his chest toward that village [where he had hoped his repentance would be accepted], and so the angels of mercy and the angels of punishment quarreled amongst themselves regarding him. God ordered the village [toward which he was going] to come closer to the man; and God ordered the village [whence he had come] to go further away. And then God ordered the angels to measure the distances between the man's body and the two villages. The result was that he was found to be one span closer to the village [he was going to]. Therefore, he was forgiven.

Sahih Muslim, Book 52, Hadith 69

Abu Hurayra reported God's Messenger as saying: "None amongst you can get into Paradise by virtue of his deeds alone." [The people] said: "Messenger of God, not even you?" Thereupon he said: "Not even I—only if God should wrap me in His grace and mercy."

Sunan Abi Dawud, Book 43, Hadith 129

Narrated by Abu Hurayra: I heard the Messenger of God say: "There were two men among the Children of Israel, who like brothers to one another. One of them would commit sin but the other would strive to do his best in the world. The man who exerted himself in worship continued to see the other in sin. He would say: 'Stop that.' One day he found him in sin and said to him: 'Stop that.' The other said: 'Leave me alone. By my Lord! Have you been sent as a watchman over me?' He said: 'I swear by God, God will not forgive you, nor will he admit you to Paradise.' Then their souls were taken back [by God], and they met together with the Lord of the worlds. He [God] said to this man who had striven hard in worship: 'Had you knowledge about Me or had you power over that which I had in My hand?' He said to the man who sinned: 'Go and enter Paradise by My mercy.' He said about the other: 'Take him to Hell.'"

Abu Hurayra himself then said: "By Him in Whose hand my soul is, he spoke a word by which this world and the next world of his were destroyed."

al-Isra wa'l-Miʿraj (The Night Journey)

Sahih al-Bukhari, Book 97, Hadith 142

Narrated by Anas bin Malik: On the night when the Messenger of God (may God bless him and grant him peace) traveled from the Mosque of the Kaʿba, three angels came to him [who had previously come to him] while he was sleeping in the Inviolable Mosque before he received revelation. The first of them [had previously] asked, "Which of them is he?" The middle one said, "He is the best of them." The last of them said, "Take the best of them." On that [earlier] night he did not see them. He only saw them on another night [that is, the night of the ascension] in which his heart saw while his eyes were asleep. His heart does not sleep. That is how it is with the prophets: their eyes sleep but their hearts do not sleep.

[The angels] did not speak to him until they carried him and placed him at the well of Zamzam and then from among them Gabriel took charge of him. Gabriel split him open between his throat and the middle of his chest and emptied out his breast and abdomen and then washed it with Zamzam water so that he cleansed his abdomen. Then a tray was brought which contained a gold vessel filled with faith and wisdom. He stuffed it into his breast and blood vessels—that is, the veins of his throat—and then he closed it.

Then [Gabriel] ascended with him to the lowest heaven. He knocked on one of its doors and the people of the heaven called out, "Who is this?" "Gabriel," he answered. They said, "Who is with you?" He replied. "Muhammad is with me." He said, "Has he been sent for?" "Yes," he answered. They said, "Welcome!" The people of heaven rejoice at him. The people of heaven do not know what God wants of him on the earth until He informs them. "He will find Adam in the lowest heaven. Gabriel will tell him, 'This is your father Adam, so greet him.'" He greeted him and Adam returned the greeting and said, "Welcome to my son! And an excellent son you are!" There in the lowest heaven are two flowing rivers and he asked, "What are these two rivers, Gabriel?" He replied, "This is the sources of the Nile and the Euphrates." Then he took him around heaven and there was another river on which was a castle of pearls and emeralds. He put his hand into it and it was very fine musk. He asked, "What is this, Jibril?" He replied, "This is Kawthar, which your Lord has stored up for you."

Then [Gabriel] took [Muhammad] up to the second heaven and the angels said to him the like of what those in the first had said, "Who is this?" He answered, "Gabriel." They asked, "Who is with you?" He replied. "Muhammad is with me." They said, "Has he been sent for?" "Yes," he answered. They said, "Welcome!"

Then he took him to the third heaven and they said to him the like of what those in the first and second had said. Then he took him to the fourth and they said the like of that. Then he took him to the fifth heaven and they said the like of that. Then he took him to the sixth heaven and they said the like of that and then he took him to the seventh heaven and they said the like of that.

Each heaven contained prophets which he named. I recall of them that Idris [Enoch] was in the second, Aaron in the fourth, another whose name I do not recall in the fifth, Abraham in the sixth, and Moses in the seventh because of the virtue of speaking directly to God. Moses said, "Lord, I did not think that You would elevate anyone above me!" Then Gabriel ascended with him above that as only God knows until he reached the Lote-Tree of the Furthest Boundary and the Compeller, the Lord of Might approached and descended until He was the distance of two bow spans from him or nearer. Part of what God revealed to him was "Fifty prayers for your community every day and night."

Then [Muhammad] descended until he met Moses, who stopped him and said, "Muhammad, what did your Lord on you?" He answered, "He enjoined on me fifty prayers every day and night." He said, "Your community will not be able to do that. Go back and ask your Lord to lighten it for you and for them." The Prophet turned to Gabriel as if he wished to consult him about that and Gabriel indicated to him, "Yes, if you wish." So he ascended to the Compeller and said while he was in his place, "O Lord, lighten it for us. My community will not be able to do this!" He reduced it by ten prayers. Then he returned to Moses who stopped him, and Moses continued to send him back to his Lord until it was five prayers. Then Moses stopped him the fifth time and said, "Muhammad, I tried as hard as I could with the tribe of Israel, my people, with less than this and they were weak and abandoned it. Your community has weaker bodies, hearts, physique, seeing and hearing. Go back and ask your Lord to lighten it for you."

Every time the Prophet turned to Gabriel so that he could advise him and Gabriel did not dislike that. So he took him up for the fifth time and he said, "O Lord, my community are weak in their bodies, hearts, hearing and physique, so lighten that for us." The Compeller said, "Muhammad!" "At Your service!" he replied. He said, "The Word with Me does not change and it is as I made it obligatory for you in the Mother of the Book." He said, "Every good action is worth ten like it and so it is fifty in the Mother of the Book while it is five for you." He returned to Moses who asked, "How did you do?" He said, "He lightened it for us and gave us ten for every good action." Moses said, "By God, I tried as hard as I could with the tribe of Israel with less than this and they abandoned it. Return to your Lord and ask him to lighten it for you more." The Messenger of God, may God bless him and grant him peace, said, "Moses, by God, I am embarrassed by the number of times I returned to my Lord." [Moses] said, "Descend in the Name of God." [Abu Hurayra] said, "[The Prophet Muhammad] woke up and he was in the Inviolable Mosque."

Note

1. Translation by Ahmad Hassan.

Part Two

Christian Perspectives on Mercy and Grace

9

Concepts of Mercy and Grace in the Catholic Tradition

An Overview

Julia A. Lamm

Interestingly, however intricately connected mercy and grace are in Christian life, theologically speaking they seem to have operated in parallel universes. In my treatment of them, therefore, I move back and forth between the two concepts. Doing so has been instructive for me, since *grace* has historically received so much theological attention that its sororal twin, *mercy*, became theologically neglected, often relegated to debates about the divine attributes or Christian moral theology. But to say that it was theologically neglected, comparatively speaking, is not to say it was neglected in Christian life. Giving *mercy* its theological due and restoring the balance between *mercy* and *grace* (as "two operations of the one divine love," to paraphrase Julian of Norwich), we Christian theologians might be able to break certain old habits and reflexes, and notice features of *grace* that have been marginalized.

Some Notes on Mercy

Mercy, of course, has multiple layers of meanings. For simplicity's sake, I want to loosely track two interrelated aspects of mercy that in Latin are conveyed as *misericordia* and *clementia.* These are not necessarily in tension with each other, but they do need to be distinguished.

Misericordia is a compound word combining "heart" and "the wretched," thereby conveying mercy as compassion and pity; it involves emotion as it moves us toward the afflicted out of tender love in order to heal, make whole, and restore. *Clementia* (clemency) is also mercy and compassion but carries more the meaning of leniency, indulgence, or forbearance; it is less associated with pathos, emphasizing calmness instead; it tends to be more forensic, although it too can be—and ideally in Christianity should be—the expression of steadfast love, compassion, and kindness.

In the history of Christian thought and practice, there are countless permutations of how mercy is exercised and understood—and, of course, also elided or distorted. The dynamics are complex: how versions of mercy get played out, emphasized, marginalized, retrieved, and recombined depends as much on local events as on larger historical trends. Here are just some of those recurring dynamics:

- *Clementia* versus *Misericordia*
- Interior disposition versus exterior action
- Spiritual versus ethical
- Institutional versus personal
- Justice versus mercy
- Local versus universal
- The move toward inclusivity versus the need to affirm boundaries and hierarchies
- The role of emotion (and its problems)
- The role of gender

Both basic meanings of mercy (as benevolent forgiveness and overflowing compassion), each capacious on its own, express the fundamental encounter with God described in the Bible as "merciful and gracious, slow to anger and abounding in steadfast love and faithfulness" (Exod. 34:6; Ps. 86:15). The biblical notion of mercy, as opposed to a juridical or political exercise of pardon, establishes and renews the covenantal relationship. God's mercy and grace uphold, sustain, and console.

The paradigmatic teachings of Christ that have informed the important role of mercy in Christian ethics throughout the ages are the parable of the Good Samaritan (Luke 10:29–37; the true neighbor is "'the one who showed him mercy.' Jesus said to him, 'Go and do likewise'"); and the Beatitudes (Matt. 5:1–12; among which is "Blessed are the merciful, for they will receive mercy").[1] Yet the underlying point to highlight is that, for Christians, Jesus Christ did not just teach about mercy. He offered it. He embodied it. Jesus Christ is mercy incarnate.[2]

Mercy in Liturgy and the Sacraments

Mercy is ubiquitous throughout Christian liturgy and the liturgical year. Those rites and prayers that acknowledge and call for God's mercy serve to remind us of who we are and what we have received. They reset—daily, weekly, seasonally—the Christian in right relation to God, to the church as community, and to all God's creation. Walter Kasper puts it well: "The culture of mercy among Christians should become concrete above all in the liturgy, in which we make God's mercy present in our celebration."[3]

Here my focus in on the Roman Catholic Mass, but the basic order of worship is similar in so-called mainline Protestant denominations. The introductory rites include the Penitential Act, in which the faithful acknowledge their sins and place their trust in God's mercy, and the recitation of the *Kyrie Eleison* ("Lord, have mercy. Christ, have mercy"). This is followed by the Liturgy of the Word. This typically includes three readings from scripture (from the Old Testament, from the New Testament Epistles, and from the Gospels), which may well convey the message of mercy; additionally, the responsorial Psalm (recited or chanted between the first two readings) will often be a plea for, or expression of gratitude for, God's mercy—especially during the season of Lent.

The second main part of the Mass, the Liturgy of the Eucharist, begins with the Lord's Prayer—which, when we think about it, is all about mercy and the grateful acknowledgment of our dependence on God: "forgive us our trespasses, as we forgive those who trespass against us." That is followed by the sign of peace, which is in turn followed by the *Agnus Dei*: "Lamb of God, who takes away the sins of the world, have mercy on us," said or sung three times, with the final iteration concluding "grant us peace." The Eucharist, as giving thanks, itself is a commemoration of Christ's merciful act of offering his own body and blood. Receiving Holy Communion is a communal act of radical inclusivity based on the experience of divine mercy.[4]

In addition to the Eucharist, the sacraments of baptism and reconciliation also confer divine mercy, and funeral rites commend the deceased to God's merciful love. Finally, the seasons of Lent and Easter feature repentance, mercy, and gratitude in countless ways.

Early Christianity

I turn now to examples of Christian writings on mercy and grace at various stages in Christianity's development.

1 Clement (ca. AD 96–97)

James Keenan identifies mercy as playing a defining role in "the social formation of the early church."[5] Supporting evidence for this can be found in the *First Letter of Clement* (third bishop of Rome), one of the earliest postapostolic texts of Christianity and, therefore, one of the first to contain citations of passages from the Jewish scriptures (what would become the Old Testament for Christians) alongside early Christian writings (specifically, the synoptic Gospels, the Pauline epistles, and Hebrews) that would come to be included in the New Testament.

Written shortly after the Domitian persecution of ca. 95, this document seamlessly integrates mercy as clemency, as compassion, and as care for the poor. In it, Clement (whose name means "mercy") quotes extensively from the Old Testament, fully expecting the church at Corinth to be well acquainted with the passages and their significance: he reminds them that David had been anointed with mercy, and David in turn called out for mercy (Ps. 89:20; Acts 13:22; Ps. 51:1–17).[6] Clement thus ties recognition and praise of God's great mercy and compassion together with forgiveness, resulting in the creation of a new heart and pure spirit. In other words, for Clement, the biblical notion of mercy is about restoration of human dignity and the proper relationship between humanity and the Creator. The "Father and Creator," Clement writes, is "free . . . from anger toward his whole creation" and has given us "his magnificent and excellent gifts of peace and kindness."[7] He emphasizes, "The all-merciful and beneficent Father has compassion on those who fear him, and with kindness and love he grants his favors to those who approach him with a sincere heart."[8]

Clement then transitions to Christology, arguing that this divine mercy manifests itself in Christ: "Thus, he showered his benefits on them all, but most abundantly on us who have taken refuge in his compassion through our Lord Jesus Christ, to whom be glory and majesty forever and ever."[9] Clement directly ties this divine mercy, incarnate in Christ, to Christ's "humbl[ing] himself."[10] With that Clement completes the movement that issues from the Father and Creator, through Jesus Christ, to the community of faith and the only proper response to such benignity.

For Clement, the Christian's response to God's mercy and kindness is threefold: gratitude expressed in moral uprightness ("We must, then, approach him with our souls holy, lifting up pure and undefiled hands to him, loving our kind and compassionate Father, who has made us his chosen portion"[11]); compassion toward others ("Let us be kind to one another in line with the compassion and tenderness of him who created us"[12]); and material care for the poor and vulnerable. The effect of mercy is therefore inherently moral—it manifests itself in how the Christian acts in the world, and in the type of community one helps build.

Nonetheless, we find in Clement an example of the tension between communal oneness and social ranking. He writes, "we must preserve our Christian body too in its entirety. . . . The strong must take care of the weak; the weak must look up to the strong. The rich must provide for the poor; the poor must thank God for giving him someone to meet his needs."[13]

Sometimes in Christianity mercy as material care for the weak calls for a radical inclusivity and identification that breaks down the larger society's social distinctions; at other times it can serve to reinforce those distinctions and foster a sense of superiority.

Justin Martyr (ca. 100–165)

Another example of mercy in early Christianity, this time mercy as clemency, is found in the work of Justin Martyr, who, as his name indicates, was not finally successful in his plea for clemency from the Roman emperor. He based his plea on the morality and reasonableness of the Christian faith as he tried to establish common ground with the best of Greco-Roman philosophy. According to Justin, clemency is aligned with justice; indeed, it is dictated by justice as it stands against tyranny. He enjoins the emperor, "Rulers similarly should give their decision as followers of piety and philosophy, not with tyrannical violence."[14] He goes so far as to identify Jesus as "Reason himself."[15] We can detect here an undercurrent of a two-part identification: on the part of Justin-the-philosopher with Jesus as "Reason" (Logos) itself; yet also on the part of Justin-the-religious-convert with Jesus as himself the victim of a merciless, unjust tyrannical system.

Justin does not fully develop the Christological implications of this, but it was a powerful theme that would continue to resurface: Jesus was shown no mercy in his trial and crucifixion, even as he continued to show mercy.[16] The effect of this on Christian ethics and spirituality was at least twofold: first, Christians ought to be both just and clement; and second, Christians who suffer unjustly for the sake of their faith are given moral and spiritual strength through the power of Christ. Mercy and grace are thus bound together Christologically. The cross is the place where justice and mercy meet. Justice as solely determined by the world—hence, as meted out with brutality and coercion—leaves no hope. Yet justice reconnected to a transcendent truth, revealed through love and mercy, and vindicated in the Resurrection does offer real hope.

The Church in Late Antiquity

Constantine famously issued the Edict of Milan in 313, granting not just new legal status but also preferential treatment to the Christian church, which just one decade earlier had suffered the Great (Diocletianic) Persecution. As a result, the church gained enormous power, wealth, and influence. Mercy came to be at play in complex exchanges between church and empire. Christian bishops practiced mercy publicly as both *misericordia* and *clementia*.

The Post-Constantinian Church on Mercy

Peter Brown, the historian who coined the term *late antiquity*, makes the case that in the post-Constantinian era Christian bishops transformed society in part through the Christian notion of *misericordia*. He explains:

> The bishops and their helpers—lay and clerical alike—are more than symptoms. They were, themselves, agents of change. To put it bluntly: in a sense, it was the Christian bishops who invented the poor. They rose to leadership in late Roman society by bringing the poor into ever sharper focus. They presented their actions as a response to the needs of an entire category of person (the poor) on whose behalf they claimed to speak.[17]

Here, arguably, the church did not so much mirror the larger Roman society as challenge it through its inclusive and integrating operations.

Where the church did absorb Roman understandings of *clementia*, it often transformed it with new applications, both politically and theologically. In their sweeping study of mercy in the Western intellectual tradition, Alex Tuckness and John Parrish show how Christian bishops "acquired the influence necessary to encourage public officials to show mercy to those convicted of crimes."[18] The institution's political stature thus rested in part on its moral claims. Theologically, the language of the church often reflected that of Roman law. Retributive justice was stressed—but it was reserved for God. Consequently, a more forensic notion of "mercy as clemency" slipped in as a counterweight to justice as conceived in the Roman political sphere. For example, Augustine emphasized divine justice as retributive, but because humans could not see through the opaqueness of the human soul, authorities should practice some leniency (and leave final judgment to God).[19]

Augustine (354–430) on Grace

In the first four centuries of Christianity, grace was a given—the general grace of creation and the specific grace of baptism in Christ—but it was not yet a discrete theological topic.[20] Grace became *the* central Christian doctrine that we know it to be during the pitched debate between Pelagius and Augustine in the second decade of the fifth century, in the aftermath of Alaric's sack of Rome in 410. It is important to keep in mind that Pelagius, a Romano-British ascetic and spiritual guide who arrived in Rome around 380, actually represented the accepted line: he was the conservative, Augustine the upstart. Yet Augustine prevailed and, as a result, his views on sin, grace, and divine sovereignty became theological orthodoxy. The subsequent history of debates about grace and free will is one of path dependency on the conditions and terminology set by Augustine.

Pelagius stressed five basic principles, all of which were meant to honor the goodness and justice of the Creator: (1) "the goodness of human nature is from God, its creator";[21] (2) our conscience and freedom of choice are existential proof that our basic goodness remains;[22] (3) the "custom of sinning" was introduced by Adam and Eve and perpetuated by imitation, but it is avoidable;[23] (4) the law acts as an aid to conscience; and (5) Christ "taught us and regenerated us."[24]

Augustine's response was initially temperate but became increasingly ferocious, to the point where he was successful in having Pelagius condemned and "Pelagianism" declared heresy. This is, of course, a long and enormously complex story, and Augustine's views shifted over the course of a decade and a half. Let me put it as succinctly as possible, with reference to the five points listed above.

1. Augustine's doctrine of original sin distinguished sharply between created (good) and fallen (corrupted) human nature—and he grew ever more pessimistic about the degree of our fallenness. Increasingly, he came to believe that we are incapable of choosing the good; free choice (*liberum arbitrium*) remains, but it is reduced merely to the ability to choose among evils.
2. Augustine focused more on the will than on reason. At first he granted that a flicker of our original desire for God remained, but he would come to deny even that.
3. Original sin is not merely a matter of social imitation and replication. It is passed on genetically through Adam's seed and is thus inherited. All humans carry the guilt of the original sin.
4. The law can only convict.
5. Augustine criticized Pelagius for reducing the work of Christ to his personal virtue and his forgiveness of sins. Christ, he insisted, is more than moral example. The question at issue here is, on the one hand, the role of human free will in achieving righteousness and, on the other hand, divine sovereignty. Augustine rejected Pelagius's view that all we need for righteousness has already been given to us by the Creator—namely, our natural capacity and the law. If that were true, he insisted, then Christ's death would have been in vain.

These commitments entailed a different understanding of grace—what it is, how it operates, what it accomplishes.

Grace brings forgiveness, but for Augustine, unlike (he claimed) for Pelagius, forgiveness is not just of past sins committed before Baptism; Christ's grace helps us to avoid future sin. Grace restores freedom (*libertas*), which is love of the good. Grace heals (one of his favorite metaphors is God as physician and grace as salve): "We are, after all, dealing with the grace of God which comes to our help as medicine through the mediator."[25] Grace is *caritas*. Probably the most important scriptural passage for Augustine's understanding of grace is Romans 5:5: "God's love has been poured into our hearts through the Holy Spirit that has been given to us." This passage not only gave him the fundamental idea of grace as *caritas*, but it also underscored the dynamic work of the Holy Spirit in individual souls. Augustine's doctrine of grace is deeply Trinitarian. According to Augustine, Pelagius separated the Creator from the Redeemer and the Holy Spirit. Grace is divine power at work in us. Augustine is keen to emphasize the sovereignty of God. He often speaks of *cooperative grace* (how we respond to God's grace), but *operative grace* (God as sole actor) was for him the primary point.

Augustine's stress on divine sovereignty, hence on *operative* or *prevenient* grace, intensified as the polemics with Pelagius grew fiercer—so much so that his critics would point out that such determinism made Augustine sound like his old Manichaean self. To his credit, he modified his view in the last decade of his life.

Medieval Christian Thought and Practice

The Middle Ages in Christianity spanned a millennium, roughly from about the fifth century through the sixteenth century. To illustrate the richness of Christian thought and practice when it came to mercy and grace during this period, I focus here on three examples from the High and Late Middle Ages—one each from the twelfth, thirteenth, and fourteenth centuries.

The Twelfth Century and Affective Spirituality

The history of mercy in the Western church took a turn in the High Middle Ages in Europe with the rise of affective spirituality. One could argue that mercy—both the heightened awareness of divine mercy revealed in the Incarnation and the imperative of merciful acts in Christian life—was at the center of that new devotion. Beginning in the twelfth century, we find a momentous shift in spirituality and religious devotion due to the confluence of several factors. Historically and socially, power in Europe was becoming consolidated, urban centers were growing, laws related to almost every aspect of life were being codified, and expanding systems of education were producing an increasingly literate populace. This went hand in hand with religious and theological changes: the so-called idea of the individual had emerged; the increase of power (secular and ecclesial) granted to religious leaders, which had been codified in canon law and the Gregorian Reform, created an ambivalence (among some) regarding such power and prompted reflections about the nature of genuine authority; the systematization regarding the seven sacraments and the priestly office contributed to increased demand for the sacraments of penance and the Eucharist; and—perhaps most important for the purposes of our discussion on mercy—new interest in the humanity of Christ dovetailed with new explorations of spiritual emotions and agency.

Allow me to digress a bit in order explain the significance of this new focus on Christ's humanity, how it expanded the repertoire of spiritual emotions, and the role that mercy played in this complex matrix of piety, theology, and iconography. In Christianity, the basic question of how the divine in Jesus Christ was related to the divine in God the Father and Creator ("the Trinitarian controversy") was resolved in the fourth century, at the Ecumenical Council of Nicaea (325) and the First Council of Constantinople (381). The debate then shifted to the question of the relation between the human and divine natures of Christ ("the Christological controversy"). The Council of Chalcedon (451) arrived at the formulation of two natures (*natura/ae*) in one person (*persona*).[26] In other words, Christ was fully human and fully divine, his two natures retaining their distinctness in their union. Although this was always affirmed in Latin Christianity, the emphasis during the first millennium tended to be on the divine nature—on *Christus Victor* (Christ the Victor), the resurrected Christ in glory. You see this theological and spiritual emphasis reflected in art up through the eleventh century: Christ depicted as king.

Beginning in the twelfth century in western Europe, however, a new emphasis emerged: an intense interest in the human nature of Christ, in his vulnerability in the nativity, in the conditions of his earthly life, in the fuller content of his teaching, and most especially in the extent of his suffering during his Passion.[27] It was in the Passion that the full significance of the Incarnation came into relief—which is to say, it was in the Passion that the depth of God's mercy was revealed. We witness this shift in emphasis increasingly in artwork from the twelfth through the fifteenth centuries: the vulnerability of Christ's humanity, expressed in depictions of his wounds that became more and more vivacious as his suffering became more graphic. This exploration of Christ's humanity prompted a simultaneous cultivation of religious emotions. Focus on Christ's nativity elicited responses of gratitude, compassion, and tenderness. Focus on Christ's Passion elicited similar responses, although arguably more intensely as they also demanded repentance and ongoing conversion. The vivid visualization of Christ's Passion—of his suffering and therefore of his love—pressed home the role of divine mercy in the history of salvation. God's mercy became personalized and internalized in new ways.

This all served to recast the Christian experience of divine love. For Augustine, God's love (*amor Dei*) remained an objective genitive: our love for God, not God's love for us.[28] This was not necessarily true for all Christian authors, but Augustine did have an outsized influence. In the twelfth century, however, there was a tidal wave of awareness of the subjective genitive: God's love for humanity as superabundant, as revealed in the Incarnation and Passion of Christ. And this established a different kind of emotional register. Notice here the difference: with emphasis on the subjective genitive comes a certain understanding of divine love—namely, of God moving toward humanity in kindness, tenderness, and mercy. This, in turn, elicited an affective response on the part of believers: gripping sorrow, deep remorse, overwhelming gratitude, and deep desire. If the Incarnation and Passion are the revelation of God's mercy and not just a generalized mercy, the individual could realize this more intensely and immediately by entering imaginatively into a gospel scene (the nativity, a moment of Christ's ministry, or his Passion), and by imitating Christ (*imitatio Christi*). This served to intensify the experience of the sacraments, especially penance and the Eucharist, both of which were objective offers of God's mercy. Here, too, we see the emergence of devotion to the sacred heart of Jesus, which is the symbol of divine mercy and compassion.[29]

With this new emphasis on the humanity of Christ, hence on divine mercy, came issues of gender (since the medieval registry of emotion associated compassion with the feminine) and challenges to the very systems of power that had been strengthened through the construction of more defined hierarchies and centralized power. Caroline Walker Bynum has done extensive work on how, for instance, abbots with considerable new authority handled their own ambivalence sometimes by viewing themselves as mothers as they simultaneously viewed Jesus as mother. Bynum also argues persuasively that medieval women, due to their identification with the bodiliness of Christ in his humanity, would incorporate that into their own self-understanding, thus potentially inverting the scales of religious power and authority.[30]

We see this sensibility taken up in the two new mendicant (or "begging") religious orders—the Franciscans and Dominicans, founded in 1209 and 1216, respectively. These mendicant friars were novel at the time in that, unlike Benedictines, they did not remain attached to their specific monasteries but went out to the cities and villages to preach the gospel to the people. They began as itinerant preachers. They were committed to a new, more radical understanding of the vow of poverty. The Franciscans, especially, were committed to identifying with and helping the poorest of the poor and the most marginalized—lepers, for example. Their ministry inspired a new evangelical understanding: a realization that the *vita apostolica* (apostolic life) can be lived by lay people living in the world and not cloistered in monasteries.

It was not just the institutional church or the religious orders that were leaders in this activity related to mercy. Christian society in the High and Late Middle Ages became organized around works of mercy in countless ways. Keenan has outlined the many medieval guilds and organizations that committed themselves to this work (although he omits the role of women mystics).[31] Similarly, beginning around 1200 in the Low Countries, groups of pious women who wished to lead lives combining contemplation and action, yet who wanted neither to marry nor to enter a convent, banded together to form a different kind of religious community where their vows could be temporary. They came to be called *beguines*, and their small cities within cities *beguinages*. Their mission was defined by mercy: they were motivated by their experience of and insight into God as Love (*Amor* in French, *Minne* in Dutch[32]) to love and serve the most vulnerable (the poor, the rejected, the marginalized, the sick). They flourished for a century and were much admired for their faith and service. When they became too threatening to bishops due to their popularity and accumulated property and independence, they were denounced by the Council of Vienne (1311–1312).[33]

What began on the level of piety took hold theologically and institutionally, only to be filtered back down to the laity at large through inscribed practices of the seven corporal works of mercy (based on the Beatitudes) and the seven spiritual works of mercy. (See heading below, "Catholicism and the Works of Mercy [Corporal and Spiritual].")

Thomas Aquinas, OP (1225–74), on Mercy

In his *Summa theologiæ*, Thomas Aquinas treated mercy under two different theological loci. This underscores the difficulty of theorizing about mercy due to its ubiquity: mercy pertains to the divine nature, salvation history, religious experience, theological anthropology, and the moral life. Therefore, to learn an author's views of mercy, one must become familiar with the entire corpus of their writings.

In Part 1 of the *Summa*, while treating the doctrine of God, Aquinas addressed the matter of whether mercy can properly be attributed to God. He highlighted two classical theological problems: first, since mercy is a passion, to attribute it to God would suggest that God can be moved and therefore would not be unchangeable; and second, the divine mercy might be seen as going against the divine justice. Aquinas's answer to the first was that "mercy is especially to be attributed to God, as seen in its effect";[34] his answer to the second was that mercy does not go against justice but does "something more than justice."[35]

Shadows of these same concerns arise again when Aquinas returned to mercy in the second part of Part 2, where the subject matter is Christian life and the virtues. Here Aquinas defined mercy as "heartfelt sympathy for another's distress, impelling us to succor him if we can. For mercy takes its name '*misericordia*' from denoting a [person's] compassionate heart [*miserum cor*] for another's unhappiness."[36] Following Augustine (but, as usual, systematizing him), Aquinas made mercy (*misericordia*) an extension of charity (*caritas*), one of the three theological virtues. Mercy, he explained, is one of three interior acts of charity, along with joy and peace (the exterior acts being beneficence, alms giving, and fraternal correction). He thus framed mercy as a state, an attitudinal stance, a way of being related to the external acts of beneficence and almsgiving without being reducible to them. (Aquinas placed clemency under the virtue of temperance.)

The implication of mercy being an extension of *caritas* is profound since our being moved by pity—hence, taking on another's distress—is the effect of love as the "union of affections."[37] In his discussion of mercy as an interior act of charity, Aquinas again faced the nagging problem that mercy is a passion and therefore might be construed as weakness because it relates to the appetitive power. He got around the problem by arguing that mercy is indeed a virtue, but only when it is subject to reason and thus is a movement of mind.

Aquinas's twofold treatment of mercy reflects the special nature of mercy as both cause and effect. God moves toward humanity in compassion—by forgiving, healing, and saving. That is grace, which then creates merciful hearts. Those merciful hearts are in turn commanded and empowered by grace to move toward others in compassion.

Thomas Aquinas on Grace

Aquinas's treatise on grace (at the end of the first part of Part 2 of the *Summa*) famously systematized an Augustinian understanding of grace with the help of Aristotelian categories and newer scholastic methods. (Again, while the Augustinian view on grace had long since been taken as orthodoxy,

"Augustinian" here has to be qualified, for there were different Augustines.) Aquinas elegantly created a third way between Pelagianism or semi-Pelagianism, on the one hand, and determinism, on the other.

Aquinas echoed Augustine in affirming that all is grace, as he also explained how we can and must cooperate with and respond to God's operative grace. Like Augustine, Aquinas distinguished between human nature as created and as fallen, but his anthropology was certainly not as bleak as Augustine's had been at the height of the attack on Pelagius in 418. Aquinas was more of a humanist in his anthropology. Although damaged by sin, we are not totally corrupt. Using the scalpel of careful scholastic definitions and distinctions, Aquinas addressed some of the thorniest questions bequeathed by Augustinian views of grace: he resolved the problem of an infinite regress of preparatory grace;[38] he distinguished between the natural and the supernatural;[39] he explained how grace operates as *motus* (movement) and as *habitus* (infused virtue), as he also clarified that grace as *habitus* is not an acquired virtue but is entirely a gift;[40] and he distinguished between *condign* and *congruous merit*.[41] In all of this, he affirmed that God alone is the cause of grace.

As for the essence of grace, Aquinas began with the common understanding of grace (modeled on a feudal relationship between a king and vassal) as three interrelated movements in our relationship with God: God looks on us with favor; God freely bestows a gift on us; and we are grateful for that gift and its benefits.[42] Aquinas proceeded to develop this basic analogy, drawing on the Augustinian understanding of grace as *caritas*:

> Therefore it is clear that every love of God is followed at some time by *a good caused in the creature*, but not co-eternal with the eternal love. And according to this difference of good the love of God to the creature is looked at differently. For one is common, whereby He loves "all things that are" (Wisdom 11:25), and thereby gives things their natural being. But the second is *a special love, whereby He draws the rational creature above the condition of its nature to a participation of the Divine good*; and according to this love He is said to love anyone simply, since it is by this love that God simply wishes the eternal good, which is Himself, for the creature.[43]

Grace, in this classical Catholic formulation, is not just forensic (not *just* clemency, not *just* a declaration) but is rather an infused quality of the soul. Aquinas explains: "inasmuch as a habitual gift is infused by God into the soul; and for this reason, that it is not fitting that God should provide less for those He loves, that they may acquire supernatural good."[44] As we have just seen, one effect of this infused grace is mercy as *misericordia*: works of mercy flow from the person who has been infused with sanctifying grace.

Julian of Norwich (ca. 1342–ca. 1406)

About a century after Aquinas died in Italy, a thirty-year-old woman in Norwich, England, received sixteen "shewings" (showings, visions, revelations) on what she thought was her death bed. She later wrote about those showings in a book now titled *Showings* or *Revelations of Divine Love*. It was the first book in the English language (Middle English) written by a woman, as far as we know. Julian would spend the next twenty years trying to understand those visions in light of scripture, a life of prayer, and the theological tradition—and in response to the existential and spiritual concerns of her fellow townspeople. She (and they) had survived several waves of the bubonic plague and witnessed the social unrest that followed, including a major revolt in 1381 and its brutal suppression; they had experienced untold grief and gross social injustice. In her *Showings*, Julian presented the message that God is love, and only love. For her that meant that God is not wrathful, God does not punish, God is not distant. Rather, God is Mother, which is to say that God is tender and compassionate; God encloses us in love; God lifts us up when we fall. Lost to history for centuries, her *Showings* has only recently received the scholarly and popular attention it deserves. Julian therefore did not have the influence of someone like Aquinas, or really any influence at all. Nevertheless, in this amazing work we can gain insight into how some Christian lay people may have understood and experienced God's mercy and grace.

Interestingly, for our present purposes, Julian theologically reunited mercy and grace. Indeed, the phrase *mercy and grace* runs as a couplet throughout the entire work. Julian's own breakthrough in her own doctrine of grace came when she questioned the couplet and began to distinguish *mercy* from *grace*, no longer allowing their conflation but not separating them either. She argued that they are not merely synonyms but are two "properties" of the one divine love. With impressive precision and confidence, Julian explained,

> For I behelde the properte of mercy, and I behelde the properte of grace, which have two maner of working in one love. Mercy is a pitteful properte, which longeth to moderhode in tender love. And grace is a wurshipful properte, which longeth to ryal lordshippe in the same love. Mercy werketh—keping, suffering, quicking, and heling—and all is of tendernesse of love. And grace werketh with mercy: raising, rewarding (endlessly

> overpassing that oure loving and our traveyle deserveth), spreding abrode, and shewing the hye, plentuouse largesse of Goddes ryal lordshippe in his mervelouse curtesy. And this is of the habundance of love. For grace werketh oure dredful failing into plentuouse and endlesse solace, and grace werketh oure shameful falling into hye, wurshippeful rising, and grace werketh oure sorowful dying into holy, blisseful life.[45]

According to Julian, mercy is not so much forgiveness as it is pity and compassion (*reuth and pitte*). The significance of this breakthrough becomes clear if we understand it in historical context: she was rejecting the common religious notion of mercy as clemency in her day, which stressed the need for forgiveness because it held forth the image of a punitive God; this notion served to control the population through fear; hence, the need for political pardon was especially acute in the wake of the failed Revolt of 1381. Against this backdrop, Julian argued that God's mercy is compassion and pity, the movement of God toward humanity, toward the individual, through means of the Incarnation. Mercy is God's tender and "kinde" love for all humanity.[46] It is no accident that it was precisely here, in her description of mercy as compassion and pity, that Julian first referred to God as Mother in *Showings*. She has become famous for her notion of God as Mother—and while most of her discussion of that is found in chapters 52–62, it is here in chapter 48, in conjunction with *mercy*, that she first introduced the idea. Again, the gendered associations of mercy come to the fore.

While Julian inherited many Augustinian insights and reflexes, she did not accept the Augustinian terms of the debate when it came to grace—for reasons, and with new theological tools, specific to the late fourteenth century:

- She put forth a much more positive anthropology, aided by her vernacular language where the word for *nature* was not the Latinate *natura* but was the Middle English *kinde* (conveying kindness, kinship, goodness, virtue).
- She did not plot her doctrine of mercy and grace along a horizontal line that presumes the need for progress as it also amplifies a sense of distance between God and us; instead, she viewed mercy and grace as two interrelated, dynamic vertical divine movements (mercy being God's movement down to us in compassion and pity right now, and grace being God's raising us up into the life of the Trinity right now) that make God present to us immediately here and now.

- She emphasized God's love for humanity—as expressed in the Incarnation, in the Passion, in Christ's eternal identification with humanity, in the understanding of God as Mother—all of which together suggest a new vision for how society should or could be restructured.

There is much more to say about this vision and her doctrine of grace, but for present purposes this example serves to remind us that a new (or renewed) understanding of mercy may well erupt in response to performances of worldly power that contradict the gospel.

Mercy and Grace in Modern Catholic Thought and Practice

The polemics over grace that sparked the Protestant Reformation in the sixteenth century would drive Catholic–Protestant (and intra-Protestant, and intra-Catholic) polemical relations for centuries. There were countless permutations and shifts (due to religious and theological differences and further fueled by the pressures placed by the rise of the modern historical consciousness, modern scientific paradigms, modern economic theories, the Industrial Revolution, political revolutions, two world wars, and so on), but the fundamentals remained identifiable up until the Second Vatican Council (1962–65) and indeed remain even now, albeit in a much more ecumenical spirit. These respective views of grace had implications for how mercy was understood and enacted in the Christian moral and spiritual life. Since in chapter 14 of this volume ("Theology of Grace in the Christian Tradition: Basic Affirmations and Debates") Veli-Matti Kärkkäinen expertly and succinctly presents those debates on grace between Catholics and Protestants (as well as the common affirmations and divergent interpretations of the Roman Catholic, Protestant, Anglican, and Eastern Orthodox traditions), I do not rehearse that same material here. Instead, I focus on the role of mercy in the Catholic tradition.

Catholicism and the Works of Mercy (Corporal and Spiritual)

Grafted into the Catholic moral consciousness are the seven corporal works of mercy (the first six of which came directly from Matt. 25:34–45): Feed the hungry, give drink to the thirsty, shelter the homeless, clothe the naked, visit the sick, visit those imprisoned, and bury the dead. These are supplemented by the seven spiritual works of mercy, which benefit the person performing them more than any recipient: instruct the ignorant, counsel the doubtful, comfort the afflicted, admonish the sinner, forgive offenses, bear wrongs patiently, and pray for the living and the dead. Keenan maintains that the integration of the works of mercy into Catholic morality and spirituality distinguishes the Catholic moral tradition: "While fellow Protestants recognize the extraordinary importance of mercy as the basic stance of our God toward us, still we Catholics have taken that insight further in terms of a long legacy of the corporal and spiritual works of mercy. Those works have distinguished us, for if there is one dimension of the Christian tradition that differentiates Protestants from Catholics, it is, precisely, 'works.'"[47]

Indeed, works of mercy shaped modern Catholic lay piety in deep and profound ways. And because mercy tends to be gendered, it is not surprising that Catholic women's ways of living the Christian life, especially, were shaped by *misericordia* and *clementia*. We have already glimpsed how this functioned in medieval society, but modern society with its own threats gave rise to new religious orders as well as lay organizations. Catholic women played a remarkable role in the United States in addressing the needs of immigrants and in demanding just laws to protect them. Let me take the most obvious example, given the name: the Sisters of Mercy. The order was founded in Ireland (officially) in 1831, after Catherine McAuley became convinced that the needs of the destitute could and should be met. She spent her inheritance and opened the first House of Mercy in Dublin to shelter and educate women and girls. The first Sisters of Mercy arrived in America in 1843. Almost two hundred years later the order is international and remains active—indeed, it is on the cutting edge of fighting poverty, injustice, and the structural systems that perpetuate them. There are similar histories and missions of other modern religious orders, such as the Sisters of St. Joseph of Carondelet, all stemming originally from the institutionalization and systematization of the works of mercy.

Contemporary Refinements of Mercy

Recently the theological tide has begun to turn back to mercy. Christian theologians are retrieving what they take to be the more radical gospel message of mercy as inclusive, as disruptive of unjust systems, and as demanding a real, sometimes uncomfortable change of heart. *Misericordia*, these Catholic scholars argue, needs to be taken more literally and actively. Jesuit liberation theologian Jon Sobrino describes mercy as the "principle" of Christianity:

> We are speaking here not of "works of mercy" but rather of the basic structure of the response to this world's victims. This structure consists in making someone else's pain our very own and allowing that pain to move us to respond. We are to be moved simply by the fact that someone

> in need has been placed along our way. Even though Jesus presents the Samaritan as an example of one who obeys the commandment to love his neighbor, there is nothing in the parable which would lead us to conclude that the Samaritan acts in order to fulfill a commandment. He was simply moved to pity. It needs also to be emphasized that mercy is not only a fundamental attitude at the root of every human interaction but also a principle which affects subsequent interactions.[48]

Along these lines, another Jesuit scholar, ethicist James Keenan of Boston College, has written extensively on mercy, which he defines as "the willingness to enter into the chaos of another," a definition which has already had a wide influence in Catholic social thought.[49] Mercy is also a theological foundation for Catholic opposition to the death penalty.[50] Walter Kasper, a German cardinal, identifies mercy as "the essence of the gospel and the key to Christian life."[51] Theologian Elizabeth Johnson, a Sister of St. Joseph, has written a book titled *Creation and the Cross: The Mercy of God for a Planet in Peril*, where she follows Pope Francis's encyclical on the environment, *Laudato Si'*, in linking social justice and environmental justice.[52] And, finally, Pope Francis himself called an extraordinary Jubilee Year of Mercy in 2015–16. Without doubt, then, mercy as concept and practice is being employed in order to meet the urgent needs of our times and challenges the status quo. In all these cases, mercy is not just a work but a way of being that stems from a profound conversion prompted by a deepened understanding of the gospel.

Conclusion

The labels these contemporary scholars have employed—principle, heart, essence, and key—fall short in conveying what their authors intend—namely, the vital importance and pervasiveness of mercy in Christian faith. A new metaphor is needed. I suggest that of the nervous system: mercy vitally connects the various organs and systems of Christian life, both individual and corporate—and it connects them precisely through conducting stimuli, communicating vital information, prompting actions, alerting, and resituating. As the nervous system of Christian life, mercy—as idea, attitude, virtue, and activity—connects Christian theology, prayer, spirituality, ethics, and worship. Within each of those areas it also plays a connective role. For instance, it connects the various theological loci in systematic theology; it runs throughout the liturgy and throughout the liturgical year; it connects prayer directly to our way of being in the world. If mercy is ubiquitous in Christian life and thought, this is not to say that it is always the same. Mercy—as experience, concept, action—emerges or erupts in sometimes unexpected ways in response to particular stimuli.

The debates over grace have not only proven divisive over the centuries; in their inevitable technical language, they have also tended to strip away the experiential dimension of grace. Furthermore, those debates have led to bifurcations, thus diminishing our understanding of grace because, ironically, they try to control what by definition exceeds our control. I suggest a better way to understand the experience of grace in the Christian tradition in terms of six distinct but interrelated forms:

1. Grace as forgiveness and liberation
2. Grace as breakthrough and shaking the foundations
3. Grace as Word and witness
4. Grace as beauty and beneficence
5. Grace as caritas and communion
6. Grace as preservation and friendship

Each form of grace is formulated as a couplet to better capture how grace, as Aquinas says, "is usually taken in three ways": the disposition of the giver, the gift itself, and the recipient's gratitude for the gift.[53] Each form also includes a social element. Mercy permeates every form of grace as it is also experienced as "gift" and effects a merciful heart.

Notes

1. The earliest followers of Jesus embraced that as they went forth to preach the gospel and build a community of believers: In the Acts of the Apostles, Paul says, "In all this I have given you an example that by such work we must support the weak, remembering the words of the Lord Jesus, for he himself said, 'It is more blessed to give than to receive'" (Acts 20:35).

2. As Pope John Paul II put it, "Christ confers on the whole of the Old Testament tradition about God's mercy a definitive meaning. Not only does He speak of it and explain it by the use of comparisons and parables, but above all He Himself makes it incarnate and personifies it. He Himself, in a certain sense, is mercy. To the person who sees it in Him—and finds it in Him—God becomes 'visible' in a particular way as the Father who is rich in mercy." John Paul II, *Dives in misericordia* §2, November 30, 1980.

3. Walter Kasper, *Mercy: The Essence of the Gospel and the Key to Christian Life* (Mahwah, NJ: Paulist, 2013), 171.

4. The Letter of James reads:

> If a person with gold rings and in fine clothes comes into your assembly, and if a poor person in dirty clothes also comes in, and if you take notice of the one wearing the fine clothes and say, "Have a seat here, please," while to the one who is poor you say, "Stand there," or, "Sit at my feet," have you not made distinctions among yourselves, and become judges with evil thoughts? Listen, my beloved brothers and sisters. Has not God chosen the poor in the world to be rich in faith and to be heirs of the kingdom that he has promised to those who love him? But you have dishonored the poor. (2:2–6)

Kasper quotes St. John Chrysostom, who expands on the point, connecting the mercy of the Good Samaritan with the Eucharistic table (see Kasper, *Mercy*, 172).

5. James F. Keenan, SJ, *A History of Catholic Theological Ethics* (New York: Paulist, 2022), 35–68.

6. See *1 Clement* 23:1, in Cyril C. Richardson, trans., *Early Christian Fathers* (New York: Macmillan, 1979), p. 55.

7. *1 Clement* 19:3, 2, p. 53.

8. *1 Clement* 23:1, p. 55.

9. *1 Clement* 19:12, p. 54.

10. *1 Clement* 16:17, p. 52. Clement here quotes Philippians 2:5–8: "Let the same mind be in you that was in Christ Jesus, who, though he existed in the form of God, did not regard equality with God as something to be grasped, but emptied himself, taking the form of a slave, assuming human likeness. And being found in appearance as a human, he humbled himself and became obedient to the point of death—even death on a cross."

11. *1 Clement* 29:1, p. 57.

12. *1 Clement* 14:3, p. 50.

13. *1 Clement* 38:1–2, p. 61.

14. Justin Martyr, *First Apology* 3, in Richardson, *Early Christian Fathers*, 243.

15. Justin Martyr, *First Apology* 5, p. 245.

16. See Luke 23:32–43:

> Two others also, who were criminals, were led away to be put to death with him. When they came to the place that is called The Skull, they crucified Jesus there with the criminals, one on his right and one on his left. Then Jesus said, "Father, forgive them, for they do not know what they are doing." And they cast lots to divide his clothing. And the people stood by watching, but the leaders scoffed at him, saying, "He saved others; let him save himself if he is the Messiah of God, his chosen one!" The soldiers also mocked him, coming up and offering him sour wine and saying, "If you are the King of the Jews, save yourself!" There was also an inscription over him, "This is the King of the Jews." One of the criminals who were hanged there kept deriding him and saying, "Are you not the Messiah? Save yourself and us!" But the other rebuked him, saying, "Do you not fear God, since you are under the same sentence of condemnation? And we indeed have been condemned justly, for we are getting what we deserve for our deeds, but this man has

> done nothing wrong." Then he said, "Jesus, remember me when you come in your kingdom." He replied, "Truly I tell you, today you will be with me in paradise."

17. Peter Brown, *Poverty and Leadership in the Later Roman Empire* (Hanover, NH: University of New England, 2002), 8–9.

18. Alex Tuckness and John M. Parrish, *The Decline of Mercy in Public Life* (New York: Cambridge University Press, 2014), 93.

19. See Tuckness and Parrish, *Decline of Mercy*, 95–108.

20. B. R. Rees well summarizes this momentous shift in the early history of Christian thought:

> The early Greek Fathers give only particular descriptions of grace and do not offer formal definitions, for which indeed no necessity arose in the Christian East. Creation, providence and redemption all fell within the province of "original" grace, and man shared in these according to his capacity to do so; for his eternal salvation he also needed the "specific" grace conferred only by baptism, which was a prerequisite for spiritual growth. The early Latin Fathers, living as they did in an age or romantic heroism, shared his belief in the saving grace of baptism and were strengthened in it by the bitter exigencies of persecution. Grace, now rendered by the Latin word *gratia*, was offered unconditionally and universally but could be appropriated only through baptism in faith. Thereafter, the Christian would be confirmed by God in the power to do good by his obedience (Tertullian) or his loyalty (Cyprian), which would be properly rewarded by the ability to withstand the trials and temptations of life.

B. R. Rees, *Pelagius: A Reluctant Heretic* (Woodbridge, Suffolk: Boydell, 1988), 30.

21. Pelagius, *Letter to Demetrias* §2, in J. Patout Burns, trans., *Theological Anthropology*, Sources of Early Christian Thought (Philadelphia: Fortress, 1981), 41.

22. See, e.g., Pelagius, *Letter to Demetrias* §§4, 7, pp. 43–44, 48–49, respectively.

23. Pelagius, *Letter to Demetrias* §8, p. 50.

24. Pelagius, *Letter to Demetrias* §8, p. 50.

25. Augustine, *On Nature and Grace* §80, in Roland J. Teske, SJ, trans., *Answer to the Pelagians* I/23, *The Works of Saint Augustine: A Translation for the 21st Century*, ed. John E. Rotelle, OSA (Hyde Park, NY: New City, 1997), 267.

26. Not all Alexandrians accepted this formulation, hence the establishment of the Coptic Orthodox Church.

27. Thomas Aquinas's systematic exploration of aspects of Christ's human nature in part 3 of his *Summa theologiæ* was relatively new territory at the time.

28. See John Burnaby, *Amor Dei: A Study of the Religion of St. Augustine* (London: Hodder & Stoughton, 1938), 99.

29. Devotion to the Sacred Heart took on more particular form in the early modern period due to Margaret Mary Alacoque (1647–90) and visions she claimed to have received.

30. Caroline Walker Bynum, *Jesus as Mother: Studies in the Spirituality of the High Middle Ages* (Berkeley: University of California Press, 1984).

31. See James F. Keenan, SJ, *The Works of Mercy: The Heart of Catholicism* (Lanham, MD: Rowman & Littlefield, 2005).

32. See, e.g., Marguerite Porete, *The Mirror of Simple Souls*, trans. Ellen L. Babinsky (New York: Paulist, 1993); and *Hadewijch: The Complete Works*, trans. Columba Hart (New York: Paulist Press, 1980), respectively.

33. See Walter Simons, Cities of Ladies: Beguine Communities in the Medieval Low Countries, 1200–1565 (Philadelphia: University of Pennsylvania Press, 2010).

34. Aquinas, *ST* 1, q. 21, art. 3. All quotations are from *The Summa Theologiæ of St. Thomas Aquinas*, Literally translated by Fathers of the English Dominican Province, 2nd and rev. ed., 1920; online ed. © 2017 by Kevin Knight, https://www.newadvent.org/summa/.

35. Aquinas, *ST* 1, q. 21, art. 3, reply to obj. 2.

36. Aquinas, *ST* II–II, q. 30, art. 1.

37. Aquinas, *ST* II–II, q. 30, art. 2.

38. See Aquinas, *ST* I–II, q. 109, art. 6, and q. 111, art. 3.

39. See Aquinas, *ST* I–II, q. 109, art. 1.

40. See Aquinas, *ST* I–II, q. 109, art. 6, and q. 111, art. 2.

41. See Aquinas, *ST* I–II, q. 114.

42. See Aquinas, *ST* I–II, q. 110, art. 1.

43. Aquinas, *ST* I–II, q. 110, art. 1, emphasis added.

44. Aquinas, *ST* I–II, q. 110, art. 2.

45. Julian of Norwich, *Revelation of Divine Love*, ed. Nicholas Watson and Jacqueline Jenkins, in *The Writings of Julian of Norwich: A Vision Showed to a Devout Woman and a Revelation of Love* (University Park: Pennsylvania State University Press, 2005), 267–69; chap. 48.

46. See Julia A. Lamm, *God's 'Kinde' Love: Julian of Norwich's Vernacular Theology of Grace* (New York: Herder & Herder/Crossroad, 2019).

47. Keenan, *Works of Mercy*, 2.

48. Jon Sobrino, *The Principle of Mercy: Taking the Crucified People from the Cross* (Maryknoll, NY: Orbis, 1994), 10. He argues that the parable of the Good Samaritan reveals that "the ideal human being, the complete human being, is the one who interiorizes, absorbs in her innards, the suffering of another . . . in such a way that this interiorized suffering becomes a part of her, is transformed into an internal principle. . . . Mercy, as re-action, becomes the fundamental action of the total human being. Thus, this mercy is more than just one phenomenon in human reality among many" (17).

49. James F. Keenan, SJ, "The Scandal of Mercy," *Zeitschrift für Katholische Theologie* 138 (2016): 277. On the influence of Keenan's definition, see, for example, Nicole Flores, "Mercy as Public Virtue," *Journal of Religious Education* 48 (2020): 458–72.

50. See Vicki Schieber, Trudy D. Conway, and David Matzko McCarthy, eds., *Where Justice and Mercy Meet: Catholic Opposition to the Death Penalty* (Collegeville, Minn.: Liturgical Press, 2013).

51. Kasper argues that "we should treat mercy not as an appendix to the exposition of God's attributes, but rather as the organizing center of God's attributes, with the other attributes grouped around it" (*Mercy*, 89). As Bill Madges notes, Kasper "prefigure[d] key elements in Pope Francis's vision of the church's mission and his own pontificate" (Preface to *Mercy*, ix).

52. Elizabeth A. Johnson, CSJ, *Creation and the Cross: The Mercy of God for a Planet in Peril* (Maryknoll, NY: Orbis, 2018).

53. Aquinas, *ST* I–II, q. 110, art. 1. Brian Gerrish argues that Calvin shares this basic framing; *Grace and Gratitude: The Eucharistic Theology of John Calvin* (Minneapolis: Fortress, 1993), 69–70n83.

10

Mercy and Grace in the Old Testament

An Introduction

Jacob Onyumbe

The Old Testament / Hebrew Bible can be considered (and rightly so) as the story of God's expression of mercy and grace toward creation, especially toward the people of Israel whom he chose to be his special possession and a channel of blessings for the rest of creation. From the moment of Creation in the book of Genesis to the last book of the Christian canon (Malachi), God shows himself to be a God who is willing and ready to forgive undeserving evildoers and outpour his love and favors on whomever he wills. This way of being of YHWH, the God of Israel, is expressed through certain terms, of which the most common are *ḥṣḏ*, *rḥm*, *ḥnn*, and *ḥml.*

That YHWH is gracious and merciful often functions as an invitation to those who believe in him to behave like God himself—that is, to bestow favors on others and be merciful toward them without taking into consideration who the beneficiary of their beneficence is.

What appears as shocking, though, is that there are instances when God forbids Israel to show mercy to other creatures, especially in the context of the entry into the land of Canaan, regarding their dealings with the nations that the Israelites are about to encounter in the Promised Land. How can YHWH, who is gracious (*ḥanun*) and merciful (*raḥûm*), forbid the practice of mercy toward some people? As will become clear through the texts that we are studying in this session, grace and mercy cannot be taken for granted, whether they are practiced by God or by humans: they are in every instance the expression of a leap beyond the expected behavior. Also, it is important to note that divine grace and mercy cannot be divorced from the requirements for justice.

In the Old Testament, the concepts of grace and mercy—since both denote God's gratuitous care for undeserved creatures—are sometimes treated as synonyms. The word *ḥṣḏ* for example, can mean both grace and mercy.

Sometimes it speaks of unmerited kindness or charity bestowed on someone (e.g., Gen. 19:19, 24:12; Josh. 2:12); somewhere else it will speak of a disposition to forgive wrongdoing (as in Ps. 51:1) or of an expression of loyalty to a friend or a partner (e.g., Gen. 20:13, 21:23; Ruth 3:10). The term *ḥnn*, even though it speaks mostly of an undeserved gift or pity for someone in a miserable condition (e.g., Gen. 6:8, 19:19; Exod. 3:21, 22:27), is also sometimes used in contexts where forgiveness is needed—and in those contexts it is often paired with the term *rḥm* or its cognates (e.g., Exod. 34:6; Neh. 9:17, 31). It is the same for the term *rḥm:* this term, often translated as *mercy* or *compassion*, can express the idea of grace and also the idea of mercy, pity, and forgiveness.[1]

In the remainder of this essay, I introduce several biblical texts dealing with the question of grace and mercy. These texts not only tell us about the character of God but also show us how and why anyone who has a relationship with this God ought to be gracious and compassionate.

God Is Gracious and Merciful

Exodus 33:1–34:7

The passage Exodus 33:1–34:7 is of critical importance in the study of the concepts of grace and mercy because it is, canonically, the first time YHWH defines himself in those terms. It is also in this passage that YHWH defines the way grace and mercy operate: their application in specific situations depends entirely on YHWH alone, and they cannot be presumed. It seems that all the texts dealing with the question of grace and mercy assume, to a certain degree, that Exodus understanding of these concepts.

Exodus 33:17–34:7 comes after the first radical breach between YHWH and the people whom he delivered from slavery in Egypt. It is a conversation between YHWH and Moses, the latter interceding for the Israelites and YHWH conceding to Moses's request but insisting that he will show mercy and grace on his own terms.

Throughout the journey from Egypt, through powerful acts of care and protection, YHWH showed the Israelites that their lives and survival depended on him, so they should rely only on him, never other deities. God performed these acts for Israel, not only because of his fidelity/loyalty to the covenant he made with Israel's ancestors (see Exod. 3:16) but also (and especially) because he is a God who hears the cries of people who have been wronged (Exod. 3:7). God assumed that Israel would not deduce behavioral requirementsfor themselves from what he did for them; so he gave them instructions for how they should behave: the Ten Commandments (literally the Ten Words). The first of those commandments deals with exclusive worship of YHWH by the Israelites:

> I am YHWH your God, who brought you out of the land of Egypt, out of the house of slavery. You shall not have other gods beside me. You shall not make for yourself an idol or a likeness of anything in the heavens above or on the earth below or in the waters beneath the earth; you shall not bow down before them or serve them. For I, YHWH, your God, am a jealous God, inflicting punishment for the ancestors' wickedness on the children of those who hate me, down to the third and fourth generation; but showing *ḥṣd* (kindness, covenant loyalty, love, compassion, mercy) down to the thousandth generation of those who love me and keep my commandments. (Exod. 20:2–6)

Following this commandment, it is clear that when the Israelites made a molten calf and called it their "god who brought you up from the land of Egypt" (Exod. 32:4), they had decided to part ways with YHWH. So God's anger and decision to destroy Israel or not to go with his people to the land of Canaan was justified. Not only had Israel forfeited the right to have God walk with her, but also, since Israel was a stubborn people, God realized that his walking with them would be lethal to them.[2] And yet, for Moses, unless God went with them, they could not leave Horeb and continue the journey to the land of Canaan.

In Exodus 33:17–34:7, God decided to go with the people and told Moses why he could do this: because he is gracious and merciful. First, Moses was granted this request because he had found favor/grace with God. In the Hebrew Bible, the expression "to find favor with *x*" often means that someone of inferior or endangered situation has been granted some protection or has been spared by a more powerful being (see Gen. 6:8; 18:3; 19:19). Most of the times, God is the one who bestows the favor on others. Sometimes (for example, in the case of Noah or Abraham) it is not clear why YHWH bestows his favor on an individual: he simply does it. Second, God told Moses that he agrees to forgive his people, but it should be made clear that YHWH does not show grace and mercy to people indiscriminately: "I will be gracious to whom I will be gracious and I will be merciful to whom I will be merciful" (Exod. 33:19). YHWH is gracious and merciful, but the modus operandi of those qualities of God cannot be foreknown by anyone.

In addition, it is YHWH who chooses when and how to apply those qualities to specific situations. It is a mistake to presume divine grace and mercy. In an amplified paraphrase of this verse, Umberto Cassuto rendered God's thought thus:

> The exercise of those qualities depends entirely on My will; you may know that I am compassionate and gracious, and that I love to go beyond the strict letter of the law, but the decision to act according to these virtues is at all times in My discretion, and it is impossible for you to know when, or if, I shall act thus. If I were constantly to let the quality of mercy prevail over justice, and were to pardon every sinner, I should not be a righteous judge, and every man would permit himself all kinds of wickedness in the assurance that he would be forgiven. I shall be gracious and compassionate if it pleases Me, when it pleases Me, and for the reasons that please Me.[3]

The point of the statement about God showing grace and mercy on his terms is that mercy and grace cannot be taken for granted; they are not God's most readily available or expected ways of behaving in every situation. In every instance when God shows mercy, his actions are shown to be unpredictable.

The same idea of the unexpected nature of God's grace and mercy are expounded in Exodus 34:6–7. Here YHWH passes by, proclaims his name, and tells Moses who he is and how he makes his grace, mercy, and justice operate. God's proclamation to Moses is made in two parts. In verse 6, God states what his attributes are: he is merciful (*raḥûm*), gracious (*ḥanun*), slow to anger (*'ereḵ 'apayim*), great (*raḇ*) in *ḥṣḏ* and truth/fidelity (*'emeṯ*). This part of the text is a verbless clause: it tells about what YHWH is. In verse 7 we have an explicative clause with three verbs: *nṭr*, *pqd*, and *nqh*. These verbs show us what the God described in verse 6 does. It appears that, from these two verses, God is both punitive and merciful. God is merciful, but punishment is the expected consequence of sin.[4] So when God forgives or takes time to punish, it is an act of pure gratuity.[5]

Nehemiah 9:16–19, 26–31

This passage from Nehemiah 9 develops the same idea of a merciful God who is also punitive. In Exodus God says who he is and how he works out his qualities. In Nehemiah, after the exile, the people have returned to the land of Judah, but life does not seem to have improved: they are still living like slaves in their own land (Nehemiah 9:36). Then the Levites implore YHWH to forgive his people by reminding YHWH of how, because he is gracious and merciful, he saved their rebellious ancestors in the past. Based on the memory of God's dealings with the ancestors, they now hope that, even though God is right to be angry with them, God can forgive and save them because of his grace and mercy. The Levites do not deny their culpability: they know that Israel has sinned, but they also know that God can give them a second chance.

Micah 7:18–20

Micah 7:18–20 (like Nehemiah 9:16–19, 26–31) is part of a prayer of supplication to YHWH. The prophet assumes that the consequence of sin is punishment, but he also knows that YHWH is able to forgive. YHWH, in this passage, is presented as unique, different from all other gods. What sets him apart from other gods are his ability to change his mind about a decided punishment and his ability to balance "the requirement for justice and a commitment to mercy and clemency."[6]

Hosea 11:8–9

In Hosea 11:8–9, God is presented as a grieved father who cannot bear destroying his own child. Israel/Ephraim is God's child for whom he cared since birth.[7] God had told his child not to put other gods before/beside him and not to swear or to mention his name in vain and to live in harmony and love with others (see Exod. 20:2–14). However, Ephraim/Israel did exactly the opposite of what God commanded: they broke all the commandments (see Hosea 4:2ff and Hosea 11:2–7).[8] God thus threatens to disown this child, to send him back to Egypt (11:5).

However, YHWH is not a man; he is God. So, he decides not to destroy his child. We see here internal conflict within God: God has to preserve justice, but he also has to preserve mercy. God's heart turns against God himself. In this passage, being God means not being packaged in one predetermined way of being and acting. It means that God will be neither always vengeful nor always merciful. YHWH's threats to destroy/punish are no jokes; but he is also able to be moved by compassion and may forgive without any reason other than that he is God. As Nogalski puts it, "The biblical God . . . is not a mechanistic deity whose actions and decisions are set forever in stone. Rather, the biblical God tempers wrath with patience and compassion."[9]

Passages from the Psalms

The passages selected from the book of Psalms for study are all prayers of supplication or statements of assurance in YHWH in situations of physical, spiritual, and psychological weakness or threat. In Psalm 23:5–6, the poet imagines a situation in which he lives among enemies. His life is in danger, and it is God's caring love/attention (*ḥṣḏ*) that protects him. *Ḥṣḏ* in this context includes certainly the idea of "pity," but the emphasis is more on what God does to shield the psalmist from surrounding dangers.

Psalm 51:1–2, traditionally called the "*miserere*" (have pity/mercy) is a prayer of supplication but not supplication from a person in danger. Traditionally, this poem is attributed to David when he, the king of Israel, slept with the wife of one of his soldiers, named Uriah, and killed the latter in order to cover up the adultery (see 2 Sam. 11–12). The poem uses the twin words *rḥm* and *ḥnn*. It begins with the imperative of *ḥnn* (show me grace, have pity on me) to emphasize the fact that he in no way deserves God's forgiveness. Then he adds that God can forgive him not because of anything else but because of God's own abundant mercy.

In Psalm 86:1–3, 15–16, as in Psalm 23, the psalmist faces dangers. However, whereas in Psalm 23 the psalmist states that he has already been protected, in Psalm 86, the pray-er is still in danger; he wants God to have mercy on him (to take care of him). Interestingly, the psalmist evokes the Exodus motif of YHWH being merciful (*raḥûm*), gracious (*ḥanun*), slow to anger (*'ereḵ 'apayim*), great (*raḇ*) in *ḥṣd* and truth/fidelity (*'emeṯ*). It seems that the psalmist at the same time wants YHWH to deliver him but also wants YHWH to remain just (punishing and forgiving wrongdoing). For a merciful, gracious, and just God, it is not enough to protect the just/poor/wronged from danger; he also has to judge (and eventually punish) the wrongdoer.

Psalm 109:10–16, 20–22, an imprecatory poem, presents God's mercy as God's ability to destroy the wrongdoer, erase his posterity, and protect the psalmist. The psalmist presents himself as poor, needy, and brokenhearted, one of those pursued by the abuser. Just like in Psalm 86:1–3, 15–16, God's *ḥṣd* involves not only taking care of a person in a miserable situation but also destroying the very root of the person's suffering.

God's Mercy toward the Nations

Jonah 1:1–4, 7, 15, 17; 2:10–4:4, 11

Jonah is one of the books of the Old Testament in which the question of how to deal with the peoples around Israel is addressed. Among the prophetic books of the Old Testament, Jonah and Nahum deal with the question of how to deal with Assyria, the archenemy of Israel and Judah in the eighth and seventh centuries BCE. In Nahum, Assyria and its people had to be obliterated from the face of the earth. And indeed, the prophet graphically depicts that imagined fall of Nineveh, drawing on his own experience of the traumatic assault of Assyria on Judah in 701 BCE.[10]

In Jonah, God invites the Israelite prophet to imagine God allowing Nineveh (Assyria) to benefit from his grace and mercy and thus survive (avoid destruction). Unlike Nahum, who claimed Nineveh had to be destroyed, Jonah claims that no people is beyond the reach of YHWH's favors and mercy, and God is not a seeker of vengeance.[11]

As Ellen Davis demonstrates, the book of Jonah is full of humor. Its very style invites us, its readers, to stretch "our imagination to entertain big new ideas about how God might be working his purpose out, with or without the cooperation of this Israelite prophet."[12] The main new big idea that we encounter in the book is that YHWH does not follow our lead. No one can try to limit God's mercy, even when he shows mercy and compassion to those believed to be less deserving.[13]

Deuteronomy 7:1–6

Deuteronomy 7: 1–6 is one of the texts that shock readers of the Bible. In this passage God forbids Israel to show mercy to the Canaanites, whom they would encounter in the land. Moreover, he commands them to go to the other extreme: to exterminate them completely. He forbids them to make treaties or intermarry with them. If God's mercy is supposed to be extended to all the nations, why then does God forbid Israel to show mercy to the nations they will encounter?

What seems to be happening here is that YHWH is preparing Israel to avoid any accommodation with Canaanite religious practices.[14] Since Israel is going to live among non-Yahwistic nations established in the land, Deuteronomy 7:1–6 intends to help Israel preserve identity within that multicultural society. And since the final redaction of this book took place around the exilic period in the sixth century BCE, it is important to understand, as Mark E. Biddle explains, that "for exilic readers, the problem of living among the nations while resisting pressures to assimilate would have only acquired new urgency: the violent eradication of foreign elements was no longer an option."[15] In addition, showing these nations mercy can undermine Israel's relationship with YHWH, who requires them exclusive loyalty.[16]

That being said, in Africa and in other formerly colonized countries, Deuteronomy 7 continues to shock its readers, even with the best explanation. It is easier to understand the need for Israel to preserve its own identity when one identifies with the Israelites. However, if one identifies with native Canaanites (as in the case of colonized nations), it is difficult to accept that the God who calls you to believe in him is also the God who commands that you be exterminated.

Do Justice, Love Mercy

Micah 6:6–8

That God is gracious, merciful, and just is an invitation to believers to imitate their God. Micah 6:6–8 speaks about what should constitute the priorities of someone who has benefited from YHWH's favor. It follows God's complaint about Israel's lack of loyalty and gratitude. God did everything good for them—since the time he delivered them from Egypt to the time he planted them in the land—but Israel's responses have been apostasy, violence, and immorality. God presents this indictment and lets Israel give a response. In 8:6–7, Israel's response is a hyperbolic description of extravagant sacrifices: the worshiper wants to offer God thousands of rams, myriad streams of oil, offer his firstborn son. The use of hyperbolic intensification intends to draw attention to the fact that the worshiper has shifted his priorities. He seems to have forgotten the essential and is wholly consumed by unnecessary extravagance. The mention of the possible sacrifice of his son is an indication that this worshiper has become a representative of pagan worship.[17] He has forgotten that firstborn children cannot be sacrificed; they have to be redeemed (Exod. 13:2). He has forgotten that, in fact, infant sacrifice was forbidden.[18] In Micah 6:6–8 we see that, for the worshiper, what matters is religious extravagance and conformity.

In Micah 7:8 the prophet corrects the worshiper's understanding of the requirements for proper relationship with YHWH. God told Israel what is essential, but its leaders had rejected it (Mic. 3:8). Here the prophet reminds the worshiper that what matters is justice and mercy, not religious performance. Right sacrifice and religious performance have to lead to a life of mercy and justice. In the context of people plotting evil in their beds and doing it once they wake up (Mic. 2:1), refocusing people's attention on the practice of mercy/compassion and justice is more than urgent.

Conclusion

The texts introduced in this essay show us that God is both merciful (or gracious) and just. We have seen that God cannot be packaged in one systematized way of being. One cannot choose the merciful nature of God over his justice or vice versa. A proper understanding of divine grace and mercy must not exclude the requirements for justice. What is true of YHWH in the Old Testament should also be a lesson for present-day readers of the Bible, especially in polarized societies where people believe they need to choose between mercy/grace and justice.

Notes

1. See Francis Brown, S. R. Driver, and Charles Briggs, *The Brown-Driver-Briggs Hebrew and English Lexicon of the Old Testament* (Peabody, MA: Hendrickson Academic, 1994), 933–34.

2. See Carol Meyers, *Exodus* (Cambridge: Cambridge University Press, 2005), 262.

3. Umberto Cassuto, *A Commentary on the Book of Exodus*, trans. Israel Abrahams (Skokie, IL: Varda Books, 2005), 436.

4. Meyers, *Exodus*, 260.

5. Note God's insistence on not clearing the guilty. Of the three verbs used in verse 7, only the last one, *nqh* (to clear the guilty), is a finite verb, and it is modified by an emphatic infinitive absolute expressing certainty. See Bill T. Arnold and John H. Choi, *A Guide to Biblical Hebrew Syntax* (Cambridge: Cambridge University Press, 2005), 75–76.

6. Jacob Onyumbe Wenyi, *Piles of Slain, Heaps of Corpses: Reading Prophetic Poetry and Violence in African Context* (Eugene, OR: Cascade, 2021), 130.

7. James D. Nogalski, *The Book of the Twelve: Hosea–Jonah* (Macon, GA: Smyth & Helwys, 2011), 157.

8. Nogalski, *The Book of the Twelve: Hosea–Jonah*, 157.

9. Nogalski, *The Book of the Twelve: Hosea–Jonah*, 163.

10. See Onyumbe, *Piles of Slain, Heaps of Corpses*, 13–15.

11. See Ellen F. Davis, *Opening Israel's Scriptures* (Oxford: Oxford University Press, 2019), 252.

12. Davis, *Opening Israel's Scriptures*, 250.

13. See Nogalski, *The Book of the Twelve: Hosea–Jonah*, 443.

14. Mark E. Biddle, *The Smyth and Helwys Bible Commentary: Deuteronomy* (Macon, GA: Smyth and Helwys, 2003), 136.

15. Biddle, *Deuteronomy*, 135.

16. Peter C. Craigie, *The Book of Deuteronomy*, 2nd ed. (Grand Rapids, MI: Eerdmans, 1976), 179.

17. See 2 Kings 3:27; 1 Kings 16:34.

18. See Deuteronomy 12:31; 2 Kings 16:3; 21:6; 23:10; Jeremiah 7:31.

11

The Old Testament on Mercy and Grace

Texts for Study

The English translation of the Bible passages presented in this chapter is according to the New Revised Standard Version, copyright 1989 by the Division of Christian Education of the National Council of the Churches of Christ in the USA (used by permission; all rights reserved).

Exodus 33:17–34:7

[17]The LORD said to Moses, "I will do the very thing that you have asked; for you have found favor in my sight, and I know you by name." [18]Moses said, "Show me your glory, I pray." [19]And he said, "I will make all my goodness pass before you, and will proclaim before you the name, 'The LORD'; and I will be gracious to whom I will be gracious, and will show mercy on whom I will show mercy. [20]But," he said, "you cannot see my face; for no one shall see me and live." [21]And the LORD continued, "See, there is a place by me where you shall stand on the rock; [22]and while my glory passes by I will put you in a cleft of the rock, and I will cover you with my hand until I have passed by; [23]then I will take away my hand, and you shall see my back; but my face shall not be seen."

[34:1]The LORD said to Moses, "Cut two tablets of stone like the former ones, and I will write on the tablets the words that were on the former tablets, which you broke. [2]Be ready in the morning, and come up in the morning to Mount Sinai and present yourself there to me, on the top of the mountain. [3]No one shall come up with you, and do not let anyone be seen throughout all the mountain; and do not let flocks or herds graze in front of that mountain." [4]So Moses cut two tablets of stone like the former ones; and he rose early in the morning and went up on Mount Sinai, as the LORD had commanded him, and took in his hand the two tablets of stone. [5]The LORD descended in the cloud and stood with him there, and proclaimed the name, "The LORD." [6]The LORD passed before him, and proclaimed,

"The LORD, the LORD,
a God merciful and gracious,
slow to anger,
and abounding in steadfast love and faithfulness,
[7]keeping steadfast love for the thousandth generation,
forgiving iniquity and transgression and sin,
yet by no means clearing the guilty,
but visiting the iniquity of the parents upon the children
and the children's children,
to the third and the fourth generation."

Deuteronomy 7:1–6

[1]When the LORD your God brings you into the land that you are about to enter and occupy, and he clears away many nations before you—the Hittites, the Girgashites, the Amorites, the Canaanites, the Perizzites, the Hivites, and the Jebusites, seven nations mightier and more numerous than you—[2]and when the LORD your God gives them over to you and you defeat them, then you must utterly destroy them. Make no covenant with them and show them no mercy. [3]Do not intermarry with them, giving your daughters to their sons or taking their daughters for your sons, [4]for that would turn away your children from following me, to serve other gods. Then the anger of the LORD would be kindled against you, and he would destroy you quickly. [5]But this is how you must deal with them: break down their altars, smash their pillars, hew down their sacred poles, and burn their idols with fire. [6]For you are a people holy to the LORD your God; the LORD your God has chosen you out of all the peoples on earth to be his people, his treasured possession.

Nehemiah 9:16–19, 26–31

[16]"But they and our ancestors acted presumptuously and stiffened their necks and did not obey your commandments; [17]they refused to obey, and were not mindful of the wonders that you performed among them; but they stiffened their necks and determined to return to their slavery in Egypt. But you are a God ready to forgive, gracious and merciful, slow to anger and abounding in steadfast love, and you did not forsake them. [18]Even when they had cast an image of a calf for themselves and said, 'This is your God who brought

you up out of Egypt,' and had committed great blasphemies, [19]you in your great mercies did not forsake them in the wilderness; the pillar of cloud that led them in the way did not leave them by day, nor the pillar of fire by night that gave them light on the way by which they should go." . . .

[26]"Nevertheless they were disobedient and rebelled against you and cast your law behind their backs and killed your prophets, who had warned them in order to turn them back to you, and they committed great blasphemies. [27]Therefore you gave them into the hands of their enemies, who made them suffer. Then in the time of their suffering they cried out to you and you heard them from heaven, and according to your great mercies you gave them saviors who saved them from the hands of their enemies. [28]But after they had rest, they again did evil before you, and you abandoned them to the hands of their enemies, so that they had dominion over them; yet when they turned and cried to you, you heard from heaven, and many times you rescued them according to your mercies. [29]And you warned them in order to turn them back to your law. Yet they acted presumptuously and did not obey your commandments, but sinned against your ordinances, by the observance of which a person shall live. They turned a stubborn shoulder and stiffened their neck and would not obey.[30]For many years you were patient with them, and warned them by your spirit through your prophets; yet they would not listen. Therefore, you handed them over to the peoples of the lands. [31]Nevertheless, in your great mercies you did not make an end of them or forsake them, for you are a gracious and merciful God."

Psalm 23:5–6

[5]You prepare a table before me
  in the presence of my enemies;
you anoint my head with oil;
  my cup overflows.
[6]Surely goodness and mercy shall follow me
  all the days of my life,
and I shall dwell in the house of the Lord
  my whole life long.

Psalm 51:1–2

[1]Have mercy on me, O God,
  according to your steadfast love;
according to your abundant mercy
  blot out my transgressions.

2Wash me thoroughly from my iniquity,
and cleanse me from my sin.

Psalm 86

1Incline your ear, O LORD, and answer me,
for I am poor and needy.
2Preserve my life, for I am devoted to you;
save your servant who trusts in you.
You are my God; 3be gracious to me, O Lord,
for to you do I cry all day long. . . .
15But you, O Lord, are a God merciful and gracious,
slow to anger and abounding in steadfast love and faithfulness.
16Turn to me and be gracious to me;
give your strength to your servant; save the child of your serving-maid.

Psalm 109:10–16, 20–22

10May his children wander about and beg;
may they be driven out of the ruins they inhabit.
11May the creditor seize all that he has;
may strangers plunder the fruits of his toil.
12May there be no one to do him a kindness,
nor anyone to pity his orphaned children.
13May his posterity be cut off;
may his name be blotted out in the second generation.
14May the iniquity of his father be remembered before the LORD,
and do not let the sin of his mother be blotted out.
15Let them be before the LORD continually,
and may his memory be cut off from the earth.
16For he did not remember to show kindness,
but pursued the poor and needy and the broken-hearted to
their death. . . .
20May that be the reward of my accusers from the LORD,
of those who speak evil against my life.
21But you, O LORD my Lord,
act on my behalf for your name's sake;
because your steadfast love is good, deliver me.
22For I am poor and needy,
and my heart is pierced within me.

Jonah 1:1–4, 7, 15, 17, 2:10–4:4, 11

Jonah Tries to Run Away from God

1Now the word of the Lord came to Jonah son of Amittai, saying, 2"Go at once to Nineveh, that great city, and cry out against it; for their wickedness has come up before me." 3But Jonah set out to flee to Tarshish from the presence of the Lord. He went down to Joppa and found a ship going to Tarshish; so he paid his fare and went on board, to go with them to Tarshish, away from the presence of the Lord.

4But the Lord hurled a great wind upon the sea, and such a mighty storm came upon the sea that the ship threatened to break up. . . . 7The sailors said to one another, "Come, let us cast lots, so that we may know on whose account this calamity has come upon us." So they cast lots, and the lot fell on Jonah. . . . 15So they picked Jonah up and threw him into the sea; and the sea ceased from its raging. . . . 17But the Lord provided a large fish to swallow up Jonah; and Jonah was in the belly of the fish for three days and three nights. . . . 2:10Then the Lord spoke to the fish, and it spewed Jonah out upon the dry land.

3:1The word of the Lord came to Jonah a second time, saying, 2"Get up, go to Nineveh, that great city, and proclaim to it the message that I tell you." 3So Jonah set out and went to Nineveh, according to the word of the Lord. Now Nineveh was an exceedingly large city, a three days' walk across. 4Jonah began to go into the city, going a day's walk. And he cried out, "Forty days more, and Nineveh shall be overthrown!" 5And the people of Nineveh believed God; they proclaimed a fast, and everyone, great and small, put on sackcloth.

6When the news reached the king of Nineveh, he rose from his throne, removed his robe, covered himself with sackcloth, and sat in ashes. 7Then he had a proclamation made in Nineveh: "By the decree of the king and his nobles: No human being or animal, no herd or flock, shall taste anything. They shall not feed, nor shall they drink water. 8Human beings and animals shall be covered with sackcloth, and they shall cry mightily to God. All shall turn from their evil ways and from the violence that is in their hands. 9Who knows? God may relent and change his mind; he may turn from his fierce anger, so that we do not perish."

10When God saw what they did, how they turned from their evil ways, God changed his mind about the calamity that he had said he would bring upon them; and he did not do it.

4:1But this was very displeasing to Jonah, and he became angry. 2He prayed to the Lord and said, "O Lord! Is not this what I said while I was still in my

own country? That is why I fled to Tarshish at the beginning; for I knew that
you are a gracious God and merciful, slow to anger, and abounding in steadfast love, and ready to relent from punishing 3And now, O Lord, please take
my life from me, for it is better for me to die than to live." 4And the Lord
said, "Is it right for you to be angry?". . . 11And should I not be concerned
about Nineveh, that great city, in which there are more than a hundred and
twenty thousand people who do not know their right hand from their left,
and also many animals?"

Hosea 6:6

For I desire steadfast love and not sacrifice,
the knowledge of God rather than burnt offerings.

Hosea 11:8–9

8How can I give you up, Ephraim?
  How can I hand you over, O Israel?
How can I make you like Admah?
  How can I treat you like Zeboiim?
My heart recoils within me;
  my compassion grows warm and tender.
9I will not execute my fierce anger;
  I will not again destroy Ephraim;
for I am God and no mortal,
  the Holy One in your midst,
  and I will not come in wrath.

Micah 6:6–8

6"With what shall I come before the Lord,
  and bow myself before God on high?
Shall I come before him with burnt offerings,
  with calves a year old?
7Will the Lord be pleased with thousands of rams,
  with tens of thousands of rivers of oil?
Shall I give my firstborn for my transgression,
  the fruit of my body for the sin of my soul?"
8He has told you, O mortal, what is good;
  and what does the Lord require of you

but to do justice, and to love kindness,
and to walk humbly with your God?"

Micah 7:18–20

God's Compassion and Steadfast Love

18Who is a God like you, pardoning iniquity
and passing over the transgression
of the remnant of your possession?
He does not retain his anger for ever,
because he delights in showing clemency.
19He will again have compassion upon us;
he will tread our iniquities under foot.
You will cast all our sins
into the depths of the sea.
20You will show faithfulness to Jacob
and unswerving loyalty to Abraham,
as you have sworn to our ancestors
from the days of old.

Sirach 29:1–2

On Lending and Borrowing

1The merciful lend to their neighbors;
by holding out a helping hand they keep the commandments.
2Lend to your neighbor in his time of need;
repay your neighbor when a loan falls due.

12

Implicit Grace and Ubiquitous Mercy

Examples in the New Testament Gospels and the Letter of James

Christopher M. Hays

In my previous home of Medellín, Colombia, every congested roundabout functioned as a center of commerce, where locals hawk chewing gum, cigarettes, and noxious energy drinks. Sometimes, when sufficiently provisioned with Marlboros and caffeine, I would politely decline an ambulant vendor's wares by saying *No, gracias,* "No, thanks," just like my mama taught me. I came to see, nonetheless, that this response slightly rankled the seller, but it was not until I watched a Colombian friend decline the offer of desiccated Chiclets that I realized my mistake: instead of saying *No, gracias,* she simply said *Gracias.* And the chap moved on without a grimace. You see, for a Colombian, simply to say *Gracias* was to decline the offer politely. The "no" was implied by the Colombian *gracias,* whereas from my linguistic context, to say nothing more than "thank you" would suggest acceptance of the offer. My inclusion of *no* before *gracias* came across as emphatic and, therefore, brusque. The key presupposition is whether "thank you" implies "yes" or "no." That is the tricky thing about presuppositions: they can remain invisible and implicit because of their deep rootedness in cultural assumptions. They are unspoken because they are ubiquitous. But if an outsider has not internalized those assumptions, then invisibility is mistaken for absence.

Such is the case with "grace" (*charis*) in the synoptic Gospels (Matthew, Mark, and Luke). While grace "abounds" in the Pauline corpus, the synoptic authors use the term but once, in Luke 2:40 (speaking of God's grace on Jesus).[1] The term *mercy* (*eleos*), by contrast, is in ample evidence in the Jesus tradition. Still, the fact that *grace* is in lexically short supply in the synoptics does not bespeak absence (it is illustrated in, for example, the parables of the two debtors, the prodigal son, and the laborers in the vineyard). The term *grace* is invisible because it is so strongly supposed, so central to the Old Testament paradigm of a covenant of *ḥesed,* of mercy. And I do not think we can properly understand grace or mercy in the New Testament unless we understand *ḥesed* in the Old.

The Hebrew term *ḥesed* requires the translator to apply a deft hand, being rendered in English as "steadfast love," "loyalty," "kindness," "faithfulness," and "mercy," precisely because the concept that *ḥesed* evokes entails all of the aforementioned notions.[2] *Ḥesed* is a quality of relationship essential to God's character, especially exemplified in the covenant (*berit*) between God and Israel, in which all parties are to act lovingly and mercifully to each other based on their mutual commitment, trust, and loyalty.[3] The covenant between Israel and her God is fundamentally a covenant of grace, a covenant that God graciously offered to Israel and that is to be characterized by *ḥesed*.[4] Because God is committed to Israel, God acts graciously and mercifully to the people: blessing, protecting, and forgiving them.[5] Because Israel has faith in God, they are loyal to God and imitate God's *ḥesed* in their relationships with their fellow humans.[6] This covenantal framework, laid out in the Torah, was paradigmatic for Second Temple Judaism, and Jesus built his theological edifice on that same foundation.[7] The texts we will study below show how Jesus elevated mercy and love as the quintessence of the will of God revealed in the Torah and summoned the disciples of Israel's Messiah to extend mercy and grace to others, especially to the most marginalized.

The *Magnificat* (Luke 1:46–55): God's Covenantal Mercy Expressed in Messianic Deliverance

We begin our brief study with the *Magnificat*, the famous hymn attributed to Mary, the mother of Jesus, in response to her miraculous conception of the Messiah. In this song, Mary construes God's sending of the Messiah as an act of "mercy [*eleos*] for those who fear him from generation to generation" (Luke 1:50; cf. Ps. 103:17).[8] Mary celebrates that the Lord has so blessed her and her people because of God's covenant relationship with Israel, saying that God "has helped his servant Israel, in remembrance of his mercy, according to the promise he made to our ancestors, to Abraham and to his descendants forever" (1:54–55; compare to Mic. 7:20; 2 Sam. 22:51).[9] In other words, God has sent the Messiah to deliver the Jews from their Roman oppressors because God had made a covenant with the patriarchs generations beforehand and would not now let the Holy People down.

Mary's invocation of the covenant framework explains why God's saving action (1:47) only counts as good news for "those who fear him," for "the lowly" and "the hungry," while being decidedly bad news for "the proud," "the powerful," and "the rich" (1:51–53). Following the tendency of the Old

Testament and postbiblical Judaism to cast the Jewish people as the poor and vulnerable who look for the salvation of the God who defends the indigent, the orphan, and the widow, Mary characterizes the arrival of the Messiah as God's deliverance of the down-trodden Jews from their oppressive Roman colonizers.[10] By calling herself God's "servant" (1:48), she specifically invokes Ps. 86 (one of our Old Testament study texts), a psalm of David in which the predecessor of the Messiah calls himself God's "servant," "poor and needy" (Ps. 86:1–2), and implores the Lord, as a "God merciful [*raḥum*] and gracious . . . abounding in *ḥesed* and *'emet* [faithfulness]" to "save the child of your serving girl" (Ps. 86:15–16).[11] In brief, Mary expects God's covenantal mercy to result in an inversion of fortunes between the Jews and their pagan overlords, elevating God's pious and vulnerable people and casting down their privileged oppressors. Thus, the *Magnificat* elegantly captures the ethnonational theological framework that Jesus would develop (and, to some degree, subvert) in his own ministry.

Matthew 9: Jesus's Messianic Ministry of Mercy

Shifting now into Jesus's own life, Matthew 9 provides a cross section of Jesus's ministerial activity and frames it as an expression of messianic mercy. The text (Matt. 9:10–13) first highlights Jesus's invitation to tax collectors and sinners (those not currently living within the religiopolitical parameters of messianically expectant Judaism) to follow him and abandon their marginality. While this invitation sticks in the craw of the Pharisees, who prided themselves on their cultic and ethnic fidelity, Jesus justifies himself by citing Hosea 6:6, "I desire mercy, not sacrifice." In this way, Jesus (like many prophets before him; see Isa. 1:10–17; Jer. 7:4–11; Mic. 6:6–8; compare to Am. 5:21–24) prioritizes divine mercy above (but not necessarily at the expense of) cultic attentiveness.[12]

Matthew 9 goes on to summarize Jesus's ministry as one of teaching, preaching, and curing diseases (Matt. 9:35), and in the latter sense he evokes the prophecy of Isaiah 35:5–6, which declared that the messianic restoration of Israel would be accompanied the healing of physical maladies. This is what makes sense of the blind men's plea for the "Son of David" to "have mercy on us" (Matt. 9:27): although the Messiah was principally expected to be a military deliverer, his kingdom was also to entail physical restoration for the handicapped.[13]

Matthew clarifies repeatedly that all these aspects of Jesus's work flowed out of his compassion (9:36) for a people who had been failed by their current leaders and left "like sheep without a shepherd" (an allusion to Ezek.

34:1–16; compare to Num. 27:17–18; 1 Kings 22:17; Zech. 10:2–3; 13:7).[14] So Jesus, the Messiah, steps in where the contemporary leaders of Israel had failed and, importantly, calls his disciples to join in his work of mercy since the work to be done is abundant "but the laborers are few" (9:37).

Luke 15 and Matthew 20: Parables of Mercy, Grace, and Warning

Perhaps the text that most poignantly depicts the divine compassion operative in Jesus's ministry is the parable of the prodigal son. Recognizing the gravity of the rebellion of people like the tax collectors and sinners (those who colluded with the Roman oppressors or debauched themselves in ways contrary to God's law), Jesus tells the story of a son who abandoned his family and squandered his inheritance only to be brought low by famine and misery. In penitent desperation he turns home, knowing that he no longer deserves to be called his father's son and hoping only for a job as a farmhand. But as he stumbles homeward, even at a distance, his father espies him and is "filled with compassion" (15:20) such that he dashes forward to embrace his son with kisses and reinstates his child's membership in the family with great celebration. This narrative thus adds pathos to Jesus's prior affirmation (for example, in Matt. 9:9–13) that he reached out to tax collectors and sinners because of God's summons to mercy. Jesus does not imply that God is morally lax, only that divine compassion overflows in forgiveness (15:19–21).

The story ends with a warning, not to the prodigals of Jesus's day but to the Jewish religious elite, the Pharisees, whom the parable evokes in the figure of the elder brother who is angered by the Father's prodigal forgiveness of the penitent son. Much like Jonah, whose bitter wrath bubbled over upon witnessing God's forgiveness of the Ninevites (Jon. 4:1, 9), the Pharisees were incensed at Jesus's forgiveness of sinners and thereby ran the risk of excluding themselves from enjoying the Father's abundant generosity (Luke 15:25–32).

Still, the Pharisees get a bad rap in Christianity; we sometimes do not appreciate how deeply committed the Pharisees were to their religion, exemplary in their attention to ritual purity, tithing, and cultic participation.[15] Knowing where they were coming from, we can perhaps understand their frustration at Jesus's inclusion of sinners who previously had made no commensurate effort at piety.

This dynamic is brought to the fore in the parable of the laborers in the vineyard. In that story, Jesus likens the kingdom of heaven to a landholder who offers work to day laborers at three-hour intervals between 6:00 a.m. and 3:00 p.m., and then finally again at 5:00 p.m., just an hour before sunset

(Matt. 20:1–7). These day laborers would have been subsistence workers, dependent on a daily wage of a denarius to put bread on the table one day at a time (Matt. 20:2). The subtext of the parable is that the landowner's odd hiring and payment practices are motivated by concern for the well-being of the laborers (more than his own agrarian requirements) such that he chooses to cover the daily needs of all who worked for him, even those who were unable to find work ("No one has hired us"; Matt. 20:7) until the last hour of the day (Matt. 20:8–10). Those who had worked since dawn (ciphers for the Pharisees) balk that they received no more than those who arrived near dusk (stand-ins for the sinners). However, the landowner insists that he enjoys the prerogative of generosity, and that providing a just wage to those who worked faithfully all day should not prevent him from extending mercy to the desperate laborers that he found only late in the afternoon.

I mentioned above that the word *grace* almost never appears in the synoptic Gospels. But parables like this one leave no doubt that divine grace is every bit as central to Jesus's theology as it was to Paul's. The parable of the laborers in the vineyard highlights divine grace to humans; the parable of the unforgiving debtor (Matt. 18:23–35), however, underscores the urgency of humans imitating that divine grace with one another.

Matthew 18: Withdrawing Mercy from the Merciless

In response to a query about how many times one should forgive the offenses of a brother or sister, Jesus asserts that God demands effectively limitless forgiveness of his people (Matt. 18:21–22). He goes on to explain in the ensuing parable that such unstintingly human forgiveness would still pale in comparison to the kindness God has shown humanity.

The extent of divine forgiveness is expressed parabolically in terms of a debt of ten thousand talents owed by a certain slave to his king (Matt. 18:24). Since this exceeded what even a powerful man could earn in a lifetime, the debtor throws himself at the feet of his king, begging for patience; the king is moved to compassion (18:27) and forgives the man's debt entirely.[16] Here, the parable depicts the same connection between divine mercy, patience, and the forgiveness of sins displayed in other Old Testament texts (Neh. 9:16–31; Ps. 51:1–2; Mic. 7:18–20).

But the parable turns rather more menacing in Matthew 18:28–34 as that very slave, having been forgiven a crushing debt, violently (18:28) demands that another slave pay him a much smaller debt of 100 denarii, refusing to show to another the same clemency he had just received. When news of this event reached the king's ears, his wrath is kindled such that he hands the unforgiving servant over to be jailed and tortured, demanding rhetorically, "Should you not have had mercy on your fellow slave, as I had mercy on you?" (18:33).[17]

In this way Jesus expresses that God's extravagant mercy to humans should generate corresponding mercy to others (both in relation to spiritual and social matters).[18] He made the same point earlier, when he taught the disciples to pray, "Forgive us our debts, as we also have forgiven our debtors" (Matt. 6:12).

Luke 6 and 10: The Commandment to Be Merciful

The social expectations underlying the parable of the unforgiving debtor are made more explicit in Luke 6:35–36. Here, in the famous sermon on the plain, when Jesus enjoins his followers, "Be merciful, just as your Father is merciful (οἰκτίρμων, *oiktirmon*)" (Luke 6:35), he speaks not only of forgiving personal offenses but, indeed, of actively *loving* enemies, doing good to others, and forgiving generous loans in ways that outstrip even the ethics lauded by Sirach 29:1–2 ("The merciful lend to their neighbors. . . . Lend to your neighbor in his time of need").[19] Such behavior is practiced both in imitation of the divine character and with the promise of an eschatological reward (Luke 6:35).

This same interconnection of mercy, generosity, and love is dramatically developed in the parable of the Good Samaritan (Luke 10:25–37), which Jesus shares with a certain scribe as a way of unpacking his interpretation the fundamental message of the Torah. Here, as elsewhere (Mark 12:28–31; Matt. 26:36–39), Jesus expresses the belief that the law can be summarized in the commandment to love one's God and neighbor (Luke 10:27)—an injunction derived from Deuteronomy 6:5 and Leviticus 19:18. The scribe then presses Jesus to weigh in on another widespread Jewish debate, to wit: who is the neighbor one is obliged to love (for example, one's family, one's fellow Jews, and so on)?[20]

Jesus nonetheless eschews the scribe's framing of the question and tells the parable of the Good Samaritan, in which a despised and heretical Samaritan—and not a priest or Levite, whom Jewish people typically esteemed for their Torah observance—fulfilled the commandment to love one's neighbor, having been moved by compassion (10:33) to care for the man left half-dead by bandits. In summarizing the point of the parable, Jesus does not ask the scribe, "Whose neighbor was the victim?" Rather, he asks (and the Greek verb here is a perfect infinitive), "Who *has become* (γεγονέναι, *gegonenai*) a neighbor to [the victim]?" To this, the scribe replies, "The one who showed him mercy" (Luke 10:36–37).[21] In other words, fulfilling the Torah—loving God and loving neighbor—means *becoming* a neighbor to whomever requires mercy.[22]

James 2: Grace to be Merciful

All the texts discussed heretofore have been from the Gospels of Matthew and Luke, being witness to the teachings of Jesus. At first blush, therefore, the decision to include the Epistle of James in this article might seem odd. Nonetheless, there is a strong argument to be made that the epistle was authored by a brother of Jesus (Matt. 13:55; Mark 6:3), who, although not one of the twelve disciples, became one of the main leaders of the earliest Christian community (Acts 12:17; 15:13; 21:18; Gal. 1:19; 2:9, 12).[23] James evinces major similarities to the teachings of Jesus (particularly in the Sermon on the Mount; Matt. 5–7[24]), attributable to either firsthand knowledge of Jesus's teachings or close familiarity with the oral tradition on which Matthew, the evangelist, would later base the Sermon on the Mount. Thus, I think it best to understand the theology of James as an early Christian reflection produced under the heavy influence of the teachings of Jesus. And although James 2 is often considered a *crux interpretum* by scholars vexed at its apparent tensions with the Pauline epistles, its teachings on mercy fit hand in glove with the witness of the synoptic Gospels.

James 2 begins by excoriating his audience for succumbing to favoritism and social prejudice as they fawned over affluent believers while disdaining the poor in their midst (Jas. 2:1–7). Against such ugly partiality, James enjoins his readers to "fulfill the royal law according to the Scripture, 'You shall love your neighbor as yourself'" (2:8). Here James channels Jesus's elevation of Leviticus 19:18 to the apex of Torah fidelity (as did Paul; see also Rom. 13:9; Gal. 5:14).[25] This maneuver allows him to argue that the marginalization of the needy amounts to a Torah violation ("if you show partiality, you commit sin and are convicted by the law as transgressors"), a point that Leviticus 19 itself made explicitly just three verses prior to the love command ("You shall not render an unjust judgment; you shall not be partial to the poor or defer to the great" [Lev. 19:15]).[26]

Anticipating the potential objection that Leviticus 19:15 is only one relatively minor Old Testament law, James affirms the unity of the Torah (a maneuver also made by Jesus, Paul, and previous Jewish interpreters[27]) so he can make the case that marginalizing the poor leaves his community members just as subject to judgment as they would have been had they committed murder (Jas. 2:10–11). "Whoever keeps the whole law but fails in one point has become accountable for all of it" (2:10). It is a sobering warning, to be sure. But then, after putting such a fine point on the rigorous observance of the divine commandments, James throws a twist into his argument, not by claiming that the disciple of Jesus is exempt from the law because Christ fulfilled it for them (as a Protestant preacher might aver) but by claiming that the law they must keep is in fact *freeing*: "so speak and so act," he says, "as those who are to be judged by the law of liberty" (2:12).[28]

What could James mean by describing the Torah as "the law of liberty"? The phraseology indicates that the law somehow conduces to or produces freedom, which seems counterintuitive if one is unaware that the phrase "the law of liberty" emerged initially in James chapter 1 (v. 25), which also described God's law as "the *implanted* word that has the power to save your souls" (1:21).[29] In other words, the reason that the law—distilled essentially as the imperative to love one's neighbor (2:8)—can produce liberty is because God sows it in the soul of the believer, effectively bringing love about in the believer. Similarly, James asserted, "Every generous act of giving, with every perfect gift, is from above, coming down from the Father of lights. . . . He gave us birth by the word of truth, so that we would become a kind of first fruits of his creatures" (1:17–18). In brief, the law produces freedom because God graciously implants love in the hearts of his people and calls upon his people to act in accordance with the work God was doing in their souls, as a result of which they will be free from God's wrath.[30]

Much in keeping with Jesus before him, James identifies that one fulfills the royal law of love not primarily through saccharine affirmations of religious affections but through the practice of mercy, especially directed toward the poor who were being marginalized in his own community.[31] Just as Jesus had said "blessed are the merciful, for they will receive mercy" (Matt. 5:7), James warns that judgment will be mercilessly doled out to the merciless (Jas. 2:13a). He promises, nonetheless, that those who have shown mercy to others will be forgiven their transgressions, for "mercy triumphs over judgment" (2:13b).[32]

It is within this framework that one should understand James's (in)famous statement "faith by itself, if it has no works, is dead" (2:17). Over against his Jewish–Christian contemporaries, who surmise that their theological orthodoxy—specifically, their monotheism—will suffice for their salvation, James asserts that the covenant with the one God always entails the imitation of that merciful deity who has "chosen the poor in the world to be rich in faith and heirs of the kingdom" (2:5). Accurate belief is not tantamount to covenant loyalty. James sarcastically chides his reader: "You believe that God is one; you do well.[33] Even the demons believe—and shudder" (2:19). While some Protestants chafe at James for denying that salvation is by faith alone (2:17), James understands that God's covenant with his people was always a covenant of *ḥesed* in which the merciful God is faithful to his oft-times faithless people, and they in turn are merciful to one another, thanks to the law of love that God planted in their hearts.

Conclusion

"Mercy" is writ large across the teachings of Jesus. His ministry offered divine mercy to the marginalized in fulfillment of the covenant with Abraham. But that same covenant called for God's people to extend mercy to the vulnerable as well—indeed, making the reception of divine mercy and forgiveness contingent upon the human practice of mercy. And there, it might *seem*, is the rub: for how can divine mercy be truly merciful if contingent on the mercy of an inconstant people?

The answer to that question lies in what is unsaid in the text, in what can be assumed by dint of its fundamental role in Jewish belief: that God is a God of grace. Yes, the word "grace" is all but absent from the synoptic Gospels, but only because, ironically, everyone knew it was pervasive. The absence of that lexeme does not bespeak the absence of the concept. The grace of God is what hires the unwanted laborers at dusk and provides them with a full wage; it forgives impossible sins; it plants the law of love in the hearts of the believers and makes it grow so that they can and do practice mercy. Some Protestant Christians might object that grace that entails and requires works is no grace at all; grace, they might say, means that no works are needed. But I think that such an objection bespeaks a failure to grasp fully what grace means.

Permit me to repurpose this essay's opening illustration. Some years ago in Colombia I mistakenly surmised that saying *gracias* to a street vendor meant saying "yes" to them rather than "no"—not understanding that what was implicit could flip a communication completely on its head. So it is with grace (or in Spanish, *gracia*). What is implicit for Jesus's conception of grace is not that God's graciousness exempts us from acting mercifully; it is that God's grace *changes* us, focuses our action in mercy, and mercifully forgives us as we extend mercy to others. According to Jesus, and according to James, it is *in* the merciful action that the grace, the *gracia*, operates and exists. *Muchísimas gracias.*

Notes

1. When the term *charis*—often translated "grace" in the Pauline Epistles—appears in Luke 6:34–36, it has the decidedly different meaning of "credit"; see Christopher M. Hays, *Luke's Wealth Ethics: A Study in Their Coherence and Character*, vol. 275, Wissenschaftliche Untersuchungen zum Neuen Testament II (Tübingen: Mohr Siebeck, 2010), 113–15.

2. See David J. A. Clines, *Dictionary of Classical Hebrew*, vol. 3 of 9 (Sheffield: Sheffield Phoenix Press, 1993–2014), 277.

3. *Ḥesed* is so intrinsic to YHWH's character that in Psalm 144:2, the Psalmist calls God "my *ḥesed*." Exodus 34:6 describes God as rich in *ḥesed* and *'emet* (truth). A covenant is basically a "sacred contract." See Peter R. Williamson, "Covenant," in *Dictionary of the Old Testament: Pentateuch*, ed. T. Desmond Alexander and David W. Baker (Downers Grove, IL: InterVarsity, 2003), 139–55. On the mutuality of *ḥesed*, see G. Johannes Botterweck and Helmer Ringgren, eds., *Theological Dictionary of the Old Testament* [hereafter, *TDOT*], vol. 5 of 8 (Grand Rapids: Eerdmans, 1974–2006), 47, 61; and Willem A. VanGemeren, ed., *New International Dictionary of Old Testament Theology and Exegesis* [hereafter, *NIDOTTE*], vol. 2 of 5 (Grand Rapids: Zondervan, 1997), 211–12, 216. This one Hebrew term, *ḥesed*, bespeaks a larger conceptual covenantal matrix, but Greek and English semantics do not line up neatly with Hebrew. Modern English speakers, like the Septuagint translators and the gospel authors, have to use a wide range of words to denote the aspect of the semantic range of *ḥesed* that is most operative in a given context.

4. "The reciprocity of *ḥesed* obligation is the content of a *berit* [covenant] (1 Sam. 20:8). . . . Since on the other side *ḥesed* denotes help of kindness as the grace of a superior, *ḥesed* can also be connected with *yeshua* [salvation], *shalom* [peace], *'ahabah* [love], and especially *raḥmim* [compassion]." Gerhard Kittel and Gerhard Friedrich, eds., *Theological Dictionary of the New Testament* [hereafter, *TDNT*], vol. 2 of 10 (Grand Rapids: Eerdmans, 1964–1976), 479. The existence of a covenant [*berit*] is not a precondition of *ḥesed* (*TDOT* 5:52), but *ḥesed* is a feature of the *berit* between YHWH and Israel.

5. On the association of *ḥesed* with forgiveness of sins, see Isaiah 54:8; Lamentations 3:31–32; Micah 7:18; and *NIDOTTE* 2:214.

6. For instances of God's demand of *ḥesed* from Israel, see Hosea 4:1; 6:6; Micah 6:8; Proverbs 19:22; and *NIDOTTE* 2:213.

7. Simeon the Just, a rabbi from the third century BCE, said, "By three things is the world sustained: by the Law, by the [Temple-]service and by deeds of loving-kindness" (*Mishnah, 'Abot* 1:2).

8. *Eleos* is used in the Septuagint especially translated *ḥesed* (Colin Brown, ed., *New International Dictionary of New Testament Theology*, vol. 2 of 4 (Grand Rapids: Zondervan, 1975–1978), 167–68, and sometimes *raḥmim* ("compassion") (*TDNT* 2:479). The Greek language here should not be taken as indication of a Greek valuation of *eleos*. Whereas the Stoics "regarded ἔλεος [*eleos*] as a sickness of the soul; as a πάθος [*pathos*], and even a form of λύπη [*lupē*]" (*TDNT* 2:478), in Judaism "*raḥmim* is never πάθος [*pathos*] in the Greek sense" (*TDNT* 2:480). In later Judaism, *ḥesed* and *raḥmim*, *eleos*, and *oiktirmos* [merciful/compassionate] are used interchangeably (*TDNT* 2:481).

9. "To speak of God remembering is a standard OT anthropomorphism, especially in the Psalms (for example, Gen 19:29; Exod 32:13; Ps 73 [74]:2; 104 [105]:8, 42; 118 [119]:49), and in Ps 24 [25]:6–7; Ps 97 [98]:3; and Hab 3:2 (compare to 2 Chr 6:42; *Pss. Sol.* 10:4) it is 'mercy' that God is called upon to remember (or celebrated as having remembered)." John Nolland, *Luke 1–9:20*, ed. Ralph P. Martin and Lynn Allan Losie, vol. 35A of *Word Biblical Commentary* [hereafter, WBC], ed. Bruce M. Metzger, David Allan Hubbard, and Glenn W. Barker (Waco, TX: Word Books, 1989), 73.

10. See Exodus 22:25–27; Psalm 12:5, 35:10, 40:17; Isaiah 3:14–15; Amos 8:4–8; and Christopher M. Hays, "Rich & Poor," in *Dictionary of Jesus and the Gospels*, ed. Joel B. Green, Jeannine K. Brown, and Nicholas Perrin (Downers Grove: IVP Academic, 2013), 800.

11. The evocation of texts like Psalm 86:15–16 is why Joel Green comments, "These terms, and especially 'mercy,' point even further back, to the nature of God himself. The God Mary praises is the covenant-making God, the God who acts out of his own self-giving nature to embrace men and women in relationship. God remembers . . . and acts." Joel B. Green, *The Gospel of Luke*, New International Commentary on the New Testament [hereafter, NICONT] (Grand Rapids, MI: Eerdmans, 1997), 105.

12. R. T. France, *The Gospel of Matthew*, in NICONT, 354; and Donald A. Hagner, *Matthew 1–13*, vol. 33A of WBC, 239.

13. Note that Jesus pronounces their healing "according to your faith" (Matt. 9:29). The instrumental role of faith in their reception of the eschatological, covenantal benefits of healing aligns with the role of covenant fidelity undergirding God's entire relationship of covenantal favor with Israel. In other words, Israel's belief is part and parcel of their commitment to the covenant with God; as a result, they received the eschatological covenant benefit of healing.

14. France, *Gospel of Matthew*, 372–73.

15. See further Lynn Cohick, "Pharisees," in *Dictionary of Jesus and the Gospels*, ed. Joel B. Green, Jeannine K. Brown, and Nicholas Perrin (Downer's Grove, IL: InterVarsity, 2013), 673–79.

16. By way of reference, Josephus (Antiquities of the Jews 17.11.4) indicates the taxes levied by King Archelaus on all of Judea, Idumea, and Samaria in the year 4 BCE amounted to six hundred talents. Hagner, *Matthew 14–28*, vol. 33B, WBC, 538.

17. In Judaism, divine mercy is the basis for the requirement of human mercy, as in Matthew 18:33; so Shabbat of the Babylonian Talmud 151b; Testament of Zebulon 5:3; and *TDNT* 2:483n91.

18. On this, see Robert W. Heimburger, Christopher M. Hays, and Guillermo Mejía-Castillo, "Forgiveness and Politics: Reading Matthew 18:21–35 with Survivors of the Armed Conflict in Colombia," *HTS Teologiese Studies/Theological Studies* 75:4 (2019): 1–9.

19. See further Hays, *Luke's Wealth Ethics*, 111–17. Exodus 34:6 uses οἰκτίρμων in its enumeration of the fundamental attributes of God.

20. On the divergent Jewish understanding of who qualifies as a "neighbor," see Hays, *Luke's Wealth Ethics*, 118n155.

21. For further detail, see Hays, *Luke's Wealth Ethics*, 117–19.

22. Joel Green makes the connection between human compassion and the divine

covenantal mercy, saying, "The Samaritan, then, participates in the compassion and covenantal faithfulness of God, who sees and responds with salvific care" (see 1:76–78; 7:13; 15:20). Green, *Luke*, 431.

23. Scot McKnight, *The Letter of James*, in NICONT, 13–38; and Douglas J. Moo, *The Letter of James*, Pillar New Testament Commentary (Grand Rapids, MI: Eerdmans, 2000), 9–22.

24. See, for example, James 1:22 / Matthew 7:26; James 2:13 / Matthew 5:7; James 2:14 / Matthew 721; James 3:18 / Matthew 5:9; James 5:17 / Luke 4:25; and Luke Timothy Johnson, *The Writings of the New Testament: An Interpretation* (London: SCM, 1999), 511.

25. See further McKnight, *James*, 208; and Martin, *James*, WBC, 67.

26. Moo, *James*, 112.

27. See, for example, Matthew 5:18–19; Galatians 5:3; 4 Maccabees 5:20–21; Moo, *James*, 114; and McKnight, *James*, 214.

28. This is not to say that a Torah-observant Jew of James's epoch would have despaired of any fate other than judgment. "The Torah itself wrote into its very fabric a mechanism that released Israelites from the demand of total perfection: that mechanism was Yom Kippur, the Day of Atonement. In other words, while the Torah demands obedience it also provides forgiveness through confession and sacrifice." McKnight, *James*, 211.

29. The construction νόμου ἐλευθερίας (*nomou eleutherias*) should most likely be interpreted as a genitive of product, indicating that liberty is what is produced by the law; see Daniel B. Wallace, *Greek Grammar Beyond the Basics: An Exegetical Syntax of the New Testament* (Grand Rapids, MI: Zondervan, 1996), 106.

30. See especially McKnight, *James*, 220. Incidentally, the only time the word *grace* occurs in this epistle is in James 4:6.

31. See also Martin, *James*, 71; and McKnight, *James*, 223.

32. The same logic is apparent in intertestamental Jewish literature, such as Sirach 28:4 ("If one has not mercy toward another like himself, can he then seek pardon for his own sins?") and Testament of Zebulon 8:1, 3 ("Have compassion toward every person with mercy, in order that the Lord may be compassionate and merciful to you. . . . To the extent that a man has compassion on his neighbor, to that extent the Lord has mercy on him"); Moo, *James*, 117.

33. Or in contemporary parlance, "Good for you!"

13

The Gospels and James on Mercy and Grace

Texts for Study

Matthew 9:9–38

[9]As Jesus was walking along, he saw a man called Matthew sitting at the tax
booth; and he said to him, "Follow me." And he got up and followed him.
[10]And as he sat at dinner in the house, many tax collectors and sinners
came and were sitting with him and his disciples. [11]When the Pharisees saw
this, they said to his disciples, "Why does your teacher eat with tax collectors
and sinners?" [12]But when he heard this, he said, "Those who are well have no
need of a physician, but those who are sick. [13]Go and learn what this means,
'I desire mercy, not sacrifice.' For I have come to call not the righteous but
sinners."
[14]Then the disciples of John came to him, saying, "Why do we and the
Pharisees fast often, but your disciples do not fast?" [15]And Jesus said to them,
"The wedding guests cannot mourn as long as the bridegroom is with them,
can they? The days will come when the bridegroom is taken away from them,
and then they will fast. [16]No one sews a piece of unshrunk cloth on an old
cloak, for the patch pulls away from the cloak, and a worse tear is made.
[17]Neither is new wine put into old wineskins; otherwise, the skins burst, and
the wine is spilled, and the skins are destroyed; but new wine is put into fresh
wineskins, and so both are preserved."
[18]While he was saying these things to them, suddenly a leader of the syn-
agogue came in and knelt before him, saying, "My daughter has just died;

but come and lay your hand on her, and she will live." [19]And Jesus got up and followed him, with his disciples. [20]Then suddenly a woman who had been suffering from hemorrhages for twelve years came up behind him and touched the fringe of his cloak, [21]for she said to herself, "If I only touch his cloak, I will be made well." [22]Jesus turned, and seeing her he said, "Take heart, daughter; your faith has made you well." And instantly the woman was made well. [23]When Jesus came to the leader's house and saw the flute players and the crowd making a commotion, [24]he said, "Go away; for the girl is not dead but sleeping." And they laughed at him. [25]But when the crowd had been put outside, he went in and took her by the hand, and the girl got up. [26]And the report of this spread throughout that district.

[27]As Jesus went on from there, two blind men followed him, crying loudly, "Have mercy on us, Son of David!" [28]When he entered the house, the blind men came to him; and Jesus said to them, "Do you believe that I am able to do this?" They said to him, "Yes, Lord." [29]Then he touched their eyes and said, "According to your faith let it be done to you." [30]And their eyes were opened. Then Jesus sternly ordered them, "See that no one knows of this." [31]But they went away and spread the news about him throughout that district.

[32]After they had gone away, a demoniac who was mute was brought to him. [33]And when the demon had been cast out, the one who had been mute spoke; and the crowds were amazed and said, "Never has anything like this been seen in Israel." [34]But the Pharisees said, "By the ruler of the demons he casts out the demons."

[35]Then Jesus went about all the cities and villages, teaching in their synagogues, and proclaiming the good news of the kingdom, and curing every disease and every sickness. [36]When he saw the crowds, he had compassion for them, because they were harassed and helpless, like sheep without a shepherd. [37]Then he said to his disciples, "The harvest is plentiful, but the laborers are few; [38]therefore ask the Lord of the harvest to send out laborers into his harvest."

Matthew 18:21–35

The Parable of the Unforgiving Servant

[21]Then Peter came and said to him, "Lord, if another member of the church sins against me, how often should I forgive? As many as seven times?" [22]Jesus said to him, "Not seven times, but, I tell you, seventy-seven times."

[23]"For this reason the kingdom of heaven may be compared to a king who

wished to settle accounts with his slaves. 24 When he began the reckoning,
one who owed him ten thousand talents was brought to him; 25 and, as he
could not pay, his lord ordered him to be sold, together with his wife and
children and all his possessions, and payment to be made. 26 So the slave fell
on his knees before him, saying, "Have patience with me, and I will pay you
everything." 27 And out of pity for him, the lord of that slave released him
and forgave him the debt. 28 But that same slave, as he went out, came upon
one of his fellow slaves who owed him a hundred denarii; and seizing him
by the throat, he said, "Pay what you owe." 29 Then his fellow slave fell down
and pleaded with him, "Have patience with me, and I will pay you." 30 But
he refused; then he went and threw him into prison until he should pay the
debt. 31 When his fellow slaves saw what had happened, they were greatly
distressed, and they went and reported to their lord all that had taken place.
32 Then his lord summoned him and said to him, "You wicked slave! I forgave
you all that debt because you pleaded with me. 33 Should you not have had
mercy on your fellow slave, as I had mercy on you?" 34 And in anger his lord
handed him over to be tortured until he should pay his entire debt. 35 So my
heavenly Father will also do to every one of you, if you do not forgive your
brother or sister from your heart."

Luke 1:46–55

Mary's Song of Praise (The Magnificat)

46 And Mary said,
"My soul magnifies the Lord,
  47 and my spirit rejoices in God my Savior,
  48 for he has looked with favor on the lowliness of his servant.
Surely, from now on all generations will call me blessed;
  49 for the Mighty One has done great things for me,
  and holy is his name.
50 His mercy is for those who fear him
  from generation to generation.
51 He has shown strength with his arm;
  he has scattered the proud in the thoughts of their hearts.
52 He has brought down the powerful from their thrones,
  and lifted up the lowly;
53 he has filled the hungry with good things,
  and sent the rich away empty.

[54]He has helped his servant Israel,
  in remembrance of his mercy,
[55]according to the promise he made to our ancestors,
  to Abraham and to his descendants for ever."

Luke 10:25–37

The Parable of the Good Samaritan

[25]Just then a lawyer stood up to test Jesus. "Teacher," he said, "what must I do to inherit eternal life?" [26]He said to him, "What is written in the law? What do you read there?" [27]He answered, "You shall love the Lord your God with all your heart, and with all your soul, and with all your strength, and with all your mind; and your neighbor as yourself." [28]And he said to him, "You have given the right answer; do this, and you will live."

[29]But wanting to justify himself, he asked Jesus, "And who is my neighbor?" [30]Jesus replied, "A man was going down from Jerusalem to Jericho, and fell into the hands of robbers, who stripped him, beat him, and went away, leaving him half dead. [31]Now by chance a priest was going down that road; and when he saw him, he passed by on the other side. [32]So likewise a Levite, when he came to the place and saw him, passed by on the other side. [33]But a Samaritan while traveling came near him; and when he saw him, he was moved with pity. [34]He went to him and bandaged his wounds, having poured oil and wine on them. Then he put him on his own animal, brought him to an inn, and took care of him. [35]The next day he took out two denarii, gave them to the innkeeper, and said, "Take care of him; and when I come back, I will repay you whatever more you spend." [36]Which of these three, do you think, was a neighbor to the man who fell into the hands of the robbers?" [37]He said, "The one who showed him mercy." Jesus said to him, "Go and do likewise."

Luke 15:11–32

The Parable of the Prodigal and His Brother

[11]Then Jesus said, "There was a man who had two sons. [12]The younger of them said to his father, 'Father, give me the share of the property that will belong to me.' So he divided his property between them. [13]A few days later the younger son gathered all he had and traveled to a distant country, and

there he squandered his property in dissolute living. 14When he had spent everything, a severe famine took place throughout that country, and he began to be in need. 15So he went and hired himself out to one of the citizens of that country, who sent him to his fields to feed the pigs. 16He would gladly have filled himself with the pods that the pigs were eating; and no one gave him anything. 17But when he came to himself he said, ‘How many of my father's hired hands have bread enough and to spare, but here I am dying of hunger! 18I will get up and go to my father, and I will say to him, “Father, I have sinned against heaven and before you; 19I am no longer worthy to be called your son; treat me like one of your hired hands.”’ 20So he set off and went to his father. But while he was still far off, his father saw him and was filled with compassion; he ran and put his arms around him and kissed him. 21Then the son said to him, ‘Father, I have sinned against heaven and before you; I am no longer worthy to be called your son.’ 22But the father said to his slaves, ‘Quickly, bring out a robe—the best one—and put it on him; put a ring on his finger and sandals on his feet. 23And get the fatted calf and kill it, and let us eat and celebrate; 24for this son of mine was dead and is alive again; he was lost and is found!’ And they began to celebrate.

25“Now his elder son was in the field; and when he came and approached the house, he heard music and dancing. 26He called one of the slaves and asked what was going on. 27He replied, ‘Your brother has come, and your father has killed the fatted calf, because he has got him back safe and sound.’ 28Then he became angry and refused to go in. His father came out and began to plead with him. 29But he answered his father, ‘Listen! For all these years I have been working like a slave for you, and I have never disobeyed your command; yet you have never given me even a young goat so that I might celebrate with my friends. 30But when this son of yours came back, who has devoured your property with prostitutes, you killed the fatted calf for him!’ 31Then the father said to him, ‘Son, you are always with me, and all that is mine is yours. 32But we had to celebrate and rejoice, because this brother of yours was dead and has come to life; he was lost and has been found.’”

James 2:8–17

8You do well if you really fulfill the royal law according to the scripture, “You shall love your neighbor as yourself.” 9But if you show partiality, you commit sin and are convicted by the law as transgressors. 10For whoever keeps the whole law but fails in one point has become accountable for all of it. 11For the one who said, “You shall not commit adultery,” also said, “You shall not murder.” Now if you do not commit adultery but if you murder, you have

become a transgressor of the law. [12]So speak and so act as those who are to be
judged by the law of liberty. [13]For judgment will be without mercy to anyone
who has shown no mercy; mercy triumphs over judgment.

[14]What good is it, my brothers and sisters, if you say you have faith but do
not have works? Can faith save you? [15]If a brother or sister is naked and lacks
daily food, [16]and one of you says to them, "Go in peace; keep warm and eat
your fill," and yet you do not supply their bodily needs, what is the good of
that? [17]So faith by itself, if it has no works, is dead.

14

Theology of Grace in the Christian Tradition

Basic Affirmations and Debates

Veli-Matti Kärkkäinen

As with most other Christian doctrines, the theology of grace is deeply and widely connected with and embedded in a number of other topics and therefore cannot be artificially isolated from them. In other words, "In order to avoid unilateral interpretations, rather than simply study the use of [the term] *grace* (*kharis,* in Greek; *gratia*, in Latin), we examine the fundamental idea of the salvation that the one God *freely* communicates by means of the Spirit of the Risen Christ in his church, an idea expressed sometimes in other words and categories."[1] For our purposes, the following three topics seem to be the most consequential:

- The question of the basis of salvation—that is, the nature and effects of the Triune God's work of "atonement."
- The question of what is wrong with us—that is, the understanding of sin and Fall.
- The question of the power of human will (or lack thereof)—that is, the capacity to make a choice for (or against) God's offer of grace.

Other theological topics could be added, not least the role of the "means of grace" (in other words, the preaching of the word and the celebration of the holy sacraments). But for the sake of time and space, I will mention the means of grace only briefly in the course of the discussion.[2]

In this essay, I first sketch the ways in which the three above-mentioned adjacent theological topics are related to our main theme in order to help frame and resource our conversation about the theology of grace in Christian tradition. Second, I consider the significant but complex issue of the relationship between divine grace and human freedom. Third, before some brief final reflections, I discuss in some detail the main concepts under which Christian tradition speaks of the reception of divine grace, including deification and justification by faith. The essay seeks, on the one hand, to outline the common affirmations and consensus among diverse Christian traditions regarding the theology of grace. On the other hand, it also highlights and considers important historical and contemporary divergences.

Grace in a Theological Matrix

Atonement and Grace

While in all Abrahamic traditions the merciful and gracious nature of God is extolled in scripture, theology, and spirituality, what is distinctively Christian regarding the communication of divine grace to sinful humanity is atonement theology. The Triune God became incarnate or human in Jesus Christ who lived, ministered, suffered and died for our sins, and in his glorious resurrection gained victory over judgment and death.

Atonement is depicted in theology biblical testimonies by a number of metaphors. Atonement refers to the gracious act of the Triune God in rescuing, renewing, and completing the destiny of humanity and the whole of creation. Beginning in New Testament times, Christian theology has spoken of the atonement and salvation brought about by the Triune God in varied and rich metaphors. Drawn both from the Torah and the Greco-Roman environment, such metaphorical language includes "the language of Jewish law (*justify*) and holy rite (*sanctify*), of medical healing and military rescue (*heal* and *save*), of kingship and its ties (*adopt, wed*), of life processes (*born* and *reborn*), [and] of commercial exchange (*redeem* and *reconcile*)."[3] In other words, the biblical vision of atonement is multicolored and employs a variety of metaphors. It is deeply embedded in the OT and Jewish world, although Christian tradition developed drastically different insights because of its Trinitarian and Christocentric foundation. This is the common affirmation of all Christian traditions.

This kind of atonement theology is of course not part of either Jewish or Islamic theology and indeed is strongly rejected by both.[4] Not only that, but notwithstanding the general foundational agreement, even in Christian tradition there is no unanimous account of the ways in which atonement theology should be best explained. As the premier Christian historian of theology J.N.D. Kelly puts it succinctly, "The development of the church's ideas of the saving effects of the incarnation was a slow, long drawn-out process. Indeed, while the conviction of redemption through Christ has always been a motive force of Christian faith, no final and universally accepted definition of the manner of its achievement has been formulated to this day."[5]

For the first millennium or so, the so-called *Christus Victor* (Christ the champion) metaphors were central, with their focus on Jesus's life in incarnation as "recapitulation" and healing of sinful humanity's path and their highlighting of resurrection as a way to overcoming death rather than the death on the cross as a way of "paying for sins." Rather than speaking of atonement mainly in terms of guilt and judgment, St. Irenaeus and Eastern theologians placed the main emphasis on overcoming corruption and mortality by virtue of participation in the divine life.

Many other metaphors of atonement emerged from the beginning of the second millennium onward, including Satisfaction theory (Anselm of Canterbury) with its focus on reestablishing the cosmic harmony that was lost due to human disobedience; Moral Example theory (Peter Abelard) with its interest in the inspiring power for love as able to overcome a selfish attitude toward others; and Penal Substitution theory which, while also building on the Anselmian legacy, focused on Christ's death on the cross, while innocent, as the way to meet the righteous demands of God to pay the penalty of sin and to deal with guilt and condemnation.

These and other interpretations are all complementary rather than alternative ways of embracing the multifaceted and rich atoning benefits of Christ's work on our behalf. The main point, once again, is that, in Christian understanding, the merciful and gracious God has in the "Word made flesh" (John 1:14) and in the power of the Holy Spirit brought about the decisive work of reconciliation between sinful humanity and holy God.

As important as the debates about the logistics, as it were, of this reconciliatory act might be, its supreme significance to Christian faith is uncontested. No Christian theology of grace and mercy can do without the divine atonement.

Sin and Grace

Not only do the Abrahamic sister faiths not share a common understanding of what is wrong with us, there is also disagreement among Christian traditions about this, notwithstanding the universal belief in sinfulness and the Fall.[6] To oversimplify a complex issue, we can describe the two main Christian interpretive traditions as follows:

1. The less "negative" interpretation is that of the Eastern Orthodox Church, in which the Fall narrative is depicted as a "stumbling" of yet-immature children (Adam and Eve). While of course an unfortunate experience, the Fall did not bring about original sin

(technically understood, as in the Latin West), and certainly not divine judgment. Rather, judgment comes only because of wrong choices and acts. The Eastern Orthodox Church understands the effects of the Fall more in terms of a wound inflicted in our nature.

2. The more "negative" interpretation is present in the traditions of the Christian West, which include Roman Catholicism, Anglicanism, and Protestant churches of various sorts. Based on St. Augustine's theology, they speak of original sin as the result of Adam's disobedience; this sinfulness, which results in divine judgment, is "inherited" from generation to generation. That said, there is a divergence within the Christian West between the two main families, and the Roman Catholic Church developed the Augustinian tradition somewhat differently from the Anglican and Protestant traditions.

In the Latin West, under the influence of St. Paul, the Genesis 3 Fall narrative came to be read through Romans 5. Under the guidance of Augustine, the *doctor gratiae*, it was believed that St. Paul had worked out a technical doctrine of the semiautomatic transmission of sin through procreation, and that guilt accrued even to infants at their birth.[7] Briefly put, when Adam sinned, we participated in it. This interpretation was supported by the faulty Vulgate translation of Romans 5:12, which translated the Greek *eph ho* as "in whom"—that is, when Adam transgressed, we, the human race, participated in his sin and inherit this fallen nature from our parents.[8] We are guilty and condemned as a result.[9]

Theological scholarship contemporary with us, however, does not agree with that classical interpretation. Even if Pauline theology traces the universality of sin back to Adam (Rom. 5:12), there is not yet any notion of sin "as a fated universal legacy that proliferates generation [by] generation like a congenital disease."[10] And although Paul teaches the universal occurrence of death (as in Rom. 5:12, an idea familiar also to Jewish tradition), he does not speak of us inheriting sin in any technical sense.

Importantly, Eastern Orthodox theology followed other Pauline and the wider New Testament traditions in understanding the example and sin of Adam as representing the whole race instead of linking this notion to the idea of the inheritance of sin. It is also highly significant that, for centuries, patristic theology (or theology of the church Fathers) did not have a developed doctrine of sin at all (other than a deep intuition of the fallen and sinful nature of humanity).

In fact, in the Christian East, the human person was regarded as mortal even *before* the Fall, and hence death in itself could not be punishment for the Fall. Human nature is intact even after the Fall and is good by virtue of existing as the image of God, and free will is not destroyed by the Fall. In this interpretation, we do not inherit sin but rather its consequences, particularly corruption and mortality. In other words, the East followed the Hebrew notion that even the concept of original sin is not a standard term. While the universality of sin is affirmed, Eastern theology often describes it in terms of woundedness or sickness.

The ensuing discussion of the freedom of will, or lack thereof, spells out the details concerning the effects of Christians' quite radically differing views of grace and its reception. That said, all Christian traditions consider the current state of humanity to be hopeless apart from God's saving grace. Whatever men and women may or may not contribute to their salvation, for all of them the source and initiative of salvation lies in what the gracious God has done for us. Indeed, there is no denying that while "no religious vision has ever esteemed humankind more highly than the Christian vision," no other tradition has also "judged it more severely."[11] In sum, all Christian traditions believe that something is fundamentally wrong with us and with the world, and that unless God in his grace and mercy stoops down to our level and saves us, we are without hope.

Human Freedom and Grace

An important corollary issue behind varying interpretations of sin and the Fall is the question of the freedom of the will. Whereas in the Greek-speaking Christian East freedom of the will was not negated by Adam's disobedience, the Latin-speaking Christian West, following Augustine, denies the power of choice apart from divine restorative grace (except for freedom to choose wrongly). Western Christians maintain that before the Fall, the human being was capable of not sinning but totally lost that capacity thereafter.[12] Protestant and Anglican churches continued affirming this Augustinian denial of freedom of the will (apart from grace), whereas in Roman Catholicism, mainly thanks to St. Thomas Aquinas, a somewhat less negative account of the will developed.

Behind the Thomist continuation and modification of the Augustinian doctrine is the "two-story" anthropology based on a nature–grace dialectic. Whereas intellect and will belong to the realm of nature, the supernatural gift of "original righteousness" (as well as supernatural "virtues" of faith, hope, and love) belong to that of grace. As a result, the latter can be removed (as happened as a result of the Fall) without destroying the "natural" endowments (even though they, too, were hampered severely because of sin). Clearly, at the center of Thomas's theology is not the Fall but rather the supernatural destiny of human nature.

Grace and Human Freedom: Vehement Debates and Disputes

Human Freedom and Responsibility

As influential as Augustine's theological legacy has been in the Christian West, it was never unanimously affirmed. His most famous opponent, Pelagius, a monk (allegedly) with a rigorous ethical-moral drive, rightly feared that the Augustinian interpretation of salvation would make Christians complacent through its seeming endorsement of total weakness of will because of the Fall and the emphasis on God's eternal divine election.[13] By contrast, Pelagius maintained that men and women are able to choose between good and evil, similarly to the Christian East.[14]

Although Pelagianism died hard, already the Council of Orange in 529 ruled that the human person is not free apart from God's grace to believe and that God's salvific response does not come as a rewarding for the best efforts of men and women.[15] That said, the defeat of Pelagianism did not in any way constitute an unconditional, let alone unreserved, establishment of the Augustinian view, which "had in many ways gone beyond even the Western theological tradition (not to mention the Eastern tradition) by positing a doctrine of predestination, including predestination to damnation, and of the irresistibility of grace."[16]

Responding to his critics, Augustine consolidated his view of the sovereignty of God and the unconditionality of divine election in eternity (although he also sought to resist pagan fatalism, as had his forebears).[17] The "double predestination" view, as it is known, taught that people are destined for condemnation unless God's sovereign choice rescues them from it.

Grace, Election, and Predestination

In both John Calvin's Reformed theology (as further developed by his ablest successor, Theodore Beza, and others) and in Anglicanism, the idea of double predestination came to its fullest fruition.[18] One of the oddities of the (ultra-)Calvinist formulation of election is that of "irresistible grace"—the idea that to whomever God has from eternity decided to grant grace will necessarily receive it, without the possibility of resistance.

Not surprisingly, the Arminian party vehemently resisted the Calvinist (Augustinian) interpretation and instead offered an alternative theology of grace and election, most notably by the Remonstrants in 1610.[19] The Arminian understanding of grace is decidedly different from the irresistible grace of Calvinism:

> That this grace of God is the beginning, continuance, and accomplishment of all good, even to the extent that the regenerate man himself, without prevenient or assisting, awakening, following and cooperative grace, can neither think, will, nor do good, nor withstand any temptations to evil; so that all good deeds or movements that can be conceived must be ascribed to the grace of God in Christ. But with respect to the mode of the operation of this grace, it is not irresistible, since it is written concerning many, that they have resisted the Holy Spirit (Acts 7, and elsewhere in many places).[20]

The five points of the TULIP, as it is known—an abbreviation for "total depravity, unconditional election, limited atonement, irresistible grace, and perseverance of the saints" formulated by the Calvinists in the Canons of Dort of 1618 to 1619—were programmatically aimed at conclusively defeating the Arminian position. No unanimity was reached, and the debates continue to this day. While on the Lutheran side of the Protestant Reformation Augustine's notion that the human will is unable to take any initiative toward salvation prevailed, the Reformed idea of double predestination was not endorsed.[21]

The Wittenberg Reformer, Martin Luther, had a famous and very consequential debate with Roman Catholics. In his 1525 pamphlet *The Bondage of the Will*, Luther's vehement rebuttal of the Catholic humanist Erasmus of Rotterdam's *The Freedom of the Will* (1524) showcased the debates of the Christian West. Whereas the latter finds all kinds of affirmations of the freedom of will in scriptural narrative (albeit at times in limited fashion), the former not only contested their meaning but also claimed to find a great deal of biblical support for the denial of all power of will in relation to God.[22] As a consequence, the Lutheran (and later Protestant mainstream) tradition considered the grace of God to be the only thing that moved the soul toward God. Regarding human life and society, men and women have been given the power to choose rightly and bear responsibility for their choices; in the Catholic understanding (at least some) responsibility also lies on the human side with real, albeit limited, powers of will to choose rightly.

Generally speaking, between Roman Catholics and Protestants, particularly Reformed Protestants, there is a marked difference in the approach to divine election. Notwithstanding Augustine's heritage, the Roman Catholic

Church does not endorse the doctrine of divine predestination or reprobation apart from human response.[23] In other words, throughout history, the continuing "stumbling block in the Augustinian view of grace" remained the doctrine of reprobation, which was variously negotiated among the medieval masters Anselm, Aquinas, Bonaventure, and others.[24] What can be seen as a "milder predestinarianism" (so named by Paul King Jewett) became the mainstream (though not the only) opinion in the Christian West, according to which election to salvation is affirmed but not reprobation.[25]

Having now considered in some detail both the common affirmations and disputes among the Christian traditions regarding the source, power, and conditions of divine grace, in the rest of the essay I delve into the question of the reception of grace.

The Reception of Divine Grace: Deification and Justification by Faith

For Orientation: Common Affirmations and Divergent Interpretations

As I explained at the outset, Christian theology of grace is not only widely and deeply intertwined with other theological topics; its reception is also expressed and defended with a variety of different terms. Generally speaking, the reception of salvation in the Christian church (and still in our day) has followed two major lines of interpretation:

1. *Theosis* (meaning deification or divinization) is the Christian East's way of speaking of the way in which the sinful human person may be saved by the grace of God.
2. *Justification by faith* (and the sequential concept of sanctification) is how Catholics, Protestants, and Anglicans typically speak of the same thing, albeit each in their own way. The main difference between Catholics and Protestants/Anglicans is Catholics' continuation of the Augustinian/Thomistic emphasis on justification as bringing about the renewal of life, whereas Protestants/Anglicans (although not, of course, denying the importance of the renewal of life) have made sanctification a "second moment" in the process of justification—and often to the point that even without many (or even any) visible signs of the renewal, justification still holds. The remainder of the Protestants, including Anabaptists and many of their "Free Church" friends, as well as the Methodist and Holiness movements, have

> emphasized the necessity of the renewal of life, although not to the detriment of the "forensic" understanding of justification by faith as the first moment. (Here the term *forensic* means the pronouncement of the sinful person as just/righteous before God, whereas sanctification, the renewal of life, is at times dubbed "effective" justification.)

In sum, "Protestants have tended to think through the categories of justification and sanctification. The Roman Catholic tradition has often seen salvation through the lens of transformation and renewal. Eastern Orthodox traditions have emphasized participation and deification."[26] As mentioned, while embracing the Protestant type of understanding of salvation, the Wesleyans (the Methodists and Holiness movements) focus on sanctification, Anabaptists on discipleship and "practical Christianity," and Pentecostals on empowerment and healing.

Before taking a closer look at some of these key traditions, it is—again—important to frame the discussion by emphasizing the importance of common or shared affirmations:

- All human beings are sinful and fallen and thus in need of divine initiative and divine offer of salvation.
- No human being can be justified or deified without the atoning work of the Triune God in the incarnation of the Son of God, in the power of the Holy Spirit.
- No human being, not even the best ones, can save themselves apart from the grace of God.
- Whatever the exact interpretation of the nature of human freedom or divine predestination, only the Triune God can ultimately begin and complete the process of salvation.
- The goal of Christian life is to grow in godlikeness, the ultimate effect of divine grace.

Of course, these principles are (for the most part) foreign to the two other Abrahamic sister faiths, even though Jews and Christians share the same Torah.

One with God: Orthodox Doctrine of Grace

The Christian East uses a number of distinctive terms and metaphors for salvation resulting from the grace of God, including participation, union, and deification. However, the most widely used is *theosis*. Briefly put, it means that the human being *becomes god* (lower case), not only *like god.* Through the Holy Spirit, the human person is "graced" to the point that there is union with God (upper case).

In this regard, the two cardinal biblical texts for the Eastern Church are 2 Peter 1:4, which speaks of becoming "partakers of the divine nature," and Psalm 82:6 (as quoted by the Johannine Jesus in John 10:34): "I said, you are gods."[27] The Petrine passage accentuates the key idea of release from the corruption and mortality caused by the evil desires of the world. That is the key soteriological motif in the East.

The roots of the doctrine of divinization go back to the beginning of Christian theology, highlighting the centrality of the incarnation of Christ. St. Irenaeus spoke of the "Word of God, our Lord Jesus Christ who because of his limitless love became what we are in order to make us what even he himself is."[28] St. Athanasius taught that "Christ became human that humans might become divine."[29] Further examples are easily found.

The fourteenth-century Gregory of Palamas helped conclusively establish the main theological ramifications of the doctrine of *theosis*. The key aspects of his teaching are (1) the creation of the human being "in the image and after the likeness of God," (2) the incarnation of the Logos of God, and (3) the human being's communion with God in the Holy Spirit. Importantly, Palamas taught that the distinction between God's essence and God's "energies" makes it possible to say that deification means participating in divine energies but not in the divine essence as such—thus avoiding pantheism. God still remains God, and humans remain human, although participating in the divine.

Differently from the West, Eastern theology does not juxtapose divine grace (and initiative) with human freedom (and responsibility). It speaks of divine–human synergy (cooperation), which is anathema to Lutherans and many other Protestants.

A central feature of Eastern Christian mentality is also cosmic orientation. This comes to the fore in embracing the whole world as the locus of God's grace, blessing, and providence.

The Christian West: Justification by Faith as the "Umbrella" Concept

While "grace was a central issue for all parties in the sixteenth-century Reformation," it was mainly, almost exclusively, expressed in the Christian West in terms of the doctrine of justification.[30] As much as Catholics, Protestants, and Anglicans might have debated about the details of the doctrine, their theology of grace came to be expressed via that framework.

With that in mind, it is important to note that patristic writers did not express the doctrine of grace and salvation under the concept of justification, even though the term is not missing.[31] Only with the rise of Pelagian "works righteousness" did the Western Church have to begin to articulate a doctrine that later became highly technically formulated.

Augustine's legacy also rules here. He considered justification as the work of the Holy Spirit. Related to this is the emphasis on love rather than "faith alone" as the primary aspect of justification (Rom. 5:5).[32] Building on the Pauline rule of "faith working through love" (Gal. 5:6), Augustine established the highly influential "faith formed by love" principle, which was followed by Catholics but strongly opposed by Protestants because they feared it would introduce the need for human merit at the expense of faith (even though Augustine understood both love and faith as divine gifts). The key to renewal is the Holy Spirit poured out as love at justification; love is nothing else but the Spirit himself.[33] Very importantly, unlike the later Protestant Reformation's separation of justification from sanctification, Augustine unambiguously taught that justification means "to make righteous."[34] Technically put, he endorsed both the "forensic" aspect (declaring the sinner righteous) and the "effective" aspect (making the sinner righteous)—in short, sanctification.[35]

Thomas Aquinas built on and developed Augustine's thought yet further. Although he held on to the two-aspect account of justification, he went further by talking about "habitual grace," meaning that the remission of sins elevates the sinner to a "state of justice."[36] In other words, justification makes something "inherent" reside in the believer.

Another key development—which Luther came to vehemently resist—is related to a pre-Reformation former teacher of his, Gabriel Biel, who formulated the famous slogan "God does not deny grace to the one who does everything in his or her power."[37] Or in modern terminology: do your best and God will take care of the rest.

While the Protestant Reformation never succeeded in providing a totally coherent, single understanding of justification, it is fair to say that, from the 1530s until the heyday of Protestant orthodoxy in the mid-eighteenth century, mainline Protestantism embraced the following tenets, which obviously represent new developments from the earlier tradition:[38]

- Justification as forensic declaration rather than a process of change;
- Consequently, a categorical distinction between justification as an initial "once-and-for-all" change of state and progressive growth in renewal (sanctification);

- And, subsequently, the vehement rejection of the idea of "habitual" grace.[39]

One of the divergences had to do with the means of grace. Whereas in Catholic theology the means of grace, particularly the sacraments, played a significant role, without in any way undermining the role of faith and the scripture, among the Protestants various types of emphases surfaced. To somewhat oversimplify a complex issue, we might speak of three "camps": the first aligned with Martin Luther's thought; the second, with that of Ulrich Zwingli; and the third, with that of John Calvin. Then something like the following serves as a heuristic device:

- For Lutherans, the means of grace—namely, Word and Sacraments—are central, thus also betraying their great debt to the mother church in Rome.
- For the Reformed in the Ulrich Zwingli camp, the role of the sacraments is marginal as they see the communication of grace mainly through the Holy Spirit in some sort of "direct" act of God. Among the Free Churches, beginning with the Baptists at the start of the seventeenth century and including scores of others later in history, the same attitude prevailed.
- For the Reformed in Calvin's camp, the relation between grace and the means of grace is ambiguous. For, on the one hand, the Spirit confers grace through preaching and sacrament as "means and instruments";[40] and, on the other hand, given God's transcendence, grace is not limited to created realities such as sacraments in the way more typical of Lutherans (and Catholics).[41]

Classic Roman Catholic Theology of Grace

The only official formulation of the doctrine of justification in the Roman Catholic Church goes back to the Council of Trent. In 1547 Catholics responded decisively to the doctrine that the Protestant Reformers articulated. Note that I said they responded—they reacted. In other words, they did not attempt to formulate their own doctrine of justification. Nonetheless, it is that response that has remained the binding formulation of what justification is for that church.

Although it takes God's gracious preparation of the will for a person to be justified or to receive justification (#6), nonetheless justification cannot happen without human consent (#4, #9).[42] Although faith is necessary for justification, without love faith does not suffice (#11, #12); based on Hebrews 11:6

("without faith it is impossible to please [God]"), they rejected the Protestant emphasis on justification as a free gift (#8). Most controversial to Protestants are the words about merit. Although, following Augustine, *merit* means God's crowning of his own work, the Council of Trent teaches that based on their inherent righteousness, Christians may merit eternal life (#16). What is probably a concession to Luther is the statement on justification as "alien," although Trent does not deny that it may be inherent righteousness as well. It is "alien" in the sense of coming from outside human efforts and resources (#16). Finally, Trent rejects the Protestant claim of assurance of salvation as well as perseverance (#9 and #16).[43]

Lutherans and Reformed on Justification by Faith

The standard account of the Lutheran—and, more widely, pan-Protestant—doctrine of justification by faith is something like this: whereas the forensic declaration of the sinner as just is something that happens "outside" the believer (in the sense that it is not conditioned on the inner change of the justified person), sanctification—the second step—is meant to refer to the improvement of life. However, as important as sanctification is, the existence or lack thereof has little or no effect on the foundational status of the sinner as justified.

As representative as that view may be among Protestants, important divergent views also emerged. Martin Luther himself did not, by and large, endorse the above (which was drafted mainly by his right-hand man, Philip Melanchthon, in the Lutheran Confessions). For Luther, Christ's presence in the believer through the Holy Spirit—in other words, union between God and the believer—is primary. He expressed it technically as *in ipsa fide Christus adest* (in faith itself Christ is present). The implication is that the distinction between forensic and efficient justification is not the key; as a result of Christ's presence, renewal begins and continues throughout one's life, even when Christians are simultaneously sinners and justified.[44]

Luther's own view points toward Calvin's Reformed interpretation. For the Genevan Reformer, both justification and sanctification stand under union with God—and surprisingly, sanctification is talked about before justification. The classic opening passage of the third book of the *Institutes*, a preamble to *ordo salutis* (the order of salvation), states "that so long as we are without Christ and separated from him, nothing which he suffered and did for the salvation of the human race is of the least benefit to us. To communicate to us the blessings which he received from the Father, he must become ours and dwell in us."[45] By stating it like this, Calvin tightly connects justification and sanctification in order to refute the charge of "cheap grace" and complaints about a lack of emphasis on good works as the fruit of salvation.[46]

Sanctification and Discipleship in Focus among Free Church Traditions

Calvin's tight linking of sanctification and justification through the concept of the union with God prepares the way for later developments in which growth in holiness and Christian life becomes a major concern. In other words, Free Church theologians were concerned about cheap grace, the apparent lapse into complacency regarding growth in Christian life and sanctification. The more the "free" offer of justification by faith was proclaimed to the masses, the graver this concern grew. At the same time, as mentioned, these diverse movements did not forget about the Reformation doctrine of the justification by faith.

In the theology and spirituality of the former Anglican John Wesley (and his brother Charles, along with John Fletcher and others) the invitation to sanctified life became the clarion call. For Methodism and for later Holiness movements, sanctification marks the "last and highest state" of progress in Christian life. Wesley at times even used the daring word *perfection*—but let us not misunderstand what he meant by it. For him, perfection did not entail perfect sinlessness. Nonetheless, it definitely marked Wesley's vision of soteriology as being outside the Protestant mainstream. It held on tightly to Jesus's admonition to "be perfect, as your heavenly Father is perfect" (Matt. 5:48). As suspicious as the desire for perfection may sound to mainstream Protestant and Anglican ears, Wesley's vision in fact aligns itself with the breadth of Christian tradition. The pursuit of perfection is evident among the Fathers (both in the East and in the West) and subsequently throughout history. It is not insignificant that Wesley read and helped to translate some of the key texts of the Eastern Fathers.[47]

Before Wesleyanism, the Radical Reformers, such as Anabaptists and Mennonites, had pushed even further the call for the holiness of life and the cultivation of piety and ethical pursuit in everyday life. These dissidents of the Reformation era became highly critical of Lutheran and Reformed Reformations for their alleged "compromise" with the earthly powers and their reluctance to preach the radical biblical message of repentance. They regarded the church as "an assembly of the righteous" rather than as a "mixed body." They believed that the true congregation of Christ consists of those "who are truly converted, who are born from above of God, who are of a regenerate mind by the operation of the Holy Spirit through the hearing of the divine Word, and have become the children of God."[48]

What are now known as the Free Churches, beginning with the Baptist churches stemming from the early seventeenth century, continue the legacy of both Anabaptism and (later) the Wesleyan and Holiness movements. As with their parent traditions, Free Churches preach the Reformation doctrine of justification by faith but with a single-minded emphasis on the need for personal faith, the pursuit of holiness in everyday life, and the importance of everyday discipleship. Among the Free Church family are also usually counted the Pentecostal movements with the added emphasis on the charismatic empowerment with spiritual gifts such as healing and prophecy, as the surplus of divine grace. Note that the terms *grace* (*kharis*) and *charism* are even linguistically from the same root. Importantly, these Pentecostal (and Charismatic) movements have grown phenomenally and, after the Roman Catholics, now represent the biggest group of Christians.

Final Reflections

This chapter has had a twofold task to accomplish. On the one hand, its goal has been to introduce, detail, and give examples of the ways in which divine grace and mercy are understood, believed, and lived out in the Christian church. An integral part of this task has been to trace some key developments in the emerging common understanding. The ultimate goal of this aspect of the chapter has been to sketch out a more or less commonly shared Christian theology of God's grace. Since this essay itself contains several summaries of these shared key tenets, there is no reason to repeat them here.

On the other hand, without in any way neglecting or undermining the commonly shared "Great Tradition" in the Christian theology of grace, I have also outlined important disputes, debates, differences, and unresolved issues and assessed their importance for our work in this interfaith process. Not unlike other living faith traditions, Christian theology does not speak with a unified voice about issues as big as human freedom, divine election, the capacity and means by which one receives God's offer of grace, or who might be saved. These are topics of ongoing and lively debate, dialogue, and further research.

Divergences and differences, and even fierce debates, among religious traditions do not necessarily have to be understood as problems—let alone as signs of lapses or deterioration in doctrinal rigor. They can also be seen as a welcome sign of vitality, insight, and the willingness to learn to articulate more carefully topics of life and death.

A suitable way for closing this brief essay on Christian theology of grace is to refer to the Vatican II document *Dei verbum*. It speaks beautifully of the ways in which the loving God reaches out to his children in an intimate way to invite them for fellowship and friendship. I cannot imagine a better synopsis for grace and mercy in my own faith tradition than the following:

> In His goodness and wisdom God chose to reveal Himself and to make known to us the hidden purpose of His will (see Eph. 1:9) by which through Christ, the Word made flesh, man might in the Holy Spirit have access to the Father and come to share in the divine nature (see Eph. 2:18; 2 Peter 1:4). Through this revelation, therefore, the invisible God (see Col. 1:15; 1 Tim. 1:17) out of the abundance of His love speaks to men as friends (see Ex. 33:11; John 15:14–15) and lives among them (see Bar. 3:37), so that He may invite and take them into fellowship with Himself.[49]

Notes

1. B. Studer, "Grace," in *Encyclopedia of Ancient Christianity*, ed. Angelo Di Berardino (Downers Grove, IL: InterVarsity Press, 2014), 168.

2. This essay gleans from and at times repeats more or less verbatim brief sections from several recent publications of mine: "Sin, Forgiveness, and Reconciliation: A Christian Perspective," in *Sin, Forgiveness, and Reconciliation. Christian and Muslim Perspectives*, ed. Lucinda Mosher and David Marshall (Washington, DC: Georgetown University Press, 2016), 3–12; "Human Action within the Sovereignty of God: Christian Perspectives" in *God's Creativity and Human Action: Christian and Muslim Perspectives*, ed. Lucinda Mosher and David Marshall (Washington, DC: Georgetown University Press, 2017), 139–47; *Christian Theology in the Pluralistic World: A Global Introduction* (Grand Rapids, MI: Eerdmans, 2019), chap. 8; "Pelastus ekumeenisessa teologiassa" [Salvation in ecumenical theology] in *Pelastus: Synodaalikirja 2022* [Salvation: Synodal book 2022], ed. Niko Huttunen, Anna-Kaisa Inkala, Kari Kopperi, Marko Marttila, Terhi Törmä (Helsinki: Kirkkohallitus/Piispainkokous, 2022), 70–94.

3. James W. McClendon Jr., *Doctrine*, vol. 2 of *Systematic Theology* (Nashville, TN: Abingdon, 1994), 106–7, emphases in original.

4. For a detailed discussion of atonement in Christian perspective, see my *Christ and Reconciliation*, vol. 1 of *A Constructive Christian Theology for the Pluralistic World* (Grand Rapids, MI: Eerdmans, 2013), part 2, "Reconciliation"; for comparison (from a Christian perspective) between Christian, Jewish, and Islamic interpretations of "salvation" (including Buddhist and Hindu traditions), see chap. 15.

5. J.N.D. Kelly, *Early Christian Doctrines*, rev. ed. (New York: Harper & Row, 1978), 163.

6. Whereas Christian theological tradition speaks of "original sin" (in the Christian West), Islamic tradition rejects such an interpretation. Furthermore, even the Jewish and Christian interpretations, based on the same scriptural materials ("Old Testament"), have widely differing theologies of sin. In Jewish theology, the "fallen" state of humanity is depicted in terms of being driven either by evil or good inclinations, and Adam plays virtually

no role at all, in contrast to the New Testament–based Christian exegesis. The obvious reason for the Jewish conclusion is that in the Old Testament Adam virtually disappears after the opening pages. One has to wait until 2 Esdras (7:48) to know that Adam's fall has universal effects (but that each individual may also win over sin, 7:57). For a detailed and more technical discussion of sin and grace, consult my treatment of sin and fall in Christianity and four other faith traditions (Judaism, Islam, Hinduism, Buddhism) in chap. 15 of *Creation and Humanity*, vol. 3 of *A Constructive Christian Theology for the Pluralistic World.*

7. Among many relevant writings, the most important in this regard is Augustine's *Treatise on the Merits and Forgiveness of Sins, and on the Baptism of Infants*. Augustine is of course not the only advocate of the traditional Western church's view. (Simply recall his mentor Ambrosius's influence.) However, he is the most prolific and authoritative witness.

8. An asset in the hereditary interpretation of sin came from the Traducianist view of the origin of soul (that is, at the moment of conception, the human being to be born receives her "nature" from both parents rather than directly from the Creator, as in the "creationist" view).

9. Augsburg Confession #2 (a key Lutheran confessional document) puts it this way: "since the Fall of Adam all humans who are propagated according to nature are born in sin"; and this: "vice of origin is truly sin, which even now damns and brings eternal death on those who are not born again through Baptism and Holy Spirit."

10. Wolfhart Pannenberg, *Anthropology in Theological Perspective*, trans. Matthew J. O'Connell (Philadelphia: Westminster, 1985), 121.

11. Paul Jewett, with Marguerite Shuster, *Who We Are: Our Dignity as Human; A Neo-Evangelical Theology* (Grand Rapids, MI: Eerdmans, 1996), 57.

12. Interesting in this regard is the fact that one of the first works of St. Augustine (prior to his battle with Pelagianism) was *On the Free Choice of the Will.*

13. For a succinct description of Pelagianism, see Kelly, *Early Christian Doctrines*, 357–61.

14. A particularly important text is Pelagius's *Commentary on St. Paul's Epistle to the Romans*, which was written before the controversy with Augustine, thus highlighting the original form of his ideas.

15. The canons (twenty-five altogether) of the Council of Orange can be found in many standard editions of the creeds and councils.

16. Jaroslav Pelikan, *The Christian Tradition: A History of the Development of Doctrine*, vol. 1, *The Emergence of the Catholic Tradition (100–600)* (Chicago: University of Chicago Press, 1971), 318. The term "semi-Pelagianism" is not favored by all scholars; yet, as a placeholder, it describes quite well the ambiguity in the theology of grace in the Latin church.

17. See Augustine, *On the Predestination of the Saints* and *On the Gift of Perseverance.*

18. Regarding Reformed theology, for the classic statement, see John Calvin, *Institutes of the Christian Religion*, 3.21.5, trans. Henry Beveridge (1845), available at the Christian Classics Ethereal Library website, www.ccel.org. In the Methodist tradition (which emerged from Anglicanism via John Wesley and some others), theology of predestination became a dividing issue as John Wesley advocated strongly Arminian views, whereas George Whitefield, gleaning from the ultra-Calvinist American Puritan Jonathan Edwards, advocated strong Calvinism, as visible in his 1754 *Freedom of the Will.*

19. See Arminius, *Writings*, vol. 1, "On Predestination," available at ccel.org. The classic texts with critical notes of *Five Points of the Remonstrants* (1610), on the Arminian side, and the *Canons of Dort* (1618–1619), on the Calvinist side, can be found in Philip Schaff's *Creeds of Christendom*, vol. 3, available at www.ccel.org.

20. Dennis Bratcher, ed., *The Five Articles of the Remonstrants* (1610), Christian Resource Institute website, https://www.crivoice.org/creedremonstrants.html.

21. See the important rejection of Calvinistic views of limited atonement and predestination for reprobation in Saxon Visitation Articles (1592), #4, Book of Concord website, http://bookofconcord.org.

22. Lutheran tradition famously makes the distinction between the human person *coram hominibus* ("in front of human beings"), the domain in which men and women can—and should—make choices between wrong and right, and *coram Deo* ("before God") with regard to which all human initiative is null.

23. *Catechism of the Catholic Church*, ##600, 1037, https://www.vatican.va/archive.

24. See Jaroslav Pelikan, *The Christian Tradition: A History of the Development of Doctrine*, vol. 3, *The Growth of Medieval Theology (600–1300)* (Chicago: University of Chicago Press, 1978), 271–84, at 275; and Jaroslav Pelikan, *The Christian Tradition: A History of the Development of Doctrine*, vol. 4, *Reformation of Church and Dogma (1300–1700)* (Chicago: University of Chicago Press, 1984), 28–35.

25. Paul King Jewett, *Election and Predestination* (Grand Rapids, MI: Eerdmans, 1985), 7, 8.

26. Richard Lints, "Soteriology," in *Mapping Modern Theology: A Thematic and Historical Introduction*, ed. Kelly M. Kapic and Bruce L. McCormack (Grand Rapids, MI: Baker Academic, 2012), 260.

27. Other texts referred to by Orthodox theologians include Exodus 34:30; Matthew 17:4; John 17:21–23; 2 Corinthians 8:9; 1 John 3:2; 4:12.

28. Irenaeus, *Against Heresies* 5, Preface, in *The Ante-Nicene Fathers: Translations of the Writings of the Fathers Down to A.D. 325*, ed. Alexander Roberts and James Donaldson et al., 9 vols. (Edinburgh, 1885–1897, www.ccel.org), 1:526.

29. Athanasius, *On the Incarnation* 54, in *A Select Library of the Nicene and Post-Nicene Fathers of the Christian Church*, 2nd ser. 14 vols., ed. Philip Schaff and Henry Wace (Edinburgh, 1886–1880, www.ccel.org), 4:65.

30. David S. Yeago, "Grace," in *The Oxford Encyclopedia of the Reformation*, ed. Hans J. Hillebrand (Oxford: Oxford University Press, 2005), online version.

31. Consider that the two-volume *Commentary on the Epistle to the Romans* by Origen neither caused debates nor offered substantially new perspectives. One of the reasons is that Pauline theology did not play the central role that it did later in medieval and Reformation debates.

32. "God's love has been poured into our hearts through the Holy Spirit which has been given to us." (RSV).

33. Augustine, *A Treatise on the Spirit and the Letter* 5, in *A Select Library of the Nicene and Post-Nicene Fathers of the Christian Church*, 1st ser. 14 vols., ed. Philip Schaff (Edinburgh, 1886–1880, www.ccel.org), 5:84–85.

34. Augustine takes the Latin word *iustificare*, rooted in *facere* (to make), in its literal, obvious meaning.

35. Augustine, *A Treatise on Grace and Free Will*, 33, in *A Select Library of the Nicene and Post-Nicene Fathers of the Christian Church*, 1st ser., 5:457–58.

36. Thomas Aquinas, *The Summa Theologica of St. Thomas Aquinas*, 2nd rev. ed., literally translated by Fathers of the English Dominican Province (1920), I–II, q. 113, online edition © 2008 by Kevin Knight, http://www.newadvent.org/summa/. See also Alister E. McGrath, *Iustitia Dei: A History of the Christian Doctrine of Justification*, 2 vols. (Cambridge: Cambridge University Press, 1986), 1:43–51.

37. McGrath, *Iustitia Dei*, 1:81–93.

38. Although debates about justification and faith became central by the time of Protestant Reformation from the beginning of the sixteenth century, it was not the only issue of contention with the Catholic Church. The nature and authority of the Church as well as the relation between scripture and tradition (and, thus, the locus of authority) were important related issues.

39. See Michael Horton, "Traditional Reformed View," in *Justification: Five Views*, ed. James K. Beilby and Paul Rhodes Eddy (Downers Grove, IL: IVP Academic, 2011), 85–91.

40. Calvin, *Institutes*, 4.14.12.

41. I am indebted to Yeago, "Grace," n.p.

42. "Decree on Justification: Sixth Session" (January 13, 1547), in Schaff, *The Creeds of Christendom*, 2:89–118. Numbers in parentheses refer to this document.

43. Gerald O'Collins, SJ, and Oliver P. Rafferty, SJ, "Roman Catholic View," in Beilby and Eddy, *Justification*, 280–81.

44. Olli-Pekka Vainio, *Justification and Participation in Christ: The Development of the Lutheran Doctrine of Justification from Luther to the Formula of Concord (1580)* (Leiden: Brill, 2008), 42–53.

45. Calvin, *Institutes*, 3.1.1.

46. Calvin, *Institutes*, 3.16.1.

47. For details and sources, consult William J. Abraham, "Christian Perfection," in *The Oxford Handbook of Methodist Studies*, ed. James E. Kirby and William J. Abraham (Oxford: Oxford University Press, 2014), 587–601.

48. Menno Simons, *Reply to Gellius Faber* (1552), in *The Complete Writings of Menno Simons (c. 1496–1561)*, ed. J. C. Wenger, trans. Leonard Verdiun (Scottdale, PA: Herald, 1956), 300.

49. From chapter 2 of the *Dogmatic Constitution on Divine Revelation Dei Verbum*, solemnly promulgated by His Holiness Pope Paul VI on November 18, 1965.

15

Paul on Mercy and Grace

Key Passages; Parallels with Teachings of Jesus

Susan Eastman

As Christopher Hays has rightly noted, the key themes of grace are central to the New Testament as a whole and, indeed, cohere with the meaning of mercy. But it is the apostle Paul who is responsible for introducing the language of grace (Greek, *charis*) into Christian theology, as it is his primary word for describing God's gift of Christ for the redemption of the world. The language of grace, and to a lesser extent, mercy (Greek, *eleos*, *oiktirmos*), pervades Paul's letters. For the sake of brevity, in what follows I focus on key passages from Romans and then name some obvious similarities with the teachings of Jesus.

The word *grace* means gift; it is Paul's way of proclaiming *mercy* to his Gentile listeners, who were very familiar with the language of *charis*. In the patronage economy of the Roman empire, benefaction funded social as well as financial capital. In contrast with anonymous charity in the contemporary Western world, in the ancient Mediterranean culture, gifts given and received always entailed relationship and obligation.[1] For this reason, grace was always reciprocal because the giving of gifts expresses a kind of relationship and creates bonds of obligation. Such a reciprocal bond meant that gifts should be given only to morally and socially fitting recipients. Roman benefactors would never bestow their gifts on someone of low status or morally questionable character; to bind oneself to such a person would besmirch one's own reputation.[2] This relational character of giving and receiving gifts, as well as its association with notions of what is fitting or appropriate, is the cultural context of Paul's use of *charis* to describe the gift of Christ. Paul both capitalizes on this cultural meaning and challenges it.

On the one hand, Paul agrees that grace, the giving and receiving of God's gift, always expresses and creates a relational bond between God and humanity. That is, God's love expresses the love God always has toward humanity and creates that bond of love from the human side. On the other hand, like Jesus, Paul thinks that God is shockingly indiscriminate in bestowing righteousness and salvation on the undeserving, and therefor divine grace binds God together with unworthy human beneficiaries. The basis for this countercultural understanding of grace is Jesus's death on a Roman cross, in which Jesus identified with the most marginalized and despised inhabitants of the ancient world. As Paul puts it, Christ "emptied himself, taking the form of a slave, being born in the likeness of human beings. And being found in the likeness of a human being, he humbled himself and became obedient to the point of death, even death by crucifixion" (Phil. 2:7–8, my translation). For Paul, to process information through the lens of Christ crucified is to have, as it were, the cross of Jesus imprinted on one's frontal lobe; it is to see the world, oneself, and others in an entirely new way.[3] As Paul puts it elsewhere, writing to the Corinthians, "Consider your call, brothers and sisters; not many of you were wise according to worldly standards, not many were powerful, not many were of noble birth; but God chose what is foolish in the world to shame the wise, God chose what is weak in the world to shame the strong, God chose what is low and despised in the world, even things that are not, to bring to nothing things that are, so that no human being might boast in the presence of God" (1 Cor. 1:26–29). Thus, the crucifixion, resurrection, and exaltation of Jesus recalibrates all human systems of worth. Indeed, the gift or grace of God is the "justification of the ungodly" (Rom. 4:5), a message that Paul's audience—again, like Jesus's audience—would have found morally offensive.

Keeping in mind this countercultural and relational character of grace, we turn briefly to our key texts in Paul's letter to the Romans.

Key Passages

Romans 3:21–26 amplifies the central theme of the letter, which is God's righteousness revealed through the death and resurrection of Jesus to make all human beings, both Jews and Gentiles, righteous and to deliver them from sin and death.[4] The lead-up to this passage is an extended exposé of universal sin, indicting both Jews and Gentiles (Rom. 1:18–3:20)—that is, all humanity. Four brief observations may aid our understanding of the passage.

First, temporal markers begin and end the text: "but now" (*nuni de*) indicates a new divine action breaking into the situation of universal human culpability and bondage under sin and death. Lest his listeners miss the point, Paul concludes, "at the present time" (*en tō nun kairō*). A better translation would be, "in the *now* time." Paul understands God's redemption through

Christ as the turning point of history; earlier in the letter he uses the verb *apokalyptō*, the verbal form of the word *apocalypse*, to describe God's righteousness breaking into the world through the gospel (Rom. 1:17).[5] God has acted in a new and decisive way to deliver all humanity from sin and death, quite apart from human law observance, yet in line with the revelation of God's righteousness in the law and the prophets. Because God's redemption happens apart from the law, it includes Gentiles as well as Jews.[6]

Second, the terminology of "righteousness" (*dikaiosynē*) and the cognate verb translated "to justify" (*dikaioō*) occurs seven times in these six verses, which stress the revelation and demonstration of God's righteousness through the gift of righteousness to those who trust in Christ. This divine gift is in line with the gospel as "the power of God for salvation" (Rom. 1:16).

Third, "faith" (*pistis*) and its cognate verb "believe" or "have faith" (*pisteuō*) figure prominently in the passage. *Pistis* and *pisteuō* denote both cognitive belief and relational trust and reliability, so that a better translation might be "trustworthiness" and "to trust."[7] Because human faith in Christ is generated by Jesus's own faithful self-giving on behalf of sinners, Jesus Christ is both the source and the object of trust.[8] Thus describing the bond of trust between believers and a trustworthy Lord, *pistis* describes God's faithfulness and the human response of trust in God, in a relational bond that mediates salvation, rather than being a prior condition of salvation. The passage from Ephesians 2 provides a clear summary of this claim: "For by grace [God's undeserved gift] you have been saved through faith, and this is not your own doing; it is the gift of God." Faith, thus, is the outworking of divine grace, the reception of a gift already given, not a precondition for the gift.

Fourth, the central point of the entire passage, the fulcrum on which it turns, is God's gracious gift of righteousness through the death of Christ, as signified by the words "in his blood" (Rom. 2:25). Paul describes the effects of Christ's death in two related terms. First, he speaks of "the redemption (*apolytrōseōs*) that is in Christ Jesus" (2:24). In common usage the term refers to deliverance from captivity due to slavery or war or from other desperate straits. Thus, in the psalms and prophets, God's righteousness frequently acts to deliver God's people. For example, in Psalm 31:1 the psalmist prays, "In you, O Lord, I seek refuge; let me never be put to shame. In your righteousness, deliver me." In Isaiah 46:13, the Lord says to Israel, "Listen to me, you stubborn of heart, you who are far from deliverance: I bring near my deliverance, it is not far off, and my salvation will not tarry."

This primary motif of deliverance governs the interpretation of Paul's second term, *hilasterion.* This word is very rare in the New Testament and is difficult to translate.[9] In the Septuagint (abbreviated LXX, the Greek translation of the Hebrew scriptures) and in Hebrews 9:5, *hilasterion* denotes the lid over the ark of the covenant in the Holy of Holies, where the high priest entered once a year to sprinkle blood for the sins of the people (Exod. 25:17)—hence the translation in our English text, "sacrifice of atonement." Other possible translations include "expiation," and "mercy seat." It is clear that Paul sees Christ's death as the means by which God has dealt with sin and thereby effected redemption by delivering humanity from the condemnation and the death that sin brings. Above all, Paul stresses the gifted quality of this divine action: "Being accounted righteous (*dikaioumenoi*) freely, as a gift (*dōrean*) by his grace (*charis*) through the redemption which is in Christ Jesus, whom God put forward as the *hilasterion* by his blood, effective through faith."

In Romans 5:1–3 righteousness and justification are again joined with faith and grace: "Therefore, since we are justified by faith, we have peace with God through our Lord Jesus Christ, through whom we have obtained access to this grace in which we stand." *Grace* here has a spatial sense, as a place where "we stand" before God. That is, it evokes a relational environment established by God's undeserved gift of righteousness through and in Christ. Notably Paul speaks in the first-person plural, highlighting the communal character of this matrix of grace, which in turn is sustained by the experience of God's love "poured into our hearts through the Holy Spirit who has been gifted to us" (5:5). This focus on grace and love begins a section of the letter in chapters 5–8, which depicts life in Christ as beginning and ending in love, such that at the end, nothing in "all creation will be able to separate us from the love of God in Christ Jesus our Lord" (8:39).

In this context, Romans 5:15–21 contrasts the power, abundance, and efficacy of grace with the debilitating and lethal effects of Adam's sin. In this passage, Adam and Christ are representative figures carrying the destiny of humanity. On the one hand, Adam's trespass opened the door to sin and its henchman, death, which thereby "came into" the world and spread to all human beings (5:12). With a tight quid pro quo logic of cause and effect, Adam's sin leads to condemnation and death (5:15, 16, 18) so that death rules over the human race as a tyrant (5:17). By creating the opportunity for sin to rampage through human history, Adam's disobedience made his heirs—all humanity—to be sinners (5:19). The law merely exacerbated this lethal situation (5:20) because the law also operates by cause and effect; it pronounces condemnation but is unable to give life.

Over against this grim picture of the human situation, Paul piles on the language of grace and gift: *charisma* (Rom. 5:15); the "grace [*charis*] of God and the gift [*dōrea*] in grace [*charis*] of the one person Jesus Christ" (5:16);

"the abundance of grace and the free gift of righteousness" (5:17). Grace abounds, even "super-abounds" (5:17, 20); grace "reigns through righteousness to eternal life through Jesus Christ our Lord" (5:21) so that those who receive this overflowing grace also will reign in life (5:17). The gift—grace—simply does not operate by the quid pro quo logic of sin, death, and the law. It overwhelms it with a different logic, the logic of God's undeserved gift of righteousness. In this way it is characterized by its surpassing, overflowing quality; its incongruity; and its power. The divine gift does not match human misdeeds but rather overturns the legacy of Adam. Herein lies its transforming power.

Thus, aware that his emphasis on grace may sound like a license to sin, in Romans 6 Paul emphasizes union with Christ's death, through baptism, and newness of life through belonging to Christ as Lord. For our purposes, the key point in Romans 6:12–14 is that grace is more powerful than sin: "For sin will not reign over you, since you are not under law but under grace" (6:14). The logic here echoes that of 5:17–21; God's gift, which is the gift of Christ, is stronger than the law in relationship to sin because the gift entails union with Christ as both liberator and Lord. It is the relationship with God, created by the gift, that has transforming and liberating power. This relationship is characterized by freedom; not freedom in a modern sense of individualistic autonomy but freedom mediated by service to God and God's rule over all.[10]

Romans 12 displays the transformation of believers through a communal life characterized by gifted belonging to God and to one another in "the body of Christ." Paul speaks "by the grace [*dia tēs charitos*] given to me"; so also he and his listeners "have gifts [*charismata*] that differ according to the grace given to us." Thus, grace ensures that the community is not characterized by conformity but rather by unity in diversity through the exercise of distinctive gifts for ministry. Paul's emphasis on God's grace undermines human boasting in individual achievements or entitlements and the corresponding competition and rivalry that can tear communities apart. Rather, he depicts a fellowship that exists only by virtue of God's undeserved generosity and thereby invites its members to welcome each other as God has welcomed them. Paul states this explicitly in Romans 15:7: "Welcome one another, therefore, as Christ has welcomed you, for the glory of God."

The opening appeal in 12:1, "by the mercies of God [*dia tōn oiktirmōn tou theou*]," builds on the revelation of God at Sinai, which Paul references in 9:14–18: "I will have mercy [*eleēsō*] on whom I have mercy [*eleō*], and I will have compassion [*oiktirēsō*] on whom I have compassion [*oiktirō*]" (Rom. 9:15, quoting Exod. 33:19). Paul thus connects his exhortation to the Roman believers with the demonstration of God's faithful mercy and compassion in the history of Israel. Just as *charis* is given without regard to the worth of its beneficiaries, so also mercy signifies God's freedom to be merciful without regard to either human virtue or wrongdoing. Paul draws out the implications of this sovereign divine mercy for human relatedness to God: "So it depends not on human will or exertion but on God who shows mercy" (9:16).[11] The history of Israel's election demonstrates this divine sovereign mercy: there was nothing in either Isaac or Jacob to merit God's election of them (9:6–13).[12]

From a human standpoint, such divine election seems arbitrary and unfair, prompting the question, "Is there injustice on God's part?" (9:14).[13] But Paul is willing to stake all on the outrageous claim that God calls, gifts, and shows mercy and grace regardless of the worth or unworthiness of human beings because ultimately everything comes from God, and God owes no one anything. As Paul puts it at the climax of this section of Romans, "Who has given a gift to God in order to be repaid? For from God and through God and to God are all things. To him be glory forever. Amen" (Rom. 11:35–36).

Parallels with the Teachings of Jesus

On the topic of mercy and grace, Paul is right in line with the teachings and actions of Jesus. Among many possible examples, I note only two. First, Paul emphasizes the indiscriminate abundance of God's generosity and love without regard to human worth. Similarly, in the Sermon on the Mount, Jesus tells his disciples and the crowds who follow him, "I say to you, love your enemies and pray for those who persecute you, so that you may be sons of your Father who is in heaven; for he makes his sun rise on the evil and the good, and sends rain on the just and on the unjust" (Matt. 5:44–45). This same generosity and indifference toward the social or moral worth of human beings threads through all of Jesus's interactions, epitomized in his response to the Pharisees who criticize him for hanging out with well-known sinners: "Those who are well have no need of a physician, but those who are sick. . . . For I have come to call not the righteous, but sinners" (Matt. 9:12–13).

Second, in Romans 5:12–21, I note the superabundance of grace in God's incongruous gift, which simply overwhelms the quid pro quo consequences of Adam's sin. One thinks of Jesus's parable of the workers in the vineyard (Matt. 20:1–16), who receive equal wages at the end of the day regardless of how long they have worked. Above all, the parable of the prodigal son (Luke 15:1–11) exemplifies God's overflowing generosity in the face of human wrongdoing. By rights, the son who has squandered his inheritance should pay the price for his actions, but instead the father simply chooses to shower him with gifts. This theme of divine abundance in overflowing gift is not unique to Jesus or Paul; for example, the Jewish philosopher Philo also emphasized God's overflowing beneficence, such that the grace of God is "boundless and illimitable wealth."[14] God's grace and mercy are never a zero-sum game. Where Jesus radicalizes this message, and Paul follows, is that God's abundance is given to the undeserving laborers and the disobedient son who have *not* earned it. No quid pro quo.

This logic of grace and mercy as God's incongruous, overflowing, proactive, and powerfully transforming love toward undeserving human beings, countering and overturning all human systems of worth, thus runs like a red thread through the Gospels and the Epistles. It is a central theme of the New Testament witness to God's redemption of humanity through Jesus Christ.

Notes

1. Philosophical and anthropological investigations of the dynamics of exchange in giving and receiving gifts are extensive. See, in particular, Marcel Mauss, "Essai sur le don: Forme et raison de l'exchange dans les sociétés archaïques," in *Sociologie et anthropologie* (Paris: Presses Universitaires de France, 1950), 145–275. Translated by W. D. Halls as *The Gift: The Form and Reason for Exchange in Archaic Societies* (London: Routledge, 1990); see also the survey of the anthropology and history of gift-giving in John M. G. Barclay, *Paul and the Gift* (Grand Rapids, MI: Eerdmans, 2015), 11–65. Summarizing Mauss's observations on the social dynamics of reciprocity, Barclay comments, "the gift represents the desire to reproduce social relations: each party to the gift-relation is in some sense 'produced' by the exchange between them" (18).

2. For discussion of gift-giving in the Roman empire, see Barclay, *Paul and the Gift*, 24–51. Barclay quotes Cicero's insistence that gifts should be given *pro dignitate*, "on the basis of worth" (Cicero, *De Off.* 1.42–45). As Barclay observes, "Nobody wants to think that they have voluntarily tied themselves to people who degrade their social capital" (39).

3. See Susan Grove Eastman, "Ashes on the Frontal Lobe: Cognitive Dissonance and Cruciform Cognition in 2 Corinthians," in *The Unrelenting God: Essays on God's Action in Scripture in Honor of Beverly Roberts Gaventa*, ed. David J. Downs and Matthew L. Skinner (Grand Rapids, MI: Eerdmans, 2013), 194–206.

4. The thematic statement for the letter is in Romans 1:16–17: "I am not ashamed of the gospel, for it is the power (*dynamis*) of God for salvation to everyone who has faith, to the Jew first and also the Greek, for in it the righteousness of God is being revealed (*apokalyptetai*) for all who believe, the righteousness of God from faith to faith, as it is written, 'The one who is righteous by faith will live.'" Each clause and even each word in this dense statement is debated by scholars.

5. J. Louis Martyn has observed that Paul uses *apocalyptō* ("to apocalypse") and *erchomai* ("to come on the scene") interchangeably in Galatians 3:23–25; God's apocalypse is both the

revelation of God and the action of God in history. See James Louis Martyn, *Galatians: A New Translation with Introduction and Commentary*, vol. 33A of *Anchor Bible* (New York: Doubleday, 1997), 99.

6. Indeed, the Torah's fundamental witness to the oneness of God shows that God is the God of Gentiles as well as Jews, as Paul says in the next paragraph (Rom. 3:29–30): "Is God the God of Jews only? Is he not the God of Gentiles also? Yes, of Gentiles also, since God is one, and he will justify the circumcised on the ground of faith, and the uncircumcised through faith."

7. For a thorough-going examination of faith/trust in the Roman empire and in the New Testament, see Teresa Morgan, *Roman Faith and Christian Faith:* Pistis *and* Fides *in the Early Roman Empire and Early Churches* (Oxford: Oxford University Press, 2015).

8. This is a major issue of interpretation in Pauline studies. The genitive case linking Christ and faith in verse 22 can be translated as "in" ("faith in Jesus Christ") or "of" (the "faith / trustworthiness of Jesus Christ"). In either case, Paul clearly also has human trust in Christ in view, as shown by the final clause, "for all who have faith." But he also has in view Christ's faithful death on behalf of sinners. For an influential discussion of this issue, see Richard B. Hays, *The Faith of Jesus Christ: The Narrative Substructure of Galatians 3:1–4:11*, 2nd ed. (Grand Rapids, MI: Eerdmans, 2002).

9. In the New Testament, *hilasterion* occurs only here and in Hebrews 9:5.

10. On this concept in both Muslim and Christian contexts, see Lucinda Mosher, ed., *Freedom: Christian and Muslim Perspectives* (Washington, DC: Georgetown University Press, 2021).

11. Grace is Paul's language for communicating God's mercy to Gentiles; in relationship to Israel, Paul more often uses the terminology of "mercy," as in Romans 9–11 and Galatians 6:16. See the discussion in Susan Grove Eastman, "Israel and the Mercy of God: A Re-Reading of Galatians 6.16 and Romans 9–11," *New Testament Studies* 56, no. 3 (July 2010): 367–95.

12. The interpretation of these verses is contested and would require a much longer chapter to elucidate. For helpful discussion, see Florian Wilk and John Ross Wagner, eds., *Between Gospel and Election: Explorations in the Interpretation of Romans 9–11* (Tübingen: Mohr-Siebeck, 2010).

13. See particularly the discussion in Barclay, *Paul and the Gift*, 526–33.

14. Philo, *Legum allegoriae* (Allegorical Interpretation) 3.163–64. For further discussion, see Barclay, *Paul and the Gift*, 70.

16

New Testament Writings on Mercy and Grace

Texts for Studying Pauline Thought

Pauline Writings

Romans 3:21–26

[21]But now, irrespective of law, the righteousness of God has been disclosed,
and is attested by the law and the prophets, [22]the righteousness of God
through faith in Jesus Christ for all who believe. For there is no distinction,
[23]since all have sinned and fall short of the glory of God; [24]they are now justified by his grace as a gift, through the redemption that is in Christ Jesus,
[25]whom God put forward as a sacrifice of atonement by his blood, effective
through faith. He did this to show his righteousness, because in his divine
forbearance he had passed over the sins previously committed; [26]it was to
prove at the present time that he himself is righteous and that he justifies the
one who has faith in Jesus.

Romans 5:15–21

[15]But the free gift is not like the trespass. For if the many died through the
one man's trespass, much more surely have the grace of God and the free gift
in the grace of the one man, Jesus Christ, abounded for the many. [16]And the
free gift is not like the effect of the one man's sin. For the judgment following
one trespass brought condemnation, but the free gift following many trespasses brings justification. [17]If, because of the one man's trespass, death exercised dominion through that one, much more surely will those who receive
the abundance of grace and the free gift of righteousness exercise dominion
in life through the one man, Jesus Christ.

[18]Therefore just as one man's trespass led to condemnation for all, so one
man's act of righteousness leads to justification and life for all. [19]For just as by
the one man's disobedience the many were made sinners, so by the one man's

obedience the many will be made righteous. [20]But law came in, with the result that the trespass multiplied; but where sin increased, grace abounded all the more, [21]so that, just as sin exercised dominion in death, so grace might also exercise dominion through justification leading to eternal life through Jesus Christ our Lord.

Romans 6:12–14

[12]Therefore, do not let sin exercise dominion in your mortal bodies, to make you obey their passions. [13]No longer present your members to sin as instruments of wickedness, but present yourselves to God as those who have been brought from death to life, and present your members to God as instruments of righteousness. [14]For sin will have no dominion over you, since you are not under law but under grace.

Romans 9:14–18

[14]What then are we to say? Is there injustice on God's part? By no means! [15]For he says to Moses,

> "I will have mercy on whom I have mercy,
> and I will have compassion on whom I have compassion."

[16]So it depends not on human will or exertion, but on God who shows mercy. [17]For the scripture says to Pharaoh, "I have raised you up for the very purpose of showing my power in you, so that my name may be proclaimed in all the earth." [18]So then he has mercy on whomsoever he chooses, and he hardens the heart of whomsoever he chooses.

Romans 12:1–8

[1]I appeal to you therefore, brothers and sisters, by the mercies of God, to present your bodies as a living sacrifice, holy and acceptable to God, which is your spiritual worship. [2]Do not be conformed to this world, but be transformed by the renewing of your minds, so that you may discern what is the will of God—what is good and acceptable and perfect.

[3]For by the grace given to me I say to everyone among you not to think of yourself more highly than you ought to think, but to think with sober judgment, each according to the measure of faith that God has assigned. [4]For as in one body we have many members, and not all the members have the same function, [5]so we, who are many, are one body in Christ, and individually we are members one of another. [6]We have gifts that differ according to the grace given to us: prophecy, in proportion to faith; [7]ministry, in ministering; the

teacher, in teaching; 8the exhorter, in exhortation; the giver, in generosity; the leader, in diligence; the compassionate, in cheerfulness.

Ephesians 2:4–10

4But God, who is rich in mercy, out of the great love with which he loved us 5even when we were dead through our trespasses, made us alive together with Christ—by grace you have been saved—6and raised us up with him and seated us with him in the heavenly places in Christ Jesus, 7so that in the ages to come he might show the immeasurable riches of his grace in kindness toward us in Christ Jesus. 8For by grace you have been saved through faith, and this is not your own doing; it is the gift of God—9not the result of works, so that no one may boast. 10For we are what he has made us, created in Christ Jesus for good works, which God prepared beforehand to be our way of life.

Selected Passages for Comparison of Paul's Thought to the Teachings of Jesus

Matthew 5:44–45

44[Jesus said:] "But I say to you, Love your enemies and pray for those who persecute you, 45so that you may be children of your Father in heaven; for he makes his sun rise on the evil and on the good, and sends rain on the righteous and on the unrighteous."

Matthew 9:12–13

12But when he heard this, [Jesus] said, "Those who are well have no need of a physician, but those who are sick. 13Go and learn what this means, 'I desire mercy, not sacrifice.' For I have come to call not the righteous but sinners."

Luke 15:1–11

The Parable of the Lost Sheep; The Parable of the Lost Coin

1Now all the tax-collectors and sinners were coming near to listen to him. 2And the Pharisees and the scribes were grumbling and saying, "This fellow welcomes sinners and eats with them."

3So he told them this parable: 4"Which one of you, having a hundred sheep and losing one of them, does not leave the ninety-nine in the wilderness and go after the one that is lost until he finds it? 5When he has found it, he lays it on his shoulders and rejoices. 6And when he comes home, he calls together his friends and neighbors, saying to them, 'Rejoice with me, for I have found my sheep that was lost.' 7Just so, I tell you, there will be more joy in heaven over one sinner who repents than over ninety-nine righteous people who need no repentance."

8 "Or what woman having ten silver coins, if she loses one of them, does not light a lamp, sweep the house, and search carefully until she finds it? 9 When she has found it, she calls together her friends and neighbors, saying, 'Rejoice with me, for I have found the coin that I had lost.' 10 Just so, I tell you, there is joy in the presence of the angels of God over one sinner who repents."[1]

Other New Testament Voices on Mercy and Grace

John 1:14–18

14 And the Word became flesh and lived among us, and we have seen his glory, the glory as of a father's only son, full of grace and truth. 15 (John testified to him and cried out, "This was he of whom I said, 'He who comes after me ranks ahead of me because he was before me.'") 16 From his fullness we have all received, grace upon grace. 17 The law indeed was given through Moses; grace and truth came through Jesus Christ. 18 No one has ever seen God. It is God the only Son, who is close to the Father's heart, who has made him known.

1 Peter 2:9–10

9 But you are a chosen race, a royal priesthood, a holy nation, God's own people, in order that you may proclaim the mighty acts of him who called you out of darkness into his marvelous light.

> 10 Once you were not a people,
>   but now you are God's people;
> once you had not received mercy,
>   but now you have received mercy.

Note

1. See also the Parable of the Prodigal and His Brother, included in chapter 13.

Part Three

Reflections

17

Mercy and Grace in Virginia

Conversations during the Twentieth Building Bridges Seminar

Lucinda Mosher

"I am really glad that, for my first experience of the Building Bridges Seminar, the theme was mercy and grace," a Christian scholar remarked. "I knew in the abstract that, in Islam, one of the names of God is *the Merciful*. However, during this convening, my Muslim colleagues have given me a much richer sense of just how pervasive the concept of mercy is in Islam; and that has moved me at a deep level. Several times this week, I have heard it said that reading a text takes us only so far. I want to underscore that! There's something about our dialogue—that conversational, that oral aspect of our learning—that I just especially love."

That conversational aspect of the Building Bridges Seminar takes three forms: exchanges in each of the four preassigned groups of seven or eight scholars, which meet for several hours each morning and afternoon and stay constant for the week; sharing of insights in plenary at the opening and closing of each day's work—not for detailed reporting from each group but rather to stimulate cross-fertilization of ideas; and interactions in the pairs or clusters that form spontaneously during meals and free time. In June 2022 the Airlie Center in beautiful, rural Northern Virginia provided an environment conducive to all three. The purpose of this chapter is to provide the reader an opportunity to overhear some of that sharing—primarily, that which took place during the evening plenary discussions. Here, then, is a thematically grouped sampler of what participants in Building Bridges 2022 had to say. As has long been the custom of the Seminar in essays of this sort, the Chatham House Rule obtains: participant remarks, queries, and musings are quoted or paraphrased without attribution.

Methodology

The Building Bridges Seminar has an established method. Typically, at the beginning of a small-group session, each participant points out a word or phrase in the texts under consideration—either because it is captivating or because it is confusing. An agenda for the session thus emerges. Yet there is flexibility. Modifications to the standard procedure were on display when, during a plenary, members of the four breakout groups compared their experiences. One scholar spoke about how his small group had begun its deliberations with etymology. They found it quite helpful to learn (or to be reminded) that the Arabic terms translated as "mercy" were linked with the womb, with connectedness, with umbilical outreach, with real mother love. Having compared notes on *grace* and *mercy* in an effort to determine distinctions between these words as technical terms, the group felt better able to interrogate the assigned texts. A Christian noted that her group had opened a session dedicated to Islamic texts by inviting one of its Muslim members to recite the portion of the Qur'an they were about to discuss. "That really was such a wonderful way to begin our engagement of the text," she said. "It allowed the text to speak as it should speak. I think that the text is meant to speak before we start to analyze it. Hearing recitation of the text was, I think, important for our reading it in translation."

Hermeneutical Keys

In her plenary lecture for the 2022 seminar's first morning session, Maria Dakake suggested that *mercy* is the primary "hermeneutical key" to the Qur'an.[1] The notion of a hermeneutical key proved to be a compelling one; the exact identity of that key was a recurring topic of conversation.

Regarding *mercy* as key, the presence of the *basmala* at the beginning of every sura of the Qur'an (except the ninth) had been cited as evidence.[2] However, when discussing this in plenary, one Muslim asserted that "the presence of the *basmala* at the beginning of a sura is not necessarily considered by the tradition as has revealed. In a sense, its status is contested anyway. Why is it that we are choosing mercy as the hermeneutical key when there might be some other aspect of the text that might be just as appropriate?"

The community of faith develops its own hermeneutic based on its reading of the text, another scholar explained. "What then is the community's responsibility as readers of scripture in choosing the interpretive key that will be a unifier in our reading of God's dealings with us? Our group considered this in depth." Someone else wondered whether the question of a hermeneutical key was a recent development. "Does it rise to prominence in a particular school of thought?" Around the table in his breakout group, he said, opinions about that had differed.

During a different plenary, someone related that, for his group, *mercy* was not the Qur'an's hermeneutical key; rather, it was *humility*. He explained: "If God is the source of all being and all good—if that is how God is—then we humans need to adopt a certain humility in how we interpret what comes from God. It contrasts with the notions of arrogance and disdain." A Christian added: "All of these ways of framing our interpretive efforts need to be under this rule of humility, which—given the little bit of Qur'an that I've read and the little I know about Islam—is a concept that seems really very much at home in the Qur'anic text."

The term *hermeneutic* was woven into every evening plenary discussion. Toward the end of the week, someone remarked that "we're accustomed to bringing a hermeneutic of suspicion to this work. During this Seminar, I get to see people from another tradition reading my scripture with a sort of hermeneutic of generosity. It is lovely; it is also inspiring. I appreciate that."

Context

Closely related to hermeneutical keys is the matter of contextuality. As one Muslim explained, contextual matters are certain to bear on our understanding of mercy: "When reading, contextual lenses will highlight certain things in the piece and make us attentive to them particularly. A central unifying lens includes the humility of knowing that there is a difference between our perception and God's reality. Context is a factor in our understanding of what is a mercy and what is a punishment. So, if the context changes, our understanding of mercy and punishment might change. It is submission to God that opens one's eyes to see mercy in a way that one wouldn't see it otherwise."

Readings about forgiving an enemy provoked deep consideration of the impact of context. As one participant observed, "colonizers read the text differently from someone who is oppressed or who is suffering. In our group, we asked, How can people who are suffering, who are oppressed, be asked to forgive or to love an enemy? We came close to an answer. We decided that individuals have their own scope of forgiveness and mercy and ability to show it. We also acknowledged that God's mercy is not always visible.

One scholar noted how significant it was for the Seminar to study the contrasts between the passages from the books of Deuteronomy and Jonah: "So in Jonah, you know, God's mercy overflows to people. But in Deuteronomy, the passage we read says to utterly destroy a people, to defeat them, and then to show them no mercy. That contrast was interesting for me—and for others in our group. I don't know how political our conversations should be; but you know, some of this is playing out in the world today. And so how do we engage a topic when our texts address it in contrasting ways?"

About studying Deuteronomy with Jonah, another scholar said: "One thought that emerged in my group was that the passage from Deuteronomy is addressing something very specific and local, whereas what we see elsewhere is something more general and global." Regarding the passage from Jonah, someone else noted that "we're given an image of God as very engaged in everything. For example, God is causing the wind upon the sea. The response of the people is to ask: is one of us to blame? This is not how people of faith respond today. So, when we read these texts, we are doing so while located in a very different kind of context. The story continues: the people cast lots, and the lot falls upon Jonah. Again, God seems to be involved in the world in ways that many of us simply cannot relate to. So what does that mean for us?"

Context matters in another way, one scholar pointed out, especially when dealing with biblical passages in which God commands the use of violence. "It is always wise to consider this question: 'When this text was read for the first time, who would have been listening?' Deuteronomy tells of God mandating the destruction of particular people. However, at the time this story was composed, that group of people had already been destroyed. Thus it may be read more as a 'why things are' story, rather than a 'what to do' guidebook. In any case, the question remains, how do we read texts in which God commends violence?"

A different option was suggested by a Christian scholar who pointed out that "the Bible itself gives us a way of responding to God when God does not do for us what we expect is good: it gives us the voice of lament. It offers multiple voices. It provides intrascriptural conversation—such that we see scripture protesting against scripture."

Resistance

As plenary conversation ensued, it became apparent that many had perceived in the study texts some sense of resistance to divine mercy. One Christian puzzled about the Qur'anic account of Adam and Eve in the Garden: "What is it in Adam and his wife that makes them enter into a kind of contested relationship with God right there? God the creator is simply being merciful and gives them life in the Garden. I find it quite tantalizing that this question of resistance to mercy came up again and again in our reading."

In some texts, another scholar noted, we find ourselves in the place of the person who is resisting grace. "The sense of resistance to mercy, particularly the Bible's parables, makes me wonder: is the real message of the parables that God's mercy can flow to the undeserving or the newly repentant or those who have not been devout in the same way as others might have? Is the real message a warning against a certain kind of stingy religiosity? Is it both?"

"And I have to say," a Muslim asserted, "that my sense of reading many of the texts selected for us is that they are conveying the idea that God is running you down to offer you mercy. So much of the Christian discourse is about God's justice counterbalancing God's mercy. You can see those components in the Islamic text, too. You see God shoving God's elbow onto the scale, you know, in order to game God's own system, in order to provide people with mercy. That was really moving."

Mercy versus Justice

"As beautiful as the parables are, there's something about them that always makes us feel uncomfortable," one scholar admitted. Her group had spent much time on the Good Samaritan, the Prodigal Son, and the Laborers. "Initially, our focus was not as much on God's mercy as it was on the perceived injustice in each case. In each story, there were things that caused us discomfort. But acknowledging that led us into a wonderful discussion on how God's mercy operates. One may not feel like one deserves mercy; but it just comes to whomsoever. Mercy comes, but it also demands."

"I was thinking of mentioning the parables as well," said another member of the Seminar. "Our group realized the need for more contextualization. We sensed the existence of a huge cultural gulf between our own experiences and what was happening in the parables. We became quite aware that there is a difference between living in an economy of scarcity and living in an economy of abundance. When God is dispensing mercy, we see an economy of abundance. However, we are so locked into a world of scarcity that abundance is hard to imagine."

A third scholar agreed that, indeed, one message Jesus's parables convey is that God lives in an economy of abundance. That abundance is available to us. Yet people dwell on what is theirs and what others cannot have. She pondered: "Are people in danger of locking themselves out of the grace of God?"

Mercy and Judgment

"It is important to read scripture passages about anger and wrath through the lens of mercy," someone asserted. "Perhaps we're uncomfortable in doing that. However, there is something profoundly telling in divine mercy in all its forms." Several individuals remarked on ways their small-group discussions had come around to connections between mercy and judgment—or, put another way, the difficulty in disconnecting them. One group had taken great interest in the law of retribution. As one member explained, "We played with the thought that judgment, in some cases, is a way to preserve community. Interestingly, the more we talked about the concept of mercy and punishment or judgment, the more it became blurry. It is so dependent upon the human perception and understanding that something you consider to be a punishment now might actually seem to be mercy from God tomorrow."

One scholar noted that, in the Psalms, God's mercy is shown by God's exercising of judgment on enemies. "The Psalms provide lots of prayers for people who are suffering from oppression. Psalm 62 indicates that God will repay everyone according to their deeds and that God's propensity to be merciful is linked to protection from our enemies. One lesson here is that God's mercy can operate in this different way. That does not mean that human beings are not to be merciful. It does mean that there is the hope that God will show mercy on those who are oppressed by acting to protect them from those who oppress them."

Another scholar replied that people in places where oppression is real may hear certain scripture texts differently. "That is why our group talked at length about why Jonah was so upset and so angry at God. It is not simply that God is forgiving indiscriminately. In the Bible's version of the Jonah story, forgiveness is directly linked with human transformation. It is just!"

Compassionateness

During the week, the Seminar had many reminders that al-Raḥmān (the Compassionate), one of God's Beautiful Names, is a defining attribute of God. Some Christian participants asked for clarification. They asked: "What permits God to be eternally compassionate? How is this related to creation? Is there an eternal creation? Or is God eternally committed to creation, even if creation is not eternal?" One Muslim replied that, within Islam, several theological explanations are available. "One option is to believe that God is just entirely free in what he does. Because God promised to be merciful, he definitely will now honor his promise. That is one option. Another option is to say that it is God's nature to be merciful. God eternally is merciful. Another is to assert that, if God is not temporal, it does not really make sense to say that God will be eternally merciful to the creation that appears in time. Whatever way one frames it, God will definitely be merciful because it is God's nature to be merciful."

What about love? Is there a distinction between love and mercy? "My group gave this a lot of thought," came a reply. "Our conclusion was that love implies a connection, whereas mercy can be completely impersonal. One can show mercy to someone to whom you have no connection at all."

Grace

Not surprisingly, thoughts about grace and mercy often were intertwined. Less was said directly about grace than about mercy. Yet at times grace was the center of attention. In one instance, for example, someone asserted: "Paul is utterly clear that when people are in the mercy of God, it is not because of something internal to them. I know that what Paul means by mercy has been disputed. This led me to ask: To what degree do Christians or Muslims really believe that the grace of God is something that is utterly unmerited? I think the right answer is that grace is utterly, totally unmerited. However, we humans have a hard time accepting that."

In another instance, a scholar reflected on grace without naming it: "I was just thinking about how the economy or logic of a gift or the logic of the gift emphasizes the sovereignty of God—because all things come from God. There is no transactional basis for relating to God because we are all recipients of God's prior gratuitousness. So in that sense the logic of the gift is tied into the logic of God's sovereign ability to give without regard to human worth. Any human merit would not be earning the gift because that would be a transactional relationship—as if God could be made to owe us something. In fact, God cannot be made to owe us something."

Confronting Scripture

A Christian noted that the Seminar had given him his first opportunity to observe how Muslims read scripture. "And I think it has changed me. I had read some parts of the Qur'an on my own. The Seminar gave me an experience of how the text is read." Indeed, the Seminar is very much about confronting scriptures (our own; each other's) dialogically. "Personally," one

Muslim indicated, "I really benefited from my group's engagement with parallels between passages in the Qur'an and the Christian scriptures. It gave a different echo to the passage that was more familiar to me."

"What I myself found fascinating," said another Muslim, "is the difference in the time frame of the development of each Holy Book. The Qur'an is the result of a very short period of revelation: twenty-three years. There may have been some legal and social development, but the theology is understood to be consistent throughout. However, when it comes to the Bible, we're dealing with writings from a huge, long historical period. And then of course, Christological elements figure prominently at the end of the collection. So, I wondered: given that they have this end goal in mind, how do Christians read this text? Does it differ from how Muslims read scripture? Through our small-group work, we have gotten thought-provoking answers to questions like these."

Another Muslim spoke up: "As I understand it, a Christian preacher must engage regularly with the Hebrew scriptures. Passages from the holy writings of Judaism come up in Christian liturgy. Within Islam, there is an absolutely clear position. We affirm the earlier scriptures of Judaism and Christianity. However, we also affirm the fact that, because of the history of those texts, the scriptures of Judaism and Christianity do not function in the liturgical life of the Muslim community. The Bible may play an increasing role in the academic life of some Muslim scholars. (Some have taken an interest in it for various reasons.) However, it does not have a role to play in Muslim worship."

So, why study the scripture of a religion one does not embrace? "As a Christian student of the Qur'an," one scholar explained, "I think it is important for Christians to consider themselves addressed by the Qur'an and challenged by the Qur'an. The Qur'an does address us by name, in fact, and takes us to task and asks us to rethink how we are expressing things. For me, it has been enormously productive theologically to take seriously the Qur'an's challenge to me. And so I read the Qur'an from within the Christian tradition, and I try to understand the Muslim traditional reading of it. It's a kind of triangulation. The fact is that, for a fifth of the world's population, it is the key text of Revelation. That means that the rest of us have to take it seriously as something that addresses us as human beings."

"I spend most of my time in a very secular space," said another Christian. "So I am appreciative of the opportunity to be with Christians and Muslims together. To be with biblical scholars who are also believers in that tradition; to read the Qur'an and Hadith with people who have known and loved them from birth: this has been a great gift."

Disagreeing Well

"One of the things we always say about the Seminar is that one of our goals is to improve the quality of our disagreements," noted a veteran participant. "We did work on that this week. We studied a number of lengthy, elaborate Qur'an passages. (In the past, we had stuck to much shorter portions of the Qur'an.) It was definitely interesting to hear those long passages unpacked. For me, it was quite a nice blessing to be the Christian in the room—listening; learning about Muslim texts; listening to Muslims disagree about aspects of the texts that we were looking at; and learning more deeply what was going on in these texts. That is always an important part of the Building Bridges Seminar. I think we learn a lot by listening to people who respect each other and who can talk well about a difficult passage from multiple perspectives. We certainly had many examples of that this week. Yet, as much as we are looking to sharpen our disagreements, I think it is surprising how much, at some deep level, we do also encounter agreements."

A twenty-first iteration of the Building Bridges Seminar is planned for 2023. Assuredly, that convening's oral aspect of learning will provide ample opportunity for more of that sharpening and encountering.

Notes

1. See chapter 3 in this volume, Maria Massi Dakake, "Mercy, Grace, and Guidance: The Meccan Suras."

2. The *basmala* is the invocation, *bi-smi llāhi r-raḥmāni r-raḥīm* (In the Name of God: the Compassionate, the Merciful).

18

Cultivating Peaceful Proximity

A Scholar-Practitioner's Engagement with the Building Bridges Seminar Book Series

Charles Tieszen

Beyond whatever value it has for its participants and their students, what has been the impact of the Building Bridges Seminar? To what uses are its publications put? Such questions have been raised from time to time. Here is one scholar's response.

I cannot remember the first time I became aware of the Building Bridges Seminar and its corresponding publications. I may have been a seminary student in New England. I was surely familiar with them by 2006, when I moved to Birmingham, England, for doctoral studies focusing on the history of Christian–Muslim relations. My supervisor, Professor David Thomas, is a historian, so he had one foot firmly planted in the academy, but as a Church of England priest, he kept his other foot in ecclesial life. A part of his ministry was helping the Anglican Communion Network for Inter Faith Concerns (NIFCON). Through David, my wife and I became involved with NIFCON too, adding some of the practical manifestations of Christian–Muslim encounter to our academic work. From then on I tried to follow along in David's footsteps, endeavoring to practice healthy interreligious relations as much as to learn from its history.

What I observed in my supervisor and read about in the published proceedings of the Building Bridges Seminar inspired my efforts to maintain this dual vocation of scholar and practitioner. In the Building Bridges Seminar publications—I have steadily acquired each of the available volumes; eighteen in all as of the date I am writing—I encountered other scholars like David. Experts in fields like history and theology, they took what they had learned and applied it to interreligious contexts for the sake of a more just world. I wondered how I could do more of the same thing.

The first copy of a Building Bridges Seminar book I acquired was the series' third volume, *Bearing the Word*.[1] According to the small note I penciled in near the spine of the book, I bought it on June 11, 2011, at what used to be Coffee by the Books—the Fuller Theological Seminary bookstore in Pasadena, California. I paid $16.00. The book was published in 2005, just a year after the Seminar's third convening took place in Washington, DC. I was clearly a bit slow in acquiring it, but I quickly took in its contents, learned new things, and tried to apply them to both my scholarship and my practice of Christian–Muslim relations.

I found Daniel Madigan's contribution, "Jesus and Muhammad," one of the most intriguing essays in the volume.[2] I was already familiar with some Christian assessments of Muhammad, such as Kenneth Cragg's *Muhammad and the Christian*.[3] I had begun to read from the wider history of Christian reflection on Muhammad and was aware of the work of a number of scholars, including Yvonne Haddad and Jane Smith.[4] Madigan's essay stood out because it struck me with the clarity and insight he offered in a relatively short span of pages. Therein he addressed many of the major pitfalls for Christian responses to Muhammad. Given the Prophet's multifaceted life, the question becomes: which part are Muslims really asking Christians to engage?[5] Since the question of a Christian response often links to a Muslim desire for reciprocity—they honor Jesus, so can Christians honor Muhammad?—how ought those who confront the issue avoid making the categorical mistake of comparing Jesus's function in Christianity with Muhammad's role in Islam?[6] Madigan raised challenges like these as a means for driving to the heart of the matter, which is really to frame the issue as a question of whether the Prophet can be taken seriously as someone who was attentive to the Word of God.[7] Looking through this frame should, so Madigan urged, inspire responses from Christians that seek to open up a path toward productive, not destructive, encounters between Muslims. Even more, it should create a larger space in which to consider what it means to listen for God.[8]

Madigan's essay left me with a sense of urgency with respect to how I, as a Christian, ought to think about Muhammad. In turn, his essay led to a series of changes in both my scholarship and practice of Christian–Muslim relations. To begin with, I started to keep track of Christian remarks about Muhammad. At first, this involved taking note of relevant comments and arguments in passages I was reading in historical texts written by Christians and Muslims. This practice became much more detailed when I joined the team responsible for *Christian–Muslim Relations: A Bibliographical History*. This project aims to catalog every known text written by Christians about Islam and by Muslims about Christianity from the seventh century until 1914. The results are published in a series of volumes and in an online database.[9]

Given the geographical and chronological scope of the project, I have made a record of relevant texts from every century since the inception of Islam and from every continent on which Christians and Muslims have lived. One of the results was my recent book, *The Christian Encounter with Muhammad*, a historical examination of how Christians interpreted the Prophet throughout history.[10]

My historical scholarship also developed theological expressions as a result of engaging the Building Bridges Seminar's publications. One example, my edited volume, *Theological Issues in Christian–Muslim Dialogue*, offers fresh theological reflection on topics of discussion that persist in the history and current state of Christian–Muslim relations.[11] Building Bridges Seminar rapporteur Lucinda Mosher and two past participants are among the contributors of essays to this anthology.

Another example is a book I am writing currently in which I offer my own Christian response to Muhammad and think about what he means for the future of Christian–Muslim encounters. Part of what I am attempting is a move beyond the category of prophecy—again, thinking about insights from Madigan's essay.[12] So I use the ways by which Muslim communities honor Muhammad as a starting point for Christian response. This move employs hagiography as a frame for understanding the Prophet. Hagiography, situated in the context of worshiping communities, often reshapes the postures of those who handle it. In turn, we approach Muhammad not as demonizers but as guests responding to an invitation to consider the possibilities the Prophet offers for defining our religious communities and engaging the world.

Even more, when we position ourselves as guests of an exemplary figure, or what some would call a saint, we open ourselves to the possibility that such an individual can be a vessel of wisdom and a signpost for grace. What grace might Muhammad wisely point us toward? Historically, and for some Christians today, he might surprisingly point us toward Christ. This is an intriguing possibility, but to add to the potential pitfalls that Madigan flagged in his essay, such a view risks colonizing Muhammad by plucking him out of his native context and making him work for Christians in ways that most Muslims do not intend. In such a case, we stop being guests and begin to interlope, however well-meaning we may be in the process. If we step back into the position of guests, then we might begin to see that discussing Muhammad draws Muslims and Christians close together at one of the precise points where they might otherwise diverge. This happens not because we accept agreement as the goal of interreligious encounter but because we discern something virtuous lying beneath our disagreement.

Even this idea of benevolent, productive disagreement reflects a posture I read about early on in Building Bridges Seminar proceedings. As Rowan Williams wrote in his contribution to *Bearing the Word*, dialogue "is about finding the appropriate language in which difference can be talked about rather than used as an excuse for violent separation."[13] In this way, differences, not merely common ground, become points at which the necessary work of cultivating peaceful proximity can occur; impasse can be synonymous with intimacy. When Muslims and Christians do this work together, we can begin to see that Muhammad points us to the recognition of each other as fellow pilgrims, friends of God walking together along the way. This recognition is hardly anything less than bearing witness to God. If one of the hopes Madigan expresses in his essay is that Christian responses to Muhammad would engender productive encounters, then this is perhaps the most fruitful outcome for which one might hope. I admit that my description of all this is terribly truncated when pressed into three paragraphs. I hope I can eventually give the concepts that the Building Bridges Seminar are inspiring in this project as clear an articulation as Madigan offered in his essay.

Madigan's essay and the Building Bridges Seminar books have also found ways of impacting my work as a teacher. Teaching Islamic studies, the history of Christian–Muslim encounter, and issues related to the practice of Christian–Muslim dialogue are perhaps the most practical expressions of my scholarship. As a way of introducing students to some of the texts and traditions of Islam, we read portions of the Qur'an, hadith literature, the Prophet's biography, tafsir commentaries, and other Islamic texts in order to see what Muslims think about Muhammad and how they arrive at these conclusions. Students report their findings in a final essay in which they answer two questions. First, what are some ways Muslims think about Muhammad? Second, what does the student say about Muhammad? Our reading of Islamic sources and investigation of global Muslim practices help us to answer parts of the first question. Madigan's essay, along with other studies like it, help us begin to form a response from our position as Christians who Muslims invite into a new theological discussion.

The results of this introduction to Muhammad and its corresponding Christian response are invariably mixed. In some cases, students who spend a semester working through long-held prejudices and releasing apologetic baggage find that, when it comes to writing about and responding to Muhammad, all the old tropes and fears return. They can only see Muhammad as a hurdle to surmount. Other students acknowledge various achievements and concede that Muhammad possibly meant well. But they conclude that Muhammad ultimately stumbled and surely did more to turn a deaf ear to God than listen to him. A few students want to question the historicity of the Islamic texts they read. In turn, they question the very existence of Muhammad. Why should they respond to him, they ask, without really knowing anything certain about him?

Many other students, however, find the learning experience thoroughly transforming. For them, the stereotypes they bring to classes are permanently abandoned. Their preconceived notions simply do not square with the sources they read, the new information they are processing, and the new frames they are using to view the world. They set aside the potential challenges of a historical Muhammad. Such a concern is not of primary importance, they argue, since Muslims are not actually asking Christians to judge a collection of facts but are instead inviting them to respond to the image of Muhammad that they cherish, with all its heroism and imperfections, in their hearts. These students explore the nature and function of prophecy and wonder, along with Madigan in his essay, if it is a sufficient category from which to offer a Christian response to Muhammad.[14] In the end, for many students Muhammad—as he is presented by the Muslim voices to whom they are listening—transforms into a fellow pilgrim on the way to God.

The new paths these students chart are productive ones. They accept their roles as guests in a series of encounters with Muhammad that Muslims and Islamic sources host and broker. The results in turn lead to fresh theological reflection, scholarship with greater precision, and more fruitful exchanges with Muslim communities. All of this is very much in the spirit of the Building Bridges Seminar and inspired by essays like the one from Daniel Madigan that I first read over a decade ago.

Notes

Charles Tieszen, PhD (University of Birmingham, England), is a Fellow of the Royal Historical Society who specializes in the history of religious thought and the encounters of Christian and Muslim communities. He is one of the editors for the ongoing project *Christian–Muslim Relations: A Bibliographical History* (21 vols.; Leiden: Brill, 2009–).

1. Michael Ipgrave, ed., *Bearing the Word: Prophecy in Biblical and Qur'ānic Perspective* (New York: Church Publishing, 2005).

2. Daniel Madigan, "Jesus and Muhammad: The Sufficiency of Prophethood," in Ipgrave, *Bearing the Word*, 90–99.

3. Kenneth Cragg, *Muhammad and the Christian: A Question of Response* (Maryknoll, NY: Orbis, 1984).

4. For example, Yvonne Yazbeck Haddad and Wadi Z. Haddad, eds., *Christian–Muslim Encounters* (Gainesville: University Press of Florida, 1995); and Jane Smith, "French

Christian Narratives Concerning Muhammad and the Religion of Islam from the Fifteenth to the Eighteenth Centuries," in *Islam and Christian-Muslim Relations* 7, no. 1 (1996): 47–61.

5. Madigan, "Jesus and Muhammad," 90–91, 94.

6. Madigan, 92–93, 95.

7. Madigan, 93.

8. Madigan, 93.

9. David Thomas, Alex Mallett, Juan Pedro Monferrer-Sala, Johannes Pahlitzsch, Barbara Roggema, Mark Swanson, Herman Teule, and John Tolan, eds., *Christian–Muslim Relations: A Bibliographical History* (Leiden: Brill, 2009–), https://referenceworks.brillonline.com/browse/christian-muslim-relations-i (for authors and works from 600 to 1500) and https://referenceworks.brillonline.com/browse/christian-muslim-relations-ii (for authors and works from 1500 to 1914).

10. Charles Tieszen, *The Christian Encounter with Muhammad: How Theologians Interpreted the Prophet* (London: Bloomsbury Academic, 2022).

11. Charles Tieszen, ed., *Theological Issues in Christian-Muslim Dialogue* (Eugene, OR: Pickwick, 2018).

12. Madigan, "Jesus and Muhammad," 97–99.

13. Rowan Williams, "Analysing Atheism: Unbelief and the World of Faiths," in Ipgrave, *Bearing the Word*, 12.

14. Madigan, "Jesus and Muhammad," 97–99.

19

A Solid Contribution

An Assessment of a Volume in the Building Bridges Seminar Book Series

Syed Atif Rizwan

Being, as it is, a record of its twentieth convening, Mercy and Grace *is therefore the twentieth book generated by the Building Bridges Seminar. How might these publications be described? How might they be used? Syed Atif Rizwan answers such questions by reviewing the Seminar's thirteenth, the themes of which are closely related to those of the present volume.*

Sin, Forgiveness, and Reconciliation: Christian and Muslim Perspectives, edited by Lucinda Mosher and David Marshall (Georgetown University Press, 2016), represents the record of the thirteenth iteration of the annual convening, held in Virginia in 2014.[1] The volume's structure provides for focusing on each of the three themes: Sin (part 2), Forgiveness (part 3), and Reconciliation (part 4)—plus an overview (part 1) and a reflection (part 5).

In the overview, Veli-Matti Kärkkäinen and Jonathan A. C. Brown provide a Christian and a Muslim perspective on sin, forgiveness, and reconciliation. Kärkkäinen offers a nuanced exposition of various Christian interpretations of the Fall and atonement theology related to themes of the annual convening.[2] His essay is particularly beneficial for individuals who may not have prior knowledge on the various Christian viewpoints on the subjects. Brown offers his perspective on some of the ways in which he believes the Qur'an engages the same themes. He does this by exploring the concepts of sin, forgiveness, and reconciliation by intertwining the vertical Divine–human relationship with the horizontal plane of human–human relationships.[3] The foundation laid down by both authors is solid and nicely sets up the next section for the reader to engage.

In part 2, Christoph Schwöbel and Ayman Shabana provide respective Christian and Muslim theological perspectives on the concept of sin.[4] Schwöbel begins by underscoring the deeply Christological dimensions of Christian concepts of sin and, specifically, the extent to which all sin is embedded within the paradigm of original or universal sin as well as the relationship of all sin to the death and resurrection of Christ. From this discussion, Schwöbel moves to scriptural exegesis. After a brief review of some of the scriptural texts that play a major role in Christian theologies of sin, Schwöbel introduces the reader to the conceptions of sin and grace in the work of Augustine, Aquinas, and Luther.[5] Finally, Schwöbel offers "three suggestions for the discussion of the problems of sin," which center on the dislocation of sin in the human–God relationship and the relocation of sin from sinners.

Shabana starts by explaining the different ways in which "sin" is expressed in Arabic as well as its classification into various categories such as "major sin" and "minor sin." He then explains the Adam-Eve-Satan-God stories in the Qur'an along with an analysis of the exegetical literature related to them. This description is followed with a discussion of how such literature sheds light on the different ways in which Muslims understand the nature of sin. It is worth noting that, as part of this discussion, Shabana engages in a useful brief excursus into the history and variety of exegetical literature in the Islamic tradition. These remarks offer the reader a general yet important foundation for how Muslim exegetical literature emerged and functions in the context of Islamic scriptural hermeneutics. Both Schwöbel and Ayman are engaging, and their respective essays leave the reader with much to think about and discuss.

In part 3, forgiveness takes center stage for Susan Eastman and Mohammed Hassan Khalil.[6] Eastman examines one of the more familiar parables of Jesus: the prodigal son. For Eastman, this parable is a scriptural set piece for Christian theologies of radical forgiveness. It serves as the foundation for the numerous ways of understanding forgiveness and invites the reader to consider her suggestions. After illustrating the lessons to be drawn from the parable, especially that of the countercultural power of forgiveness, Eastman briefly shifts to a discussion of Romans 8:1–4. She does this to show that this passage sheds light on the Christian understanding of "redemption." She concludes her treatment of forgiveness and redemption with a synthesis of the possible ways in which the two concepts of forgiveness and redemption can be understood in the context of interpersonal relationships.

Khalil begins his essay by referencing a Qur'an verse according to which the power of forgiveness rests with God. He then shifts his attention to *shirk*—that is, "associating partners with God"—to establish a lens for constructing an Islamic theology of forgiveness in light of religious pluralism and interreligious dialogue. He draws upon exegetical commentaries of well-known theologians such as al-Ghazālī (d. 1111 CE) as well as the legal opinions of prominent medieval Muslim jurists such as Ibn Tamiyya (d. 1328 CE) to articulate propositions about salvation, including for non-Muslims. In the case of Muslim–Christian dialogue, the discussion brings into sharp focus the consideration of salvation for Christians, who, according to some Muslims, appear to commit a form of *shirk* in their embrace of the trinitarian doctrine. In the final section of his essay Khalil provides his articulation of forgiveness. Part 3 is intrinsically important. But there is a certain imbalance between Eastman's approach, which does not engage how Christian theologies of forgiveness might address those who reject the divinity of Christ, and Khalil's own approach, which gives substantial consideration to how an Islamic theology might address those who proclaim the divinity of Jesus. It may be that Eastman naturally and exclusively focused on the theme of part 3 whereas Khalil used the allotted space to discuss an interrelated matter.

In part 4, Philip Sheldrake and Asma Afsaruddin discuss reconciliation based on scriptural texts.[7] Sheldrake draws on the parable in the Gospel of Matthew involving the debt between three men to elucidate lessons about reconciliation. In his piece he makes a reference to the letter addressed to the Ephesians (2:11–22). He cites this passage to illustrate how forgiveness, when initiated by the offended party rather than the offender, can be a viable pathway toward achieving reconciliation. Sheldrake offers a constructive perspective on hospitality by providing an array of insightful scriptural references and drawing practical guidance from them. Finally, he uses the *Rule of Saint Benedict* and the Eucharist to develop a theology of reconciliation as hospitality.

Afsaruddin shares valuable insights on reconciliation in the Qurʾan by presenting the relevant verses and their interpretation by renowned exegetes. It's a great opportunity to gain a deeper understanding of this important aspect of the Qurʾan. For those who are unable to access the primary sources, Afsaruddin's piece is invaluable. Moreover, she has a remarkable ability to convey the intricacies of Qurʾanic theology to a group of scholarly theologians who possess expertise in various religious traditions. By the same token, however, Afsaruddin's prowess in synthesizing how *other* Muslim scholars interpret the verses under discussion leaves this reader eager to hear more directly how *she* interprets them. Nevertheless, her presentation on the subject matter is a testament to her proficiency in this field, and her efforts in promoting interfaith understanding and dialogue should be commended.

Each part of the volume ends with selected passages from Christian and Islamic scriptures. All biblical citations are taken from the New Revised Standard Version English translation. As for English translations of the Qurʾan, part 1 uses Abdullah Yusuf Ali's, whereas the other two use M.A.S. Abdel Haleem's. It is unclear as to why two different translations are used, given that each has its own distinct style. For those unfamiliar with the Qur'an, consistency across all sections would helpful.

On the whole, the Muslim perspectives in this volume appear to be Sunni-centric. It would be beneficial for the reader to see the (possible) different ways in which non-Sunnis approach issues of sin, forgiveness, and reconciliation, especially since the reader is provided with various Christian perspectives. Still, this is an excellent resource for those interested in interreligious dialogue and studies. The depth of insight and value in each contribution is noteworthy, offering an excellent foundation for meaningful contemplation and stimulating discussion. The material is detailed but accessible, which makes it useful to academicians and lay persons alike. The referenced verses are especially helpful for those unfamiliar with the other's texts. In sum, this edited volume makes an important contribution to material on interreligious studies and dialogue. It should be welcomed in the classroom as well as by theologians and religious studies scholars interested in this area of research.

Notes

Syed Atif Rizwan, PhD, is assistant professor of Islamic and interreligious studies, director of the Catholic–Muslim studies program, and chair of the department of intercultural studies and ministry at the Catholic Theological Union in Chicago, Illinois.

1. Lucinda Mosher and David Marshall, eds., *Sin, Forgiveness, and Reconciliation: Christian and Muslim Perspectives* (Washington, DC: Georgetown University Press, 2016); the volume received third place in its category in the 2017 Catholic Press Association Book Awards.

2. Veli-Matti Kärkkäinen, "Sin, Forgiveness, and Reconciliation: A Christian Perspective," in Mosher and Marshall, *Sin, Forgiveness, and Reconciliation*, 6.

3. Jonathan A. C. Brown, "Sin, Forgiveness, and Reconciliation: A Muslim Perspective," in Mosher and Marshall, *Sin, Forgiveness, and Reconciliation*, 14 and following.

4. Christoph Schwöbel, "Changing Places: Understanding Sin in Relation to a Graceful God," in Mosher and Marshall, *Sin, Forgiveness, and Reconciliation*, 23–39; and Ayman Shabana, "The Concept of Sin in the Qur'an in Light of the Story of Adam," in Mosher and Marshall, *Sin, Forgiveness, and Reconciliation*, 40–65.

5. For discussion of Augustine, Aquinas, and Luther in *Sin, Forgiveness, and Reconciliation*, see pages 31, 32, and 33, respectively.

6. Susan Eastman, "Forgiveness and Redemption in Christian Understanding," in Mosher and Marshall, *Sin, Forgiveness, and Reconciliation*, 75–82; and Mohammad Hassan Khalil, "Divine Forgiveness in Islamic Scripture and Thought," in Mosher and Marshall, *Sin, Forgiveness, and Reconciliation*, 83–89.

7. Philip Sheldrake, "Reconciliation between People: Christian Perspectives," in Mosher and Marshall, *Sin, Forgiveness, and Reconciliation*, 97–106; and Asma Afsaruddin, "Reconciliation and Peacemaking in the Qur'an," in Mosher and Marshall, *Sin, Forgiveness, and Reconciliation*, 107–17.

Index

Note: A separate index follows for Scriptural Citations.

Scriptural Citation Index

The Apocryphal/Deuterocanonical Books

The New Testament

Qur'an

About the Editor

Professor Lucinda Allen Mosher is rapporteur of the Building Bridges Seminar; director of the Master of Arts in Interreligious Studies program and an affiliate of the Duncan Black Macdonald Center for the Study of Islam and Christian–Muslim Relations at Hartford International University for Religion and Peace; and senior editor of the *Journal of Interreligious Studies*. She is the author or editor of more than twenty books and many essays on multireligious matters—among them, *The Georgetown Companion to Interreligious Studies* (2022) and ten previous volumes of the Building Bridges Seminar series. She received her doctorate in theology from the General Theological Seminary of the Episcopal Church (New York City).